A Bibliographic Guide to American Colleges and Universities

From Colonial Times to the Present

Mark Beach

GREENWOOD PRESS
Westport, Connecticut • London, England

Library of Congress Cataloging in Publication Data

Beach, Mark.
  A bibliographic guide to American colleges and universities.

  Includes index.
  1. Universities and colleges—United States—Bibliography. I. Title.
  Z5815.U5B4   [LA227.3]   016.37873   74-11704
  ISBN 0-8371-7690-5

Copyright © 1975 by Mark Beach

All rights reserved. No portion of this book may be reproduced, by any process or technique, without the express written consent of the author and publisher.

Library of Congress Catalog Card Number: 74-11704
ISBN: 0-8371-7690-5

First published in 1975

Greenwood Press, a division of Williamhouse-Regency Inc.
51 Riverside Avenue, Westport, Connecticut 06880

Printed in the United States of America

Contents

Introduction	*vi*
Alabama	3
Alaska	6
Arizona	7
Arkansas	8
California	11
Colorado	24
Connecticut	28
Delaware	35
District of Columbia	37
Florida	42
Georgia	45
Hawaii	52
Idaho	53
Illinois	55
Indiana	68
Iowa	76
Kansas	85
Kentucky	89
Louisiana	96
Maine	98
Maryland	101
Massachusetts	106
Michigan	126

Minnesota	138
Mississippi	144
Missouri	147
Montana	154
Nebraska	155
Nevada	159
New Hampshire	160
New Jersey	163
New Mexico	170
New York	172
North Carolina	199
North Dakota	207
Ohio	209
Oklahoma	221
Oregon	224
Pennsylvania	228
Puerto Rico	243
Rhode Island	244
South Carolina	247
South Dakota	251
Tennessee	254
Texas	260
Utah	268
Vermont	270
Virginia	272
Washington	282
West Virginia	286
Wisconsin	289
Wyoming	295
Index	296

Introduction

For a number of years there has been a need for better bibliographical sources about the history of colleges and universities in the United States. In the absence of one comprehensive source, scholars have had to rely upon lists of citations found in general histories of higher education, in histories of specific topics and institutions, and occasionally in journals.

The present volume is an effort to bring together in one source citations of major books, articles, and dissertations relating to the history of specific institutions of higher learning in this country. It is organized to meet two needs. First, it should help persons who want to learn about the history of a particular college or university. Second, through its index it includes a subject guide to historical writing about higher education.

All of the entries are listed alphabetically under the names of institutions to which they refer. The only exception to the alphabetical arrangement is the "major entry," the book which I considered the most important work for an institution and which, therefore, is listed first for the school to which it refers. The institutions themselves are listed alphabetically within each state in the same order as used in standard guides such as Cass and Birnbaum's *Guide to American Colleges.*

All of the citations in the text are numbered sequentially from 1 through 2806. Entries in the index are by these sequential text rather than by conventional page numbers. That procedure allows a citation listed under one school to be cross-listed for other institutions, names, or topics.

The references in this bibliography were drawn from a wide

variety of sources. The initial pool consisted of materials I encountered during ten years of research and teaching about the history of higher education. After the decision was made to publish the bibliography in its present form, that pool was systematically checked and expanded by consulting: (1) footnotes and citations in the standard texts on the history of higher education in this country and in bibliographies prepared for graduate courses on the topic; (2) all of the issues of the American Historical Association's *Guide to Historical Writing;* (3) guides to periodical literature in the *Journal of American History, American Quarterly, New England Quarterly,* and *William and Mary Quarterly;* (4) indices to the major state historical magazines and quarterlies; (5) issues of *Dissertation Abstract* and related subject guides published by University Microfilms through the end of 1972; (6) the *Dictionary of American Bibliography* for purposes of obtaining at least one useful reference for every academic person whose institutional affiliation I could identify. Additional information was secured from college and university librarians in response to a request for citations mailed to every four year institution in the country. That survey was conducted by Professor Frederick Gardner of Rochester Institute of Technology, whose generosity with the results of his inquiry added several dozen institutions to this bibliography.

In every case I have tried to include only those historical materials that describe the growth of a specific school or one of its units, portray the life of an individual closely affiliated with the institution, or describe the relationship between the school and one of its constituencies. Contemporary polemical or journalistic treatments that could be considered primary sources are, therefore, not included. The only exceptions were made in the cases of materials written by students or very recent graduates, materials which are seldom published and which in my view are underrepresented in the sources used for research into the history of higher education.

No work of the nature can exist without some errors and omissions. I hope any person who finds a mistake or knows of a reference that should have been included will mail me that information. That kind of cooperation is essential if scholarship about higher education is to have a better bibliographic basis in the future.

Rochester, New York
November 1974

A Bibliographic Guide to American Colleges and Universities

Alabama

GENERAL REFERENCES

1 Clark, Willis G. <u>History of Education in Alabama, 1702-1889</u>.
   Washington, D.C.: U.S. Government Printing Office, 1889.

2 Owen, Marie B. <u>The Story of Alabama: A History of the State</u>.
   5 vols. New York: Lewis, 1949.

INSTITUTIONAL HISTORIES

ALABAMA, UNIVERSITY OF

3 Sellers, James B. <u>History of the University of Alabama, 1818-1902</u>. University: University of Alabama Press, 1953.

4 Echols, Edward C. "Say Something Nasty About Pittsburgh." In <u>The New Professors</u>, edited by Robert O. Bowen, pp. 202-218. New York: Holt, Rinehart, and Winston, 1960. [Author is Professor of Greek and Latin.]

5 Owen, Thomas M. "The Genesis of the University of Alabama." <u>Alabama Historical Quarterly</u> 2 (1940): 163-188.

AUBURN UNIVERSITY

6 Auburn University. <u>Auburn's First 100 Years, 1856-1956</u>. Auburn: n.p., 1956.

7 Brown, William Leroy. <u>Dr. William Leroy Brown</u>. Compiled by Thomas C. Brown. New York: Neale, 1912.

BIRMINGHAM SOUTHERN COLLEGE

8   Parks, Joseph H., and Weaver, Oliver C., Jr. Birmingham-Southern College, 1856-1956. Nashville, Tenn.: Parthenon Press, 1957.

9   Perry, Wilbur D. A History of Birmingham-Southern College, 1856-1931. Nashville, Tenn.: Methodist Publishing House, 1931.

FLORENCE STATE UNIVERSITY

10 Vaughn, Susan K. The History of the State Teachers College, Florence, Alabama. Florence: Alabama State Teachers College, 1931.

HOWARD COLLEGE

11 Garrett, Mitchell B. Sixty Years of Howard College, 1842-1902. Birmingham: Howard College, 1927.

12 Pate, James A. "The Development of the Instructional Program at Howard College, 1842-1957." Doctoral dissertation, University of Alabama, 1959.

HUNTINGDON COLLEGE

13 Ellison, Rhoda Coleman. History of Huntingdon College, 1854-1954. University: University of Alabama Press, 1954.

ST. BERNARD COLLEGE

14 Reger, Ambrose. The Benedictines in Alabama. Baltimore: Kreuzer Bros., 1898.

SPRING HILL COLLEGE

15 Kenny, Michael. Catholic Culture in Alabama: Centenary Story of Spring Hill College, 1830-1930. New York: American Press, 1931.

ALABAMA

16 Smith, Andrew C. *The Phoenix and the Turtle, Some Highlights on the History of Spring Hill College.* Mobile: Spring Hill College Press, 1957.

17 Vollenweider, Roy W. "Spring Hill College: The Early Days." *Alabama Review* 7 (1954): 127-135.

TALLEDEGA COLLEGE

18 Kimball, Solon T. *The Talledega Story: A Study in Community Process.* University: University of Alabama Press, 1954.

TROY STATE UNIVERSITY

19 Bannon, Michael F. "A History of State Teachers College, Troy, Alabama." Doctoral dissertation, George Peabody College, 1955.

TUSKEGEE INSTITUTE

20 Harlan, Louis R. *Booker T. Washington: The Making of a Black Leader, 1856-1901.* New York: Oxford University Press, 1972.

21 Citro, Joseph F. "Booker T. Washington's Tuskegee Institute: Black School-Community, 1900-1915." Doctoral dissertation, University of Rochester, 1972.

22 Hughes, William Hardin, and Patterson, Frederick D., eds. *Robert Russa Moton of Hampton and Tuskegee.* Chapel Hill: University of North Carolina Press, 1956.

23 Stokes, Anson P. *Tuskegee Institute: The First 50 Years.* Tuskegee: Tuskegee Institute Press, 1931.

24 Thrasher, Max B. *Tuskegee and Its Work.* Boston: Small and Maynard, 1901.

25 Walker, Anne K. *Tuskegee and the Black Belt.* Richmond, Va.: Dietz, 1945.

26 Washington, Booker T. *Up from Slavery.* New York: Doubleday, 1901.

27 Washington, Booker T. *Working with the Hands.* New York: Doubleday, 1904.

28 Whiting, Joseph. *Shop and Class: A Definitive Story of the Tuskegee Correlation Technique.* Boston: Chapman, 1940.

Alaska

GENERAL REFERENCES

29 Poole, Charles P. "Two Centuries of Education in Alaska." Doctoral dissertation, Washington University, 1949.

INSTITUTIONAL HISTORIES

ALASKA, UNIVERSITY OF

30 Patty, Earnest. *North Country Challenge*. New York: McKay, 1969.

SHELDON JACKSON COLLEGE

31 Hinckley, Ted C. "Sheldon Jackson College: Historic Nucleus of the Presbyterian Enterprise in Alaska." *Journal of Presbyterian History* 49 (1971): 59-79.

Arizona

GENERAL REFERENCES

32 Peplow, Edward H. *History of Arizona*. New York: Lewis, 1953.

33 Gustafson, Alburn M. "A History of Teachers Certification in Arizona." Doctoral dissertation, University of Arizona, 1955.

34 Hondrum, Jon O. "The Historical Development of Teacher Education in Arizona." Doctoral dissertation, Yale University, 1953.

INSTITUTIONAL HISTORIES

ARIZONA STATE UNIVERSITY

35 Hopkins, Ernest J., and Thomas, Alfred, Jr. *The Arizona State University Story*. Phoenix: Southwest Publishing Co., 1960.

ARIZONA, UNIVERSITY OF

36 Martin, Douglas D. *Lamp in the Desert: The Story of the University of Arizona*. Tucson: University of Arizona Press, 1960.

Arkansas

GENERAL REFERENCES

37 Conklin, E.P. "Higher Education." In <u>Arkansas and Its People,</u> edited by David Thomas, vol. 4, pp. 483-495. New York: American Historical Society, 1930.

38 Cole, Tommie J. "The Historical Development of Junior Colleges in Arkansas." Doctoral dissertation, University of Arkansas, 1955.

39 Lee, Lurline Mahan. "The Origin, Development, and Present Status of Arkansas' Program of Higher Education for Negroes." Doctoral dissertation, Michigan State University, 1954.

40 Payne, John W. "Poor-Man's Pedagogy: Teachers' Institute in Arkansas (1875-1931)." <u>Arkansas Historical Quarterly</u> 14 (1955): 195-206.

INSTITUTIONAL HISTORIES

ARKANSAS AGRICULTURAL, MECHANICAL, AND NORMAL COLLEGE

41 Chambers, Fredrick. <u>Historical Study of Arkansas Agricultural, Mechanical, and Normal College, 1873-1943.</u> Muncie, Ind.: Ball State University, 1970.

ARKANSAS COLLEGE

42 Herold, Amos Lee. <u>I Chose Teaching: A Life Record of Self-Reliance and Devotion to Scholarship and Democracy.</u> San Antonio: Naylor Co., 1958.

ARKANSAS, UNIVERSITY OF, AT FAYETTEVILLE

43 Leflar, Robert Allen. *The First One Hundred Years: Centennial History of the University of Arkansas*. Fayetteville: University of Arkansas Foundation, 1972.

44 Atkinson, James H. "Memoirs of a University Student, 1906-1910." *Arkansas Historical Quarterly* 30 (1971): 213-241.

45 Bridges, Hal. "D.H. Hill and Higher Education in the New South." *Arkansas Historical Quarterly* 15 (1956): 107-124. [President, 1877-1884.]

46 Gatewood, Willard B., Jr. "Woodrow Wilson and the University of Arkansas." *Arkansas Historical Quarterly* 30 (Summer 1971): 83-94.

47 Harrison, Hale. *University of Arkansas, 1871-1948*. Fayetteville: University of Arkansas Alumni Association, 1948.

48 Leflar, Robert Allen. "Legal Education in Arkansas: A Brief History of the Law School." *Arkansas Historical Quarterly* 21 (1962): 99-131.

49 Leflar, Robert Allen. "The University's Semi-Centennial in 1922." *Arkansas Historical Quarterly* 25 (Autumn 1966): 197-213.

50 Reynolds, John Hugh, and Thomas, David Yancey. *History of the University of Arkansas*. Fayetteville: University of Arkansas, 1910.

51 Rothrock, Thomas. "The University of Arkansas's Old Main." *Arkansas Historical Quarterly* 30 (Spring 1971): 1-52.

ARKANSAS, UNIVERSITY OF, AT LITTLE ROCK

52 Atkinson, J.H. *Little Rock Junior College, the First Ten Years 1927-1937*. Little Rock: Pulaski County Historical Society, 1959.

CANE HILL COLLEGE

53 Basham, Robert H. "A History of Cane Hill College in Arkansas." Doctoral dissertation, University of Arkansas, 1969.

COMMONWEALTH COLLEGE

54　Cobb, William H. "From Utopian Isolation to Radical Activism: Commonwealth College, 1925-1935." <u>Arkansas Historical Quarterly</u> 32 (Summer 1973): 132-147.

HARDING COLLEGE

55　Atteberry, James L. <u>The Story of Harding College</u>. Searcy: n.p., 1966.

56　Croom, Adlai Stevenson. <u>The Early History of Harding College</u>. Searcy: n.p., 1954.

HENDERSON STATE COLLEGE

57　Hall, John Gladden. <u>Henderson State College: The Methodist Years, 1890-1929</u>. Forthcoming.

HENDRIX COLLEGE

58　Propps, J.J. "Memories of Hendrix College." <u>Arkansas Historical Quarterly</u> 28 (Spring 1969): 49-71.

JOHN BROWN UNIVERSITY

59　Williams, Earl Richard. "John Brown University; Its Founder and Its Founding, 1919-1957." Doctoral dissertation, University of Arkansas, 1971.

OZARKS, COLLEGE OF THE

60　Henry, Mary Hollowell. <u>History of the College of the Ozarks</u>. Clarksville: College of the Ozarks Printing Department, 1940.

PHILANDER SMITH COLLEGE

61　Gibson, De Lois. "Philander Smith College, 1877-1969." Doctoral dissertation, University of Arkansas, 1972.

California

GENERAL REFERENCES

62 Bilow, Melvin L. "A History of the Trade and Industrial Education in California." Doctoral dissertation, University of California at Los Angeles, 1949.

63 Comm, Walter. "A Historical Analysis of Vocational Education: Land-Grant Colleges to California Junior Colleges, 1862-1940." Doctoral dissertation, University of Southern California, 1968.

64 Coons, Arthur Gardiner. Crises in California Higher Education; Experience Under the Master Plan and Problems of Coordination, 1959 to 1968. Los Angeles: Ritchie, 1968.

65 Diederich, Alphonsus Francis. "A History of Accreditation, Certification and Teacher Training in Catholic Institutions of Higher Learning in California." Doctoral dissertation, University of California at Los Angeles, 1958.

66 Gardner, David. The California Oath Controversy. Berkeley: University of California Press, 1967.

67 Gerth, Donald. An Invisible Giant. San Francisco: Jossey Bass, 1971.

68 Harney, Paul John. "A History of Jesuit Education in American California." Doctoral dissertation, University of California at Berkeley, 1944.

69 Hurley, Rev. Mark J. "Church-State Relationships in Education in California." Doctoral dissertation, Catholic University of America, 1950.

70 Kenneally, Sinbar, O.S.M. "The Catholic Seminaries of California as Educational Institutions 1840-1950." Doctoral dissertation, University of Toronto, 1957.

71 Merlino, Masine Ollie. "A History of the California State Normal Schools-Their Origin, Growth, and Transformation into Teachers Colleges." Doctoral dissertation, University of Southern California, 1961.

72 Reid, Alban E. "A History of the California Junior College Movement." Doctoral dissertation, University of Southern California, 1965.

73 Ryan, James Edwin. "The History of Manual Training Teacher Education in the California State Normal Schools." Doctoral dissertation, University of California at Los Angeles, 1964.

74 Shipp, Frederic T. "The Junior College in Its Relationship to the State College in California." Doctoral dissertation, Stanford University, 1949.

75 Stanton, Charles Michael. "Student Activism on Three California Campuses During the Years 1930-1940, 1955-1965." Doctoral dissertation, Stanford University, 1966.

76 Toto, Charles, Jr. "A History of Education in California 1800-1850." Doctoral dissertation, University of California at Berkeley, 1966.

77 Welch, Frank Gardner. "Freedom of Teaching in California 1920-1930." Doctoral dissertation, University of California at Los Angeles, 1964.

INSTITUTIONAL HISTORIES

ATTUDAC COLLEGE

78 Porter, Rebecca N. "The College Nobody Knows." *Scribner's* 43 (March 1929): 342-346.

CALIFORNIA BAPTIST COLLEGE

79 Brown, Olie T., and Nelson, Lawrence E. *It's a Great Day: A History of California Baptist College--Its First Twenty Years*. Riverside: California Baptist College Press, 1970.

CALIFORNIA INSTITUTE OF TECHNOLOGY

80 DuBridge, Lee. *Frontiers of Knowledge: Seventy-Five Years at the California Institute of Technology*. New York: Newcomen Society in North America, 1967.

81 Millikan, R.A. *The Autobiography of Robert A. Millikan.* New York: Prentice-Hall, 1950. [President.]

CALIFORNIA STATE COLLEGE AT LONG BEACH

82 Wiley, Sawyer E., ed. "The First Decade of Long Beach State College, 1949-1959." Mimeographed. Long Beach: Long Beach State College, 1960.

CALIFORNIA STATE POLYTECHNIC COLLEGE AT SAN LUIS OBISPO

83 Smith, Morris Eugene. "A History of California State Polytechnic College, the First Fifty Years, 1901-1951." Doctoral dissertation, University of Oregon, 1958.

CALIFORNIA, UNIVERSITY OF, AT BERKELEY

84 Stadtman, Verne A. *The University of California 1868-1968.* New York: McGraw-Hill, 1970.

85 Adams, Ansel, and Newhall, Nancy. *Fiat Lux: The University of California.* New York: McGraw-Hill, 1967.

86 Armes, William D., ed. *Autobiography of Joseph LeConte.* New York: D. Appleton Co., 1903. [LeConte was Professor of Geology, 1869-1896.]

87 Conmy, Peter T. *History of Entrance Requirements of Liberal Arts Colleges of the University of California, 1860-1927.* University of California Publications in Education, vol. 2, pt. 4. Berkeley: University of California Press, 1928.

88 Cutter, Charles H. "Michael Reese, Parsimonius Patron of the University of California." *California Historical Society Quarterly* 42 (June 1963): 127-144.

89 Daniels, Roger. "Workers' Education and the University of California, 1921-1941." *Labor History* 4 (Winter 1963): 32-50.

90 Ferrier, William W. *Origin and Development of the University of California.* Berkeley: The Sathergate Bookshop, 1930.

91 Heirich, Max. *The Beginning: Berkeley, 1964.* New York: Columbia University Press, 1968.

92 Heirich, Max. "The Demonstrations at Berkeley, 1964-65." Doctoral dissertation, University of California, 1967.

93 Jones, W. Carey. The Illustrated History of the University of California, 1868-1901. Berkeley: Students' Cooperative Society, 1901.

94 Kroeber, Theodora. Alfred Kroeber: A Personal Configuration. Berkeley: University of California Press, 1970. [Kroeber was Professor of Anthropology.]

95 Lunsford, Terry F. The "Free Speech" Crises at Berkeley, 1964-1965. Berkeley: University of California Center for Research and Development in Higher Education, 1965.

96 Ouellette, Vernon A. "Daniel Coit Gilman's Administration of the University of California." Doctoral dissertation, Stanford University, 1952. [Gilman was President, 1871-1876.]

97 Pettitt, George A. Twenty-Eight Years in the Life of a University President. Berkeley: University of California Press, 1966.

98 Pickerell, Albert G., and Dornin, May. The University of California: A Pictorial History. Berkeley: The Regents of the University of California, 1968.

99 Sibley, Robert. The Romance of the University of California. San Francisco: H.S. Crocker, 1928.

100 Smith, Dora. History of the University of California Library to 1900. Rochester, N.Y.: University of Rochester Press, 1954.

101 Steffens, Joseph Lincoln. The Autobiography of Lincoln Steffens. New York: Harcourt, Brace, 1936. [Steffens was a Student.]

102 Stone, Irving, ed. There was Light: Autobiography of University of California at Berkeley, 1868-1968. New York: Doubleday, 1971.

103 Thwing, Charles F. "Benjamin Ide Wheeler." School and Society 33 (1931): 181-188.

104 Watson, James E. "A History of Political Science at the University of California, 1875-1960." Doctoral dissertation, University of California, 1960.

CALIFORNIA, UNIVERSITY OF, AT LOS ANGELES

105 Hamilton, Andrew, and Jackson, John B. UCLA on the Move During Fifty Golden Years, 1919-1969. Los Angeles: Ritchie, 1969.

106 Ackerman, William C. My Fifty Years Love-In at UCLA. Los Angeles: Fashion Press, 1969.

107 Florell, David M. "Origin and History of the School of Education, University of California, Los Angeles." Doctoral dissertation, University of California at Berkeley, 1946.

108 King, Kermit C. "The Historical Development of University Extension at the University of California, with Particular Reference to Its Organization in the Southern Area." Doctoral dissertation, University of California at Los Angeles, 1947.

109 Moore, Ernest C. I Helped Make a University. Los Angeles: Dawson, 1952.

110 Nystrom, Richard Kent. "UCLA, an Interpretation Considering Architecture and Site." Doctoral dissertation, University of California at Los Angeles, 1969.

111 Richard, Virginia. Origin and Development of Graduate Education at UCLA, 1933-1964. Los Angeles: University of California at Los Angeles Graduate Division, 1965.

112 Treacy, Robert. "Progressivism and Corinne Seeds: UCLA and the University Elementary School." Doctoral dissertation, University of Wisconsin, 1972.

CALIFORNIA, UNIVERSITY OF, AT SANTA BARBARA

113 Ellison, William H. "Antecedents of the University of California, Santa Barbara, 1891-1944." Unpublished manuscript, n.d.

114 Ellenwood, Theodore S. "A Study of the Anna S.C. Blake Manual Training School from 1891 to 1909." Doctoral dissertation, University of California at Los Angeles, 1960.

115 O'Reilly, Edmund. "A History of Santa Barbara State Teachers' College." Master's thesis, Stanford University, 1928.

CALIFORNIA, UNIVERSITY OF, AT SANTA CRUZ

116 Members of the Cowell History Workshop 144G. Solomon's House. Felton: Big Trees Press, 1970.

117 Trombley, William. "Three California Institutions...And a Fourth." Change 2 (1970): 54-60.

CALIFORNIA, UNIVERSITY OF, MEDICAL SCHOOL AT LOMA LINDA

118 Otto, Leroy Walter. "An Historical Analysis of the Origin and Development of the College of Medical Evangelists." Doctoral dissertation, University of Southern California, 1961.

CHAPMAN COLLEGE

119 Sayre, Arlene Reasoner. Chapman Remembers; A History of Chapman College. Orange: n.p., 1969.

CHICO STATE COLLEGE

120 Moore, Gail Everett. "History of Chico State College." Doctoral dissertation, Oregon State University, 1939.

CLAREMONT MEN'S COLLEGE

121 Benson, Mabel Gibberd, ed. An Idea Becomes a College. Claremont Men's College, the First Ten Years. Claremont: Claremont Men's College, 1958.

122 Clary, William W. The Claremont Colleges: A History of the Development of the Claremont Group Plan. Claremont: Claremont Men's College, 1970.

CONCORDIA TEACHERS COLLEGE

123 Freitag, Alfred J. "A History of Concordia Teachers College, 1864-1965." Doctoral dissertation, University of Southern California, 1965.

FRESNO STATE COLLEGE

124 Rowland, Eugenia. "Origin and Development of Fresno State College." Doctoral dissertation, University of California at Berkeley, 1949.

GOLDEN GATE COLLEGE

125 Sharpe, D.R., and Miner, Nagel. History of Golden Gate College. San Francisco: Golden Gate University, 1971.

HOLY NAMES, COLLEGE OF THE

126 Perry, Mary Dorothea. A History of the Educational Work of the Sisters of the Holy Names of Jesus and Mary in California from 1868 to 1920. San Rafael: Catholic University of America, Pacific Coast Branch, 1954.

IMMACULATE HEART COLLEGE

127 Real, James. "Immaculate Heart of Hollywood." Change 3 (1971): 48-53.

MENLO JUNIOR COLLEGE

128 Howard, Lowry S. The Story of Menlo. Menlo: Menlo Junior College, 1931.

MILLS COLLEGE

129 Keep, Rosalind. Fourscore and Ten Years. Oakland: Mills College, 1946.

130 Hadley, George. Aurelia Henry Reinhardt; Portrait of a Whole Woman. Oakland: Mills College, 1961.

131 James, Elias Olan. The Story of Cyrus and Susan Mills. Stanford: Stanford University Press, 1953.

132 Wittenmyer, Clara K. The Susan Lincoln Mills Memory Book. San Francisco: Hancock Bros. Press, 1915. [Author was President, 1890-1909.]

NOTRE DAME, COLLEGE OF

133 McNamee, Mary Dominica. Light in the Valley, the Story of California's College of Notre Dame. Berkeley: Howell-North, 1967.

OCCIDENTAL COLLEGE

134 Rolle, Andrew F. Occidental College, the First Seventy-Five Years--1887-1962. Los Angeles: Occidental College, 1962.

135 Cleland, Robert Glass. The History of Occidental College, 1887-1937. Los Angeles: Ritchie, 1937.

PACIFIC COLLEGE

136 Stanbrough, Amos Colfax. "History of Pacific College." Master's thesis, University of Oregon, 1933.

PACIFIC UNION COLLEGE

137 Utt, Walter C. *A Mountain, a Pickax, a College: A History of Pacific Union College*. Angwin: Alumni Association, 1968.

PACIFIC, UNIVERSITY OF THE

138 Hunt, R.D. *History of the College of the Pacific, 1851-1951*. Stockton: College of the Pacific, 1951.

139 Stuart, Reginald Ray, and Stuart, Grace D. *Tully Knoles of Pacific: Horseman, Teacher, Minister, College President, Traveler, and Public Speaker*. Stockton: College of the Pacific, 1956.

PASADENA COLLEGE

140 Knott, James Proctor. *History of Pasadena College*. Pasadena: Pasadena College, 1960.

POMONA COLLEGE

141 Brackett, Frank P. *Granite and Sagebrush: Reminiscences of the First Fifty Years of Pomona College*. Los Angeles: Ritchie, 1944.

142 Sumner, Charles Burt. *The Story of Pomona College*. Boston: Pilgrim Press, 1914.

REDLANDS, UNIVERSITY OF

143 Nelson, Lawrence Emerson. *Redlands: Biography of a College*. Redlands: University of Redlands, 1958.

CALIFORNIA

SACRAMENTO STATE COLLEGE

144 Moore, D.E. *The History of Sacramento State College: Twenty Years of Higher Education*. Sacramento: Associated Students of Sacramento State College, 1967.

145 Moore, D.E. *Sacramento State College: The First Eighteen Years*. Sacramento: Sacramento State College, 1965.

SAINT JOHN'S COLLEGE

146 Weber, Francis J. *A Guide to Saint John's Seminary, Camarillo, California*. Los Angeles: Westernlore Press, 1966.

SAINT MARY'S COLLEGE OF CALIFORNIA

147 McDevitt, Herbert Addis. *The Early Years of St. Mary's College, 1859-1879*. Moraga: St. Mary's College, 1968.

148 McDevitt, Herbert Addis. *The Late Years of St. Mary's College, 1879-1969*. Moraga: St. Mary's College, 1971.

SAN DIEGO STATE COLLEGE

149 Lesley, Lewis B., ed. *San Diego State College: The First Fifty Years, 1897-1947*. San Diego: San Diego State College, 1947.

SAN FRANCISCO STATE COLLEGE

150 Barlow, William. *An End to Silence: The San Francisco State College Study Movement in the Sixties*. New York: Pegasus, 1971.

151 Insel, Shepard A. "The Education Counselor." In *The New Professors*, edited by Robert O. Bowen, pp. 125-154. New York: Holt, Rinehart, and Winston, 1960. [Author is Professor of Psychology.]

152 Smith, Robert. *By Any Means Necessary*. San Francisco: Jossey-Bass, 1970.

153 Summerskill, John. *President Seven*. New York: World Book Co., 1971. [Author was President, 1967-1970.]

154 Wilner, Herbert, and Litwak, Leo. *College Days in Earthquake Country: Ordeal at San Francisco State*. New York: Random House, 1972.

SAN JOSE STATE COLLEGE

155 Gilbert, Benjamin Franklin. *Pioneers for One Hundred Years: San Jose State College, 1857-1957.* San Jose: San Jose State College, 1957.

156 Greathead, Sarah Estelle. *The Story of an Inspiring Past. Historical Sketch of the San Jose State Teachers College from 1862 to 1928.* San Jose: San Jose State Teachers College, 1928.

157 *Historical Sketch of the State Normal School at San Jose, California.* Sacramento: State Printer, 1889.

SAN LUIS OBISPO JUNIOR COLLEGE

158 Jones, Ivan Livingston, Jr. "San Luis Obispo Junior College: Demise and Rebirth." Doctoral dissertation, University of California at Los Angeles, 1967.

SANTA CLARA, UNIVERSITY OF

159 McKevitt, Gerald. "History of Santa Clara College; A Study of Jesuit Education in California, 1851-1912." Doctoral dissertation, University of California at Los Angeles, 1972.

SCRIPPS COLLEGE

160 Scripps College. *The Humanities at Scripps, 1927-1952.* Los Angeles: Ritchie, 1952.

SCRIPPS INSTITUTION OF OCEANOGRAPHY

161 Raitt, Helen, and Moulton, Beatrice. *Scripps Institution of Oceanography.* Los Angeles: Ritchie, 1967.

SONOMA STATE COLLEGE

162 Lipman, Robert S. *Sonoma State College, 1960-1970: The First Decade.* Rohnert Park: Sonoma State College, 1970.

CALIFORNIA 21

SOUTHERN CALIFORNIA, UNIVERSITY OF

163 Servin, Manuel P., and Wilson, Iris H. Southern California and Its University: A History of USC, 1880-1964. Los Angeles: Ritchie, 1969.

164 Gaw, Allison. A Sketch of the Development of Graduate Work in the University of Southern California, 1910-1953. Los Angeles: University of Southern California Press, 1935.

165 Gay, Leslie F. "Founding of the University of Southern California." Southern California Historical Society Publication No.8, Pts.1 & 2 (1911): 37-50.

166 Hungerford, Curtiss Randall. "A Study in University Administrative Leadership: Rufus B. Kleinsmid and the University of Southern California, 1921 to 1935." Doctoral dissertation, University of Southern California, 1967.

167 Hunt, Rockwell Dennis. The First Half-Century; University of Southern California. Los Angeles: University of Southern California Press, 1930.

168 Levitt, Leon. "A History to 1953 of the School of Education of the University of Southern California." Doctoral dissertation, University of Southern California, 1970.

STANFORD UNIVERSITY

169 Mirrielees, Edith R. Stanford: The Story of a University. New York: Putnam, 1959.

170 Bronson, Alice Oakes. Clark W. Hetherington (1870-1942), Scientist and Philosopher. Salt Lake City: n.p., 1958. [Hetherington was Professor of Physical Education.]

171 Burns, Edward M. David Starr Jordan, Prophet of Freedom. Stanford: Stanford University Press, 1953. [Jordan was First President.]

172 Clark, George Thomas. Leland Stanford, War Governor of California, Railroad Builder and Founder of Stanford University. Stanford: Stanford University Press, 1931.

173 Clark, George Thomas. Stanford University History. Stanford: Stanford University Press, 1931.

174 Clausen, Henry C. Stanford's Judge Crothers. San Francisco: George E. Crothers Trust, 1967.

175 Elliott, Ellen Coit. *It Happened This Way: American Scene*. Stanford: Stanford University Press, 1940.

176 Elliott, Orrin L. *Stanford University: The First Twenty-Five Years*. Stanford: Stanford University Press, 1937.

177 Fairclough, Henry Rushton. *Warming Both Hands: The Autobiography of Henry Rushton Fairclough*. Stanford: Stanford University Press, 1941. [Author was Professor of Latin and Greek, 1893-1927.]

178 Griggs, Edward Howard. *The Story of an Itinerant Teacher*. Indianapolis: Bobbs-Merrill, 1934. [Author was Professor of Ethics and Education, 1893-1898.]

179 Guerard, A. *Personal Equation*. New York: Norton, 1948. [Author was Professor of Literature.]

180 Henderson, Adin D. "The Life of Elwood Paterson Cubberley." Doctoral dissertation, Stanford University, 1953. [Cubberley was first Dean, College of Education.]

181 Hoyt, Edwin P. *Leland Stanford*. New York: Abelard Schuman, 1968.

182 Jordan, David Starr. *The Days of a Man...* 2 vols. Yonkers-on-Hudson: World Book Co., 1922.

183 Kimball, Alice Windsor. *The First Year at Stanford: Sketches of Pioneer Days at Leland Stanford, Jr. University*. San Francisco: S. Taylor Co., 1905.

184 McDonald, Emanuel B. *Sam McDonald's Farm: Stanford Reminiscences by Emanuel B. "Sam" McDonald*. Stanford: Stanford University Press, 1954.

185 Mirrielees, Edith R., and Zelver, Patricia F., eds. *Stanford Mosaic*. Stanford: Stanford University Press, 1962.

186 Mitchell, John P. *Stanford University, 1916-1941*. Stanford: Stanford University Press, 1958.

187 Mohr, James C. "Academic Turmoil and Public Opinion: The Ross Case (1900) at Stanford." *Pacific Historical Review* 39 (1970):39-61.

188 Sears, Jesse B. *Jesse Brundage Sears, An Autobiography*. Palo Alto: Stanford University Press, 1959. [Author was Professor of Education.]

189 Sears, Jesse B., and Herderson, A.D. *Cubberley of Stanford and His Contribution to American Education*. Stanford: Stanford University Press, 1957.

CALIFORNIA

190 Starr, Kevin. *California and the American Dream*. New York: Oxford University Press, 1973.

191 Stavely, Martha Rowena. "A History of Stanford's Program in Education for Women during the Last Fifty Years." Doctoral dissertation, Stanford University, 1945.

192 Taylor, Katherine Ames. *The Story of Stanford*. San Francisco: H.S. Crocker Co., 1935.

193 Weinberg, Julius. *Edward Alsworth Ross and the Sociology of Progressivism*. Madison: State Historical Society of Wisconsin, 1972. [Ross was Professor of Economics.]

WEST LOS ANGELES COLLEGE

194 Horn, Larry. "History of West Los Angeles College." Doctoral dissertation, University of Southern California, 1971.

WHITTIER COLLEGE

195 Cooper, Charles W. *Whittier: Independent College in California*. Los Angeles: Ritchie, 1967.

196 Feeler, William Henry. "History of Whittier College." Master's thesis, University of Southern California, 1919.

197 Harris, Herbert Eugene. *The Quaker and the West: The First Sixty Years of Whittier College*. Whittier: n.p., 1948.

198 Wright, D. Sands. "Whittier College Days." *Palimpsest* 10 (1929): 421-432.

Colorado

GENERAL REFERENCES

199 McGiffert, Michael. The Higher Learning in Colorado, an Historical Study, 1860-1940. Denver: Sage Books, 1964.

200 Gerber, Daniel R. "The Public Junior College Movement in Colorado: A History 1920-1967." Doctoral dissertation, University of Denver, 1969.

201 Hafen, LeRoy, ed. Colorado and Its People. New York: Lewis, 1948.

202 LeRossignol, James E. History of Higher Education in Colorado. Washington, D.C.: U.S. Bureau of Education, 1903.

INSTITUTIONAL HISTORIES

ADAMS STATE COLLEGE

203 Cottle, Thomas J. "Run to Freedom: Chicanos and Higher Education." Change 4 (1972): 34-41.

COLORADO COLLEGE

204 Hershey, Charlie Brown. Colorado College, 1874-1949. Colorado Springs: Colorado College, 1952.

COLORADO STATE UNIVERSITY

205 Hartman, William F. "The History of Colorado State College of Education--the Normal School Period--1890-1911." Doctoral dissertation, Colorado State University, 1939.

COLORADO, UNIVERSITY OF

206 Davis, William Eugene. Glory Colorado! A History of the University of Colorado, 1858-1963. Boulder: Pruett Press, 1965.

207 Baker, James Hutchins. Of Himself and Other Things. Denver: Bradford-Robinson, 1922. [Author was President, 1892-1914.]

208 Darley, Ward. The University of Colorado, Eighty Years! 1876-1956. New York: Newcomen Society in North America, 1956.

209 Davis, William Eugene. "A History of the University of Colorado, 1861-1963." Doctoral dissertation, University of Colorado, 1963.

210 Mandel, Siegfried, and Shipley, Margaret. Proud Past--Bright Future; A History of the College of Engineering at the University of Colorado, 1893-1966. Boulder: University of Colorado College of Engineering, 1966.

211 Mumey, Nolie. Joseph Addison Sewall, 1830-1917; Pioneer Physician, Educator and the First President of the University of Colorado. Denver: Old West, 1965.

212 Riddles, Willard P. "The Doctoral Program in Education at the University of Colorado, 1941-1956." Doctoral dissertation, University of Colorado, 1960.

213 Sewall, Jane. Jane, Dear Child. Boulder: University of Colorado Press, 1957.

DENVER, UNIVERSITY OF

214 Angel, Donald Earl. "A History of the University of Denver, 1880-1900." Master's thesis, University of Denver, 1961.

215 Connor, Donald B. "The University of Denver: The Butchtel Chancellorship, 1900-1920." Master's thesis, University of Denver, 1961.

216 Datz, Terry, ed. Woodstock West: Fine Days of Freedom. Littleton: Matchless, 1970.

217 Denver, University of. Information in Support of the Candidacy of the University of Denver for a Chapter of Phi Beta Kappa. Denver: University of Denver, 1930.

218 Dunleavy, Jeannette Joan. "Early History of Colorado Seminary and the University of Denver." Master's thesis, University of Denver, 1935.

219 Harrop, Arthur Henry. <u>The Story of Ammi Bradford Hyde</u>.
Cincinnati: Jennings and Graham, 1912.

220 Holland, Ralph. "A Study of Objectives, Faculty, and Curriculum of the College of Arts and Science at the University of Denver." Doctoral dissertation, University of Denver, 1970.

221 Kelsey, Harry E. <u>Frontier Capitalist; The Life of John Evans</u>.
Denver: State Historical Society of Colorado, 1969. [Evans was Founder.]

222 Knittel, Bernard J. "John Evans, Speaker and Empire Builder." Doctoral dissertation, University of Denver, 1950.

223 Mayer, Gerard Eugene. "A History of the University of Denver, 1920-1940." Master's thesis, University of Denver, 1963.

224 Norland, Jim. <u>The Summit of a Century; A Pictorial History of University of Denver, 1864-1964</u>. Denver: University of Denver, 1963.

225 Porter, R. Russell. <u>The University of Denver Centennial; Its Philosophy, Preparation, Presentation</u>. Denver: Big Mountain Press, 1965.

TEMPLE BUELL COLLEGE

226 Farrell, Harry C. "Temple Junior College, Its Founding, Growth, and Development, 1926-1964." Doctoral dissertation, Colorado State University, 1965.

TRINIDAD STATE JUNIOR COLLEGE

227 Ross, William R. "The History of the Trinidad State Junior College from 1869 to 1939." Doctoral dissertation, Colorado State University, 1939.

UNITED STATES AIR FORCE ACADEMY

228 Miller, Ed Mack. <u>Wild Blue U</u>. New York: Macmillan, 1972.

229 Miller, Edward. "The Founding of the Air Force Academy: An Administrative and Legislative History." Doctoral dissertation, University of Denver, 1970.

230 Shelburne, James C. "Factors Relating to the Establishment of the Air University." Doctoral dissertation, University of Chicago, 1954.

COLORADO

231 Woodyard, William Truman. "A Historical Study of the Development of the Academic Curriculum of the United States Air Force Academy." Doctoral dissertation, University of Denver, 1964.

Connecticut

GENERAL REFERENCES

232 Pratte, Richard N. "A History of Teacher Education in Connecticut from 1639-1939." Doctoral dissertation, University of Connecticut, 1966.

233 Steiner, Bernard. <u>History of Education in Connecticut</u>. Washington, D.C.: U.S. Bureau of Education, 1893.

INSTITUTIONAL HISTORIES

CENTRAL CONNECTICUT STATE COLLEGE

234 Fowler, Herbert E. <u>A Century of Teacher Education in Connecticut: The New Britain Normal School and Teachers College of Connecticut, 1849-1949</u>. New Britain: Central Connecticut State College, 1949.

235 Camp, David N. <u>Recollections of a Long and Active Life</u>. New Britain: Privately Printed, 1917. [Author was Professor and Principal, 1849-1866.]

CONNECTICUT COLLEGE

236 Nye, Irene. <u>Chapters in the History of Connecticut College During the First Three Administrations, 1911-1942</u>. New London: n.p., 1943.

CONNECTICUT

CONNECTICUT, UNIVERSITY OF

237 Stemmons, Walter. *The Connecticut Agricultural College, A History*. Storrs: n.p., 1931.

238 Wyllie, Robert Hugh. "Historical Development of Branches of the University of Connecticut." Doctoral dissertation, University of Connecticut, 1962.

LITCHFIELD LAW SCHOOL

239 Fisher, Samuel H. *The Litchfield Law School, 1775-1833*. Hartford: Tercentenary Commission of the State of Connecticut, 1934.

240 Forgeus, Elizabeth. "Letters Concerning Some Litchfield Law School Notebooks." *Law Library Journal* 32 (1939): 201-205.

241 Kilbourn, Dwight C. "The Litchfield Law School." In *History of the Bench and Bar of Litchfield County, Connecticut*, pp. 179-214. Litchfield: By the Author, 1909.

TRINITY COLLEGE

242 Weaver, Glenn. *The History of Trinity College*. Hartford: Trinity College Press, 1967.

243 Proctor, Charles H. *The Life of James Williams, Better Known as Professor Jim, for Half a Century a Janitor at Trinity College*. Hartford: Trinity College Press, 1873.

UNITED STATES COAST GUARD ACADEMY

244 *The U.S. Coast Guard Academy*. Washington, D.C.: U.S. Government Printing Office, 1939.

WESLEYAN UNIVERSITY

245 Price, Carl Fowler. *Wesleyan's First Century*. Middletown: Wesleyan University, 1932.

246 Dutcher, George M. *An Historical and Critical Survey of the Curriculum of Wesleyan University and Related Subjects.* Middletown: Wesleyan University, 1948.

247 Markle, David H. "Wilbur Fisk, Pioneer Methodist Educator." Doctoral dissertation, Yale University, 1935. [Fisk was First President, 1830-1839.]

YALE UNIVERSITY

248 Kelley, Brooks M. *Yale: A History.* New Haven: Yale University Press, 1974.

249 Bagg, Lyman H. *Four Years at Yale.* New Haven: C.C. Chatfield & Co., 1871. [A full account of student customs and societies. One of the most instructive contemporary portraits of American student life.]

250 Bailey, William B. "A Statistical Study of Yale Graduates, 1701-92." *Yale Review* 16 (1908): 400-426.

251 Bainton, Roland H. *Yale and the Ministry.* New York: Harper, 1957.

252 Brown, Charles Reynolds. *My Own Yesterdays.* New York: Century, 1936. [Author was Dean of Divinity School.]

253 Brubacher, John S. *The Development of the Department of Education at Yale University, 1891-1958.* New Haven: Yale University Press, 1960.

254 Canby, Henry Seidel. *Alma Mater; The Gothic Age of the American College.* New York: Farrar & Rinehart, 1936.

255 Chadwick, G.W. *Horatio Parker.* New Haven: Yale University Press, 1921. [Parker was Professor of Music.]

256 Chittenden, Russell H. *History of the Sheffield Scientific School of Yale University, 1846-1922.* 2 vols. New Haven: Yale University Press, 1928.

257 Cowie, Alexander. *Educational Problems at Yale College in the Eighteenth Century.* New Haven: Yale University Press, 1936.

258 Cross, Wilbur Lucius. *Connecticut Yankee, An Autobiography.* New Haven: Yale University Press, 1943. [Author was Professor of English.]

259 Dexter, Franklin B. *Biographical Sketches of the Graduates of Yale College, with Annals of the College History.* 6 vols. New Haven: Yale University Press, 1912.

CONNECTICUT

260 Dexter, Franklin B., ed. Documented History of Yale University, 1701-45. New Haven: Yale University Press, 1916.

261 Dexter, Franklin B. Sketch of the History of Yale University. New York: Holt, 1887.

262 Dexter, Franklin B. "Student Life at Yale, 1795-1817." American Antiquarian Society Proceedings, n.s. 27 (1917): 318-335.

263 Dwight, Timothy. Memories of Yale Life and Men, 1845-1899. New York: Dodd, Mead, 1903. [Author was President, 1886-1899.]

264 Forgeus, Elizabeth. The History of the Storrs Lectureship in the Yale Law School: The First Three Decades, 1890-1920. New Haven: Yale University Press, 1940.

265 Fulton, J.F., and Thomson, E.H. Benjamin Silliman, 1779-1864: Pathfinder in American Science. New York: Henry Schuman, 1947. [Silliman was Professor of Chemistry and Natural History, 1802-1856.]

266 Furniss, Edgar S. The Graduate School of Yale: A Brief History. New Haven: Yale University Graduate School, 1965.

267 Gabriel, Ralph H. Religion and Learning at Yale; The Church of Christ in the College and University, 1757-1957. New Haven: Yale University Press, 1958.

268 Gilman, Daniel C. Life of James Dwight Dana. New York: Harper & Bros., 1899. [Dana was Professor of Natural History and Geology, 1849-1890.]

269 Grebstein, Sheldon. "The Education of a Rebel: Sinclair Lewis at Yale." New England Quarterly 28 (September 1955): 372-382.

270 Hadley, Morris. Arthur Twining Hadley. New Haven: Yale University Press, 1948. [A.T. Hadley was President, 1899-1921.]

271 Hicks, Frederick C. Yale Law School: The Founders and the Founders' Collection. New Haven: Yale University Press, 1935.

272 Hicks, Frederick C. The Yale Law School, Including the County Court House Period. New Haven: Yale University Press, 1937.

273 Hicks, Frederick C. Yale Law School: From the Founders to Dutton, 1845-1869. New Haven: Yale University Press, 1936.

274 Hicks, Frederick C. The Yale Law School, 1895-1915. New Haven: Yale University Press, 1938.

275 Holden, Reuben A. Yale. New Haven: Yale University Press, 1967.

276 Jackson, Fred. H. "Simeon E. Baldwin and the Clerical Control of Yale." American Historical Review 57 (July 1952): 909-918. [Baldwin was Professor of Law, 1869-1919.]

277 Johnson, James G. "The Yale Divinity School, 1899-1928." Doctoral dissertation, Yale University, 1934.

278 Keller, A.G. Reminiscences of William Graham Sumner. New Haven: Yale University Press, 1933. [Sumner was Professor of Sociology, 1872-1910.]

279 Kingsley, William L. Yale College: A Sketch of Its History. 2 vols. New York: Holt, 1879.

280 Knoff, Gerald E. "The Yale Divinity School, 1858-1899." Doctoral dissertation, Yale University, 1935.

281 Kuslan, Louis I. "The Founding of the Yale School of Applied Chemistry." Journal of the History of Medicine and Allied Sciences 24 (1969): 430-451.

282 Lever, Janet. Women at Yale; Liberating a College Campus. Indianapolis: Bobbs-Merrill, 1971.

283 Lewis, Wilmarth Sheldon. One Man's Education. New York: Knopf, 1967.

284 McKeehan, Louis W. Yale Science: The First Hundred Years, 1701-1801. New York: H. Schuman, 1947.

285 Morgan, Edmund S. "Ezra Stiles: The Education of a Yale Man." Huntington Library Quarterly 17 (1953-1954): 251-268.

286 Morgan, Edmund S. The Gentle Puritan; A Life of Ezra Stiles, 1727-1795. New Haven: Yale University Press, 1962. [Stiles was President, 1777-1795.]

287 Murdock, Kenneth B. "Cotton Mather and the Rectorship of Yale College." Colonial Society of Massachusetts Transactions 25 (1922): 388-402.

288 Nissenbaum, Stephen, ed. The Great Awakening at Yale College. Belmont, Calif.: Wadsworth, 1972.

289 Northrop, Cyrus. "Yale in Its Relation to the Development of the Country." U.S. Bureau of Education Report 2 (1902): 588-594.

290 Notestein, Robert B., Jr. "William G. Sumner." Doctoral dissertation, University of Wisconsin, 1954.

291 Osborne, Elizabeth A., ed. From the Letter Files of Samuel W. Johnson. New Haven: Yale University Press, 1913. [Johnson was Professor of Agricultural Chemistry, 1856-1896.]

CONNECTICUT

292 Oviatt, Edwin. *The Beginnings of Yale, 1701-1726*. New York: Arno Press, 1969.

293 Phelps, William Lyon. *Autobiography*. New York: Oxford University Press, 1939. [Author was Professor of Literature.]

294 Pierson, George W. *Yale College: An Educational History, 1871-1921*. New Haven: Yale University Press, 1952.

295 Pierson, George W. *Yale: The University College, 1921-1937*. New Haven: Yale University Press, 1955.

296 Porter, John A., ed. *Sketches of Yale Life: Being Sketches, Humorous and Descriptive, from College Magazines and Newspapers*. Washington, D.C.: Arlington Publishing Co., 1886.

297 Powell, H.W.H. *Walter Camp, the Father of American Football*. Boston: Little, Brown, 1926.

298 Pratt, Anne S. *Isaac Watts and His Gifts of Books to Yale College*. New Haven: Yale University Press, 1938.

299 Rodes, Harold P. "Educational Factors Affecting the Entrance Requirements of Yale College." Doctoral dissertation, Yale University, 1948.

300 Rukeyser, Muriel. *Willard Gibbs*. New York: Doubleday, 1942. [Gibbs was Professor of Physics, 1871-1903.]

301 Sherman, Charles P. *Academic Adventures: A Law School Professor's Recollections and Observations*. New Haven: Tuttle, Morehouse & Taylor, 1944.

302 Stokes, Anson Phelps. *Memorials of Eminent Yale Men: A Biographical Study of Student Life and University Influences During the Eighteenth and Nineteenth Centuries*. 2 vols. New Haven: Yale University Press, 1914.

303 Totaro, Joseph V. "Curricular Changes in Higher Education: A Case Study of Modern Language Teaching at Nineteenth Century Yale." Doctoral dissertation, Syracuse University, 1957.

304 Tucker, Louis L. *Puritan Protagonist: President Thomas Clap of Yale College*. Chapel Hill: University of North Carolina Press, 1962. [Clap was President, 1739-1766.]

305 Urofsky, Melvin I. "Reforms and Response: The Yale Report of 1828." *History of Education Quarterly* 5 (March 1965): 53-67.

306 Warch, Richard. "Yale College: 1701-1740." Doctoral dissertation, Yale University, 1968.

307 Welch, Lewis Sheldon, and Camp, Walter. *Yale: Her Campus, Class-Rooms, and Athletics*. Boston: L.C. Page & Co., Inc., 1899. [An extended account of all forms of student activity.]

Delaware

GENERAL REFERENCES

308   Powell, Lyman P. <u>History of Education in Delaware</u>. Washington, D.C.: U.S. Government Printing Office, 1893.

309   Powell, Walter A. <u>A History of Delaware</u>. Boston: Christopher, 1928. [Part 2 about higher education.]

INSTITUTIONAL HISTORIES

DELAWARE MILITARY ACADEMY

310   Cooling, B. Franklin, III. "Delaware Military Academy, 1859-1862." <u>Delaware History</u> 14 (1971): 177-187.

DELAWARE STATE COLLEGE

311   Watneck, Walter Joseph. "The History of the Origins and Development of the Delaware State College and Its Role in Higher Education for Negroes in Delaware." Doctoral dissertation, New York University, 1962.

DELAWARE, UNIVERSITY OF

312   Cramton, Willa G., and Moore, Norman W., Jr. "A Forerunner to Delaware College and Its Popular Rejection." <u>Delaware History</u> 12 (1966): 121-146.

313   Ryden, George H. "The Newark Academy of Delaware in Colonial Days." <u>Pennsylvania History</u> 2 (1935): 205-224.

314 Ryden, George H. "The Relation of the Newark Academy of Delaware to the Presbyterian Church and to Higher Education in the American Colonies." *Delaware Notes* 9 (1935): 7-42.

District of Columbia

INSTITUTIONAL HISTORIES

AMERICAN UNIVERSITY

315 Osborn, Albert. John Fletcher Hurst. New York: Eaton & Mains, 1905. [Hurst was Founder and First President, 1891-1901.]

CATHOLIC UNIVERSITY OF AMERICA

316 Ellis, John T. The Formative Years of the Catholic University of America. Washington, D.C.: American Catholic Historical Association, 1946.

317 Ahern, Patrick H. The Catholic University of America, 1887-1896. Washington, D.C.: Catholic University of America Press, 1949.

318 Barry, Colman J. The Catholic University of America 1903-1909: The Rectorship of Denis J. O'Connell. Washington, D.C.: Catholic University of America Press, 1950.

319 Defferrari, Roy Joseph. A Layman in Catholic Education; His Life and Times. Boston: St. Paul Editions, 1966.

320 Defferrari, Roy Joseph. Memoirs of the Catholic University of America. Boston: Daughters of St. Paul, 1962.

321 Dixon, Blase. "The Catholic University of America, 1909-1928: The Rectorship of Thomas Joseph Ryan." Doctoral dissertation, Catholic University of America, 1972.

322 Hogan, Peter Edward. The Catholic University of America, 1896-1903: The Rectorship of Thomas J. Conaty. Washington, D.C.: Catholic University of America Press, 1949.

323 Kuntz, Frank Anthony. <u>Undergraduate Days, 1904-1908; The Catholic University of America</u>. Washington, D.C.: Catholic University of America Press, 1958.

324 Popes. <u>The Popes and the Catholic University of America; A Collection of Papal Statements on the National Pontifical University</u>. Washington, D.C.: Catholic University of America Press, 1959.

325 Ryan, James Augustine. <u>Social Doctrine in Action: A Personal History</u>. New York: Harper, 1941.

326 Ward, J. <u>Thomas Edward Shields: Biologist, Psychologist, Educator</u>. New York: Scribner's, 1947. [Shields was Professor of Psychology, 1902-1921.]

327 Watrin, Rita. <u>The Founding and Development of the Program of Affiliation of the Catholic University of America: 1912 to 1939</u>. Washington, D.C.: Catholic University of America Press, 1966.

328 Will, Allen S. <u>The Life of Cardinal Gibbons, Archbishop of Baltimore</u>. New York: E.P. Dutton, 1922. [Gibbons was Chairman of Board of Trustees from Founding until 1921.]

329 Willis, H. Warren. "The Reorganization of the Catholic University of America During the Rectorship of James H. Ryan, 1928-1935." Doctoral dissertation, Catholic University of America, 1972.

COLUMBIAN INSTITUTION

330 Rathbun, Richard. <u>The Columbian Institution of Washington, D.C., 1816-38</u>. Washington, D.C.: U.S. Government Printing Office, 1917.

FEDERAL CITY COLLEGE

331 Dunham, E. Alden. <u>Colleges of the Forgotten Americans</u>. New York: McGraw-Hill, 1969.

332 Miller, Stephen S. "The Emergence of Comprehensive Public Higher Education in the District of Columbia: The Establishment of Federal City College." Doctoral dissertation, Catholic University of America, 1970.

GALLAUDET COLLEGE

333 Atwood, Albert William. <u>Gallaudet College, Its First One Hundred Years</u>. Lancaster, Pa.: Intelligencer, 1964.

DISTRICT OF COLUMBIA

334 Alpha Sigma Pi. *Gallaudet College, Washington, D.C.--Historical Sketches of Gallaudet College.* Washington, D.C.: Gallaudet College Press, 1953.

335 Boatner, Maxine T. *Voice of the Deaf: A Biography of Edward Miner Gallaudet.* Washington, D.C.: Public Affairs Press, 1959.

336 Gallaudet College Alumni Association, Centennial Souvenir Book Committee. *Our Heritage, Gallaudet College Centennial.* Washington, D.C.: Graphic Arts Press, 1964.

337 Kowsky, Frank. *The Nineteenth Century Buildings on the Campus of Gallaudet College, Washington, D.C.* Buffalo: State University of New York, 1970.

338 Stickney, William, ed. *The Autobiography of Amos Kendall.* Boston: Lee and Shepard, 1872. [Kendall was Sponsor.]

GEORGE WASHINGTON UNIVERSITY

339 Kayser, Elmer L. *Bricks Without Straw: The Evolution of George Washington University.* New York: Appleton-Century-Crofts, 1971.

340 Wiley, Harvey Washington. *An Autobiography.* Indianapolis: Bobbs-Merrill, 1930. [Author was Professor of Chemistry.]

GEORGETOWN UNIVERSITY

341 Durkin, Joseph T. *Georgetown University: First in the Nation's Capital.* Garden City: Doubleday, 1964.

342 Daley, John M. *Georgetown University: Origin and Early Years.* Washington, D.C.: Georgetown University Press, 1957.

343 Durkin, Joseph T. *Georgetown University: The Middle Years: 1840-1900.* Washington, D.C.: Georgetown University Press, 1963.

344 Easby-Smith, James S. *Georgetown University in the District of Columbia.* New York: Lewis, 1907.

345 Friant, John R., et al. *Glimpses of Old Georgetown, Presented by John R. Friant, Thomas A. Rover and Edwin M. Dahill, Jr., of the Class of 1941, to the Alumni.* Washington, D.C.: Undergraduate History Department of Georgetown University, 1939.

346 Guilday, Peter K. *Life and Times of John Carroll, Archbishop of Baltimore (1735-1815)*. New York: Encyclopedia Press, 1922. [Carroll was a Founder.]

347 McLaughlin, J. Fairfax. *College Days at Georgetown*. Philadelphia: J. B. Lippincott, 1899.

348 Purcell, Richard J. "Judge William Gaston: Georgetown University's First Student." *Georgetown Law Journal* 27 (1939): 839-883.

349 Shea, John Gilmary. *Memorial of the First Centenary of Georgetown College, D.C., Comprising a History of Georgetown University*. New York: P.F. Collier, 1891.

350 Smith, James S. *Georgetown University in the District of Columbia, 1789-1907*. 2 vols. New York: n.p., 1907.

351 Tondorf, Francis A. *Biography and Bibliography of George M. Kober*. Washington, D.C., 1920. [Kober was Dean of Medical School, 1901-1928.]

HOWARD UNIVERSITY

352 Logan, Rayford W. *Howard University--The First One Hundred Years, 1867-1967*. New York: New York University Press, 1968.

353 Dyson, Walter. *Founding the School of Medicine at Howard University, 1868-73*. Washington, D.C.: Howard University Press, 1930.

354 Dyson, Walter. *Howard University: The Capstone of Negro Education*. Clifton, N.J.: Kelly, 1973.

355 Holmes, Dwight O. "50 Years of Howard University." *Journal of Negro History* 3 (1918): 128-138; 368-380.

356 McFeely, William S. *Yankee Stepfather: General O.O. Howard and the Freedmen*. New Haven: Yale University Press, 1968. [Howard was Founder and First President, 1869-1873.]

357 Meier, August. "The Racial and Educational Philosophy of Kelly Miller." *Journal of Negro Education* 29 (1960): 121-127. [Miller was Dean.]

PROVIDENCE HOSPITAL SCHOOL OF NURSING

358 Voss, Sister Rita. *The History of the Providence Hospital School of Nursing, Washington, D.C.* Washington, D.C.: Catholic University of America Press, 1940.

DISTRICT OF COLUMBIA

TRINITY COLLEGE

359 Butler, Mary Patricia. *An Historical Sketch of Trinity College, Washington, D.C. 1897-1925. By a Sister of Notre Dame*. Baltimore: Read Taylor Co., 1926.

Florida

GENERAL REFERENCES

360 Adams, Alfred Hugh. "A History of Public Higher Education in Florida: 1821-1961." Doctoral dissertation, Florida State University, 1962.

361 Dovell, Junius D. *Florida: Historic, Dramatic, Contemporary*. New York: Lewis, 1952.

362 Goulding, Robert L. "The Development of Teacher Training in Florida." Doctoral dissertation, George Peabody University, 1933.

363 Hale, Morris Smith, Jr. "A History of Florida Junior Colleges." Doctoral dissertation, George Peabody University, 1966.

364 Rhodes, Francis A. "The Legal Development of State Supported Higher Education in Florida." Doctoral dissertation, University of Florida, 1949.

INSTITUTIONAL HISTORIES

BETHUNE-COOKMAN COLLEGE

365 Peare, Catherine O. *Mary McLeod Bethune*. New York: Vanguard Press, 1951. [Bethune was Founder.]

FLORIDA AGRICULTURAL AND MECHANICAL UNIVERSITY

366 Spellman, Cecil L. *Rough Steps on My Stairway: The Life History of a Negro Educator*. New York: Exposition Press, 1953.

FLORIDA

FLORIDA PRESBYTERIAN COLLEGE

367 Weirman, Billy O., and Jacobson, John H. "Florida Presbyterian College: The First Ten Years." Educational Record 52 (1971): 81-86.

FLORIDA STATE UNIVERSITY

368 Campbell, Doak Sheridan. A University in Transition. Florida State College for Women and Florida State University, 1941-1957. Tallahassee: Florida State University, 1964.

369 Dodd, William George. Florida State College for Women, Notes on the Formative Years (1905-1920)--With a "Postscript: The Twenties; The Thirties"; and "Epilogue: The Forties 1940-1944". Tallahassee: n.p., 1958-1959.

370 Dodd, William George. West Florida Seminary, 1857-1901; Florida State College, 1901-1905. Tallahassee: n.p., 1952.

FLORIDA, UNIVERSITY OF

371 Cobb, Arthur. Go Gators! Official History, University of Florida Football, 1889-1967. Pensacola: Sunshine, 1967.

372 Crow, C.L. "Florida University, 1883." Florida Historical Quarterly 15 (1936): 96-112.

373 Proctor, Samuel. "The University of Florida: Its Early Years, 1853-1906." Doctoral dissertation, University of Florida, 1956.

JACKSONVILLE UNIVERSITY

374 Bald, Ralph D., Jr. A History of Jacksonville University: The First Twenty-Five Years, 1934-1959. Jacksonville: Ambrose, 1959.

ROLLINS COLLEGE

375 Hanna, Alfred Jackson. The Founding of Rollins College. Winter Park: Rollins College, 1935.

STETSON UNIVERSITY

   376 Hubbard, Elbert. <u>A Little Journey to the Home of John Batterson Stetson</u>. East Aurora, N.Y.: Roycrofters, 1911.

   377 Suhrie, Ambrose Leo. <u>Teacher of Teachers</u>. Rindge, N.H.: R.R. Smith, 1955.

Georgia

GENERAL REFERENCES

378 Bassett, Victor H. "A Georgia Medical Student in the Year 1800." Georgia Historical Quarterly 22 (1938): 331-368.

379 Cook, James, Jr. "Politics and Education in the Talmadge Era: The Controversy of the University System of Georgia, 1941/42." Doctoral dissertation, University of Georgia, 1972.

380 Cooper, Walter. The Story of Georgia. New York: American Historical Society, 1938.

381 Hicky, Louise M. "Georgia College Students, 1819-1845." Georgia Review 6 (Fall 1953): 319-330.

382 Krafka, Joseph. "One Hundred Years of Medical Education in Georgia." Association of American Medical Colleges Journal 14 (1939): 368-374.

383 Levy, John W. "Relations Between Social Changes and Curricular Trends in Georgia's Four Year State Colleges, 1948-1968." Doctoral dissertation, University of Georgia, 1970.

384 McCaul, Robert L., Jr. "A Documentary History of Education in Colonial Georgia." Doctoral dissertation, University of Chicago, 1954.

385 McCaul, Robert L., Jr. "Whitefield's Bethesda College Project and Other Attempts to Found Colonial Colleges." Georgia Historical Quarterly 44 (1960): 263-277 and 381-398.

386 Mathews, Forrest D. "The Politics of Education in the Deep South: Georgia and Alabama, 1830-1860." Doctoral dissertation, Columbia University, 1965.

387 Morgan, John William. *The Origin and Distribution of the Graduates of the Negro Colleges of Georgia.* Milledgeville: Privately Printed, 1940.

388 Ness, George T., Jr. "Georgia's Early Graduates of West Point." *Georgia Historical Quarterly* 28 (1944): 80-92.

389 Range, Willard. *The Rise and Progress of Negro Colleges in Georgia, 1865-1949.* Athens: University of Georgia Press, 1951.

390 Satterfield, Virginia. "College Libraries in Georgia." *Georgia Historical Quarterly* 25 (1941): 16-38.

INSTITUTIONAL HISTORIES

AGNES SCOTT COLLEGE

391 Agnes Scott College. *Quarto Centennial Celebration.* 3 vols. Decatur: Agnes Scott College, 1914.

ALBANY STATE COLLEGE

392 Holley, Joseph Winthrop. *You Can't Build a Chimney from the Top; The South Through the Life of a Negro Educator.* New York: William-Frederick Press, 1948.

ARMSTRONG STATE COLLEGE

393 Ashmore, Henry L. *Hypocrisy in Academia? A Case Study of an AAUP Investigation.* New York: Vantage, 1973.

ATLANTA MEDICAL COLLEGE

394 Calhoun, F. Phinizy. "The Founding and the Early History of the Atlanta Medical College." *Georgia Historical Quarterly* 9 (1925): 34-54.

395 Murphy, Gregory. "The Controversy Between Dr. T.S. Powell and the Faculty of Atlanta Medical College." *Georgia Historical Quarterly* 24 (1940): 336-352.

ATLANTA UNIVERSITY

396 Bacote, Clarence A. *The Story of Atlanta University: A Century of Service 1865-1965.* Atlanta: Atlanta University Press, 1969.

GEORGIA

397 Adams, Myron W. *A History of Atlanta University*. Atlanta: Atlanta University Press, 1930.

398 Summersette, John F. "The Structure of Atlanta University Center." Doctoral dissertation, Stanford University, 1952.

EMORY UNIVERSITY

399 English, Thomas Hopkins. *Emory University, 1915-1965: A Semi-centennial History*. Atlanta: Emory University, 1966.

400 Bullock, Henry M. *A History of Emory University*. Nashville, Tenn.: Parthenon Press, 1936.

GEORGIA INSTITUTE OF TECHNOLOGY

401 Wallace, Robert B., Jr. *Dress Her in White and Gold; A Biography of Georgia Tech and of the Men Who Led Her*. Atlanta: Georgia Tech Foundation, 1969.

402 Brittain, Martin Luther. *The Story of Georgia Tech*. Chapel Hill: University of North Carolina Press, 1948.

GEORGIA, UNIVERSITY OF

403 Brooks, Robert P. *The University of Georgia Under Sixteen Administrations, 1785-1955*. Athens: University of Georgia Press, 1956.

404 Adams, O. Burton. "Yale Influence on the Formation of the University of Georgia." *Georgia Historical Quarterly* 51 (1967): 175-185.

405 Bailes, Sue. "Eugene Talmadge and the Board of Regents Controversy." *Georgia Historical Quarterly* 53 (1969): 409-423.

406 Burks, John Bascom. "The College of Education, University of Georgia, and the Development of Teacher Education, 1908-1958." Doctoral dissertation, University of Georgia Press, 1959.

407 Coulter, Ellis Merton. "The Birth of a University, a Town, and a County." *Georgia Historical Quarterly* 46 (June 1962): 113-150.

408 Coulter, Ellis Merton. *College Life in the Old South.* 2d ed. Athens: University of Georgia Press, 1951.

409 Coulter, Ellis Merton. "Franklin College as a Name for the University of Georgia." *Georgia Historical Quarterly* 34 (1950): 189-194.

410 Coulter, Ellis Merton. "Why John and Joseph LeConte Left the University of Georgia, 1855-1856." *Georgia Historical Quarterly* 53 (1969): 18-40.

411 Diener, Thomas J. "A Junior College Idea at the University of Georgia in 1857." *Georgia Historical Quarterly* 56 (1972): 83-91.

412 Flanders, Bertram Holland. *A New Frontier in Education: The Story of the Atlanta Division, University of Georgia.* Atlanta: Atlanta Division, University of Georgia, 1955.

413 Goodrich, William H. *History of the Medical Department of the University of Georgia.* Augusta: Ridgely-Tidwell Co., 1928.

414 Hargrell, Lester. "Student Life at the University of Georgia in the 1840's." *Georgia Historical Quarterly* 9 (1924): 49-59.

415 Jacobs, Dr. Joseph. *Andrew Adgate Lipscomb, Chancellor of the University of Georgia, 1860-1874.* Athens: University of Georgia Press, 1929.

416 McClary, Ben H. "The First Professorship of English Literature in the United States." *Georgia Historical Quarterly* 57 (Summer 1973): 274-276.

417 Martin, S. Walter. "Contributions of the University of Georgia to Higher Education in Florida During the Nineteenth Century." *Georgia Historical Quarterly* 37 (1953): 265-277.

418 Mathis, G. Ray. "Correspondence Concerning Chancellor (William E.) Boggs' Decision to Leave the University of Georgia." *Georgia Historical Quarterly* 54 (1970): 419-428.

419 Mathis, G. Ray. "Walter B. Hill: Chancellor, University of Georgia, 1899-1905." Doctoral dissertation, University of Georgia, 1967.

420 Reed, Thomas Walter. *David Crenshaw Barrow (1852-1929).* Athens: By the Author, 1935.

421 Russell, Richard B. "The Legal History of the University of Georgia." *Georgia Bar Association Proceedings* 44 (1938): 256-309.

GEORGIA

422 Stephenson, Wendell H. "Ulrich B. Phillips: The University of Georgia and the Georgia Historical Society." Georgia Historical Quarterly 41 (1957): 103-125.

423 Townsend, Sara Bertha. "The Admission of Women to the University of Georgia." Georgia Historical Quarterly 43 (1959): 156-169.

424 Tuck, Henry C. Four Years at the University of Georgia, 1877-1875. Athens: Privately Printed, 1937.

LA GRANGE COLLEGE

425 Birdson, Irene B. "The History of LaGrange College." Master's thesis, University of Georgia, 1955.

426 Watts, Charles. "Student Days at Old LaGrange, 1844-45." Alabama Review 24 (1971): 63-76.

MERCER UNIVERSITY

427 Dowell, Spright. A History of Mercer University, 1833-1953. Macon: Mercer University, 1958.

428 Dagg, John Leadley. Autobiography... Rome: J.F. Shanklin, 1886. [Dagg was President, 1844-1856.]

MOREHOUSE COLLEGE

429 Brawley, Benjamin G. History of Morehouse College. Atlanta: Morehouse College, 1917.

430 Keeton, Morris, and Hilberry, Conrad. Struggle and Promise: A Future for Colleges. New York: McGraw-Hill, 1969, pp. 369-392.

431 Mays, Benjamin. Born to Rebel. New York: Scribner's, 1971. [Author was President.]

432 Torrence, R. The Story of John Hope. New York: Macmillan, 1948. [Hope was President, 1906-1929.]

MORRIS BROWN COLLEGE

433 Ponton, Mungo Melanchthon. Life and Times of Henry M. Turner. Atlanta: A.B. Caldwell, 1917. [Turner was Chancellor.]

OGLETHORPE UNIVERSITY

434 Tankersley, Allen P. <u>College Life at Old Oglethorpe</u>. Athens: University of Georgia Press, 1951.

435 Jacobs, Thornwell. <u>Step Down, Dr. Jacobs</u>. Atlanta: Westminister, 1945. [Author was President, 1915-1945.]

436 Thompson, William S. "Oglethorpe University, 1869-1875." <u>Atlanta History Bulletin</u> 2 (1937): 36 ff.

PAINE COLLEGE

437 Clary, George E. "The Founding of Paine College--A Unique Venture in Interracial Cooperation in the New South." Doctoral dissertation, University of Georgia, 1964.

438 Johnson, Alandus C. "The Growth of Paine College (Augusta, Georgia): A Successful Interracial Venture, 1903-1946." Doctoral dissertation, University of Georgia, 1970.

PIEDMONT COLLEGE

439 Rountree, George Wilburn. "Piedmont College: Its History, Resources, and Programs." Doctoral dissertation, University of Georgia, 1965.

SHORTER COLLEGE

440 Gardner, Robert G. <u>On the Hill: The Story of Shorter College</u>. Kingsport, Tenn.: Kingsport Press, 1972.

441 Sheppard, Lydia Dixon. "The History of Shorter College." Master's thesis, Emory University, 1941.

SPELMAN COLLEGE

442 Read, F.M. <u>The Story of Spelman College</u>. Atlanta: n.p., 1961.

TIFT COLLEGE

443 Stone, Eugenia Wootton. <u>Yesterday at Tift</u>. Doraville: Foote & Davies, 1969.

GEORGIA

VALDOSTA STATE COLLEGE

   444 Hambrick, Thera. "VSC: The First Fifty Years." Unpublished manuscript, 1961.

WEST GEORGIA COLLEGE

   445 English, Mildred E. College in the Country; A Program of Education for Adults. Athens: University of Georgia Press, 1959.

Hawaii

INSTITUTIONAL HISTORIES

HAWAII, UNIVERSITY OF

446   Nickerson, Thomas. <u>The University of Hawaii: 1907-1957, Higher Education in the Pacific</u>. Honolulu: University of Hawaii, 1957.

447   Dean, Arthur. <u>Historical Sketch of the University of Hawaii</u>. Honolulu: University of Hawaii, 1927.

448   Kittelson, David. "The History of the College of Hawaii." Master's thesis, University of Hawaii, 1966.

449   Smedley, Margaret A. "A History of the East-West Cultural and Technical Interchange Center Between 1960 and 1966." Doctoral dissertation, Catholic University of America, 1970.

Idaho

GENERAL REFERENCES

450 Hawley, James, ed. *A History of Idaho*. Chicago: S.J. Clarke, 1920.

451 Young, Virgil Monroe. "The Development of Education in Idaho Territory; 1863-1890." Doctoral dissertation, University of Idaho, 1968.

INSTITUTIONAL HISTORIES

BOISE STATE COLLEGE

452 Chaffee, Eugene B. *Boise College: An Idea Grows*. Boise: Syms-York, 1970.

453 Keener, Keith. "History of Boise Junior College, 1913 to 1941." Seminar paper, Boise State College, 1962.

IDAHO STATE UNIVERSITY

454 Beal, Merrill D. *History of Idaho State College*. Pocatello: n.p., 1952.

IDAHO, UNIVERSITY OF

455 Gibbs, Rafe. *Beacon for Mountain and Plain*. Moscow: University of Idaho, 1962.

RICKS COLLEGE

    456 Anderson, John M. "The Development of a Community Music Program Through the Cooperation of Ricks College and the People of Upper Snake River Valley, Idaho." Doctoral dissertation, Columbia University Teachers College, 1953.

Illinois

GENERAL REFERENCES

457 "Early History of Education in Illinois--The Three Oldest Colleges: Illinois College; McKendree College; Shurtleff College." In <u>Blue Book of the State of Illinois</u>, pp. 301-334. Springfield: n.p., 1929.

458 Hamilton, Hallie J. "The Role of the Weekly Press in the Proliferation of Colleges in Illinois 1830-60." Doctoral dissertation, University of Indiana, 1969.

459 Hildner, Ernest G. "Colleges and College Life in Illinois One Hundred Years Ago." <u>Illinois History and Transactions</u> (1942): 19-31.

460 Hildner, Ernest G. "Higher Education in Transition, 1850-1870." <u>Journal of the Illinois State Historical Society</u> 56 (Spring 1963): 61-73.

461 Smith, Melvin. "The Legal Development of the Illinois Public Junior College--1901-1968." Doctoral dissertation, Indiana University, 1970.

462 Wickiser, Ralph L. "The Development of a Public Education Policy in Illinois 1818-1868." Doctoral dissertation, George Peabody University, 1939.

INSTITUTIONAL HISTORIES

AUGUSTANA COLLEGE

463 Albrecht, Esther A. "Gustav Andreen and the Growth of Augustana College." Master's thesis, University of Illinois, 1950. [Andreen was President, 1901-1935.]

AUGUSTANA HOSPITAL SCHOOL OF NURSING

464 Schjolberg, Amy O. *A History of the Augustana Hospital School of Nursing, 1884-1938.* Chicago: n.p., 1939.

BLACKBURN COLLEGE

465 Rinaker, Thomas. "Gideon Blackburn, the Founder of Blackburn University." *Journal of the Illinois State Historical Society* 17 (1924): 398-410.

BRADLEY UNIVERSITY

466 *Bradley Polytechnic Institute--The First Decade: 1897-1907.* Peoria: Bradley Press, 1908.

467 Carter, Asa. "History of Bradley Polytechnic Institute as a Junior College." Master's thesis, University of Chicago, 1930.

468 Wyckoff, Charles Truman. "Four Decades: A Historical Sketch of Bradley Polytechnic Institute, with Personal Recollections and Impressions; Also Some Miscellany and a Bit of Autobiography." Unpublished. Peoria, 1936.

CANTON COLLEGE

469 Eversole, Mildred. "Canton College--An Early Attempt at Higher Education." *Journal of the Illinois State Historical Society* 34 (1941): 334-343.

CARTHAGE COLLEGE

470 Spielman, W.C. *The Diamond Jubilee History of Carthage College, 1870-1945.* Carthage: Carthage College Historical Society, 1945.

CHICAGO STATE COLLEGE

471 Heffron, Ida C. *Francis Wayland Parker: An Interpretive Biography.* Los Angeles: Deach, 1934.

472 McManis, John T. *Ella Flagg Young and a Half-Century of the Chicago Public Schools.* Chicago: A.C. McClurg, 1916.

473 Tostberg, Robert Eugene. "Educational Ferment in Chicago 1883-1904." Doctoral dissertation, University of Wisconsin, 1960.

ILLINOIS

CHICAGO THEOLOGICAL SEMINARY

474 Taylor, Graham. *Pioneering on Social Frontiers.* Chicago: University of Chicago Press, 1930.

CHICAGO, UNIVERSITY OF

475 Storr, Richard J. *Harper's University: The Beginnings. A History of the University of Chicago.* Chicago: University of Chicago Press, 1966.

476 Conger, George R. "Leonard Z. Koos: His Contribution to American Education During Half a Century." Doctoral dissertation, Florida State University, 1968. [Koos was Professor of Education.]

477 Dard, Harris Jeremiah. *The Life and Works of Herbert Ellsworth Slaught (1861-1937).* Nashville, Tenn.,: George Peabody University, 1948. [Slaught was Professor of Mathematics, 1892-1937.]

478 DePencier, Ida B. *The History of the Laboratory Schools of the University of Chicago, 1896-1965.* Chicago: Quadrangle, 1967.

479 Dorfman, Joseph. *Thorstein Veblen and His America.* New York: Viking, 1935. [Veblen was Professor of Economics, 1891-1906.]

480 Engle, Gale W. "William Rainey Harper's Conceptions of the Structuring of the Functions Performed by Educational Institutions." Doctoral dissertation, Stanford University, 1955. [Harper was First President, 1891-1906.]

481 Fairchild, H.L. "Thomas Chrowder Chamberlin--Teacher, Administrator, Geologist, Philosopher." *Science* 68 (1928): 610.

482 Goodspeed, T.W. *A History of the University of Chicago.* Chicago: University of Chicago Press, 1916.

483 Goodspeed, T.W. *William Rainey Harper, First President of the University of Chicago.* Chicago: University of Chicago Press, 1928.

484 Goodspeed, T.W., ed. *The University of Chicago Biographical Sketches.* 2 vols. Chicago: University of Chicago Press, 1922-1925.

485 Gould, Joseph E. "William Rainey Harper and the University of Chicago." Doctoral dissertation, Syracuse University, 1951.

486 Herbst, Jurgen. "From Moral Philosophy to Sociology: Albion Woodbury Small." *Harvard Educational Review* 29 (1959): 237-244. [Small was Professor of Sociology and Dean, 1892-1924.]

487 Holmgren, Daniel. "Edward W. Bemis, Reformer." Doctoral dissertation, Western Reserve University, 1965. [Remis was Professor of Economics, 1892-1895.]

488 Humphreys, Joseph A. "Changes in Certain Aspects of the College of the University of Chicago Following the Inauguration of the New Plan." Doctoral dissertation, University of Chicago, 1933.

489 Lovett, R.M. *All Our Years*. New York: Viking, 1948. [Author was Professor of English and Dean of Junior Colleges, 1893-1920.]

490 Moulton, William F. *Richard Gree Moulton*. London: Epworth Press, 1926. [R.G. Moulton was Professor of Literature, 1892-1919.]

491 Rodgers, Andrew D. *John Merle Coulter: Missionary in Science*. Princeton: Princeton University Press. [Coulter was Professor of Biology, 1896-1925.]

492 Schlichting, Harry F. "The Nature and Extent of Educational Research in the Laboratory Schools of the University of Chicago, 1903-28." Doctoral dissertation, University of Chicago, 1953.

493 Stagg, Amos A. *Touchdown*. New York: Longmans, Green, 1927. [Author was Football Coach, 1892-1933.]

494 Stevens, David Harrison. "Life and Work of Trevor Arnett (1870-1955)." *Phylon* 16 (1955): 127-140. [Arnett was Vice-President, 1899-1926.]

495 Stumph, Wipperte A. "A Comparative Study of Certain Aspects of the Old and the New Plan at the University of Chicago." Doctoral dissertation, University of Chicago, 1942.

496 Talbot, Marion. *More Than Lore*. Chicago: University of Chicago Press, 1936. [Author was Professor of Home Economics and Dean of Women, 1892-1925.]

497 Wallace, Elizabeth. *The Unending Journey*. Minneapolis: University of Minnesota Press, 1952.

498 Ware, Lowry P. "The Academic Career of William E. Dodd." Doctoral dissertation, University of South Carolina, 1956.

499 Winnik, Herbert. "Science and Morality in Thomas C. Chamberlin." *Journal of Historical Ideas* 31 (1970): 441-456.

500 Wright, Helen. *Explorer of the Universe: A Biography of George Ellery Hale*. New York: E. P. Dutton, 1966. [Hale was Professor of Astronomy, 1892-1905.]

ILLINOIS

501 Zunzer, Robert F. "Robert Maynard Hutchins' Conceptions of the Functions and Structures of Higher Education." Doctoral dissertation, Stanford University, 1952. [Hutchins was President, 1929-1945.]

CONCORDIA TEACHERS COLLEGE

502 Freitag, Alfred J. College with a Cause: A History of Concordia Teachers College. River Forest: Concordia Teachers College, 1964.

EASTERN ILLINOIS UNIVERSITY

503 Coleman, Charles Hubert. Eastern Illinois State College: Fifty Years of Public Service. Charleston: Eastern Illinois University, 1950.

504 McKinney, Isabel. Mr. Lord: The Life and Words of Livingston C. Lord. Urbana: University of Illinois Press, 1937. [Lord was President, 1899-1933.]

ELMHURST COLLEGE

505 Denman, William F. "Elmhurst: Developmental Study of a Church-Related College." Doctoral dissertation, Syracuse University, 1966.

EUREKA COLLEGE

506 Eureka College. A History of Eureka College. St. Louis: Christian Publishing Co., 1894.

GEORGE WILLIAMS COLLEGE

507 Austin, James R. "A History of the Young Men's Christian Association College, Chicago." Unpublished. Chicago, 1915.

508 Fiftieth Anniversary, George Williams College, March 1-2-3, 1940. Chicago: George Williams College, 1940.

ILLINOIS BENEDICTINE COLLEGE

509 Mizera, Peter Francis. Czech Benedictines in America, 1877-1901. Lisle: Center for Slav Culture, St. Procopius College, 1969.

ILLINOIS COLLEGE

510 Rammelkamp, Charles Henry. Illinois College: A Centennial History 1829-1929. New Haven: Yale University Press, 1928. [Author was President, 1905-1932.]

511 Barlow, Merrill M., et al. "Charles Henry Rammelkamp, 1874-1932." Journal of the Illinois State Historical Society 25 (1932): 190-232.

512 Carriel, Mrs. Mary (Turner). The Life of Jonathan Baldwin Turner. Jacksonville: n.p., 1911. [Turner was Professor of Literature, 1833-1847.]

513 Rammelkamp, Charles H. "The Reverberations of the Slavery Conflict in a Pioneer College." Mississippi Valley Historical Review 14 (1928): 447-461.

514 Sturtevant, Julian M. An Autobiography. New York: F.H. Revell Co., 1896. [Author was President, 1844-1876.]

ILLINOIS INSTITUTE OF TECHNOLOGY

515 Peebles, James Clinton. A History of Armour Institute of Technology--Describing the Circumstances of Its Founding in 1896 and Providing a Chronological Narration of Events Until Its Merger in 1940 with Lewis Institute to Form Illinois Institute of Technology. Chicago: n.p., 1956.

ILLINOIS STATE UNIVERSITY

516 Marshall, Helen E. Grandest of Enterprises: Illinois State Normal University, 1857-1957. Normal: Illinois State University, 1956.

517 Cook, John W., and McHugh, James V. A History of the Illinois State Normal University, Normal, Illinois. Normal: Illinois State University, 1882.

518 Evjen, Henry O. "Illinois State University, 1852-1868." Journal of the Illinois State Historical Society 31 (1938): 54-71.

519 Evjen, Henry O. "Scandinavian Students at Illinois State University." Norwegian-American Studies and Records 11 (1940): 17-29.

520 Harper, Charles A. Development of the Teachers College in the United States, with Special Reference to the Illinois State Normal University. Bloomington: McKnight and McKnight, 1935.

521 Hurst, Homer. "Illinois State Normal University and the Public Normal School Movement." Doctoral dissertation, George Peabody University, 1947.

522 Marshall, Helen E. The Eleventh Decade: Illinois State University, 1957-1967. Normal: Illinois State University, 1967.

523 Semi-Centennial History of Illinois State Normal University, 1857-1907. Normal: Illinois State University, 1907.

ILLINOIS, UNIVERSITY OF

524 Solberg, Winton U. The University of Illinois, 1867-1894: An Intellectual and Cultural History. Urbana: University of Illinois Press, 1968.

525 Bevier, Isabel. "Recollections and Impressions of the Beginnings of the Department of Home Economics at the University of Illinois." Journal of Home Economics 32 (1940): 291-297.

526 Dilliard, Irving. "When Woodrow Wilson Was Invited to Head the University of Illinois." Journal of the Illinois State Historical Society 60 (1967): 357-382.

527 Ebert, Roger, ed. An Illini Century; One Hundred Years of Campus Life. Urbana: University of Illinois Press, 1967.

528 Girling, Katherine P. Selim H. Peabody, 1829-1903. Urbana: University of Illinois Press, 1923. [Peabody was President, 1880-1891.]

529 Hatch, Richard A., comp. Some Founding Papers of the University of Illinois. Urbana: University of Illinois Press, 1967.

530 Horner, Harlan. Life and Work of Andrew Sloan Draper. Urbana: University of Illinois Press, 1936. [Draper was President, 1891-1904.]

531 Illinois, University of. Illini Years; A Picture History of the University of Illinois, 1868-1950. Urbana: University of Illinois Press, 1950.

532 Illinois, University of. Library School. Fifty Years of Education for Librarianship. Urbana: University of Illinois Press, 1943.

533 Illinois, University of. *Semi-Centennial History of the University of Illinois.* Urbana: University of Illinois Press, 1918.

534 Johnson, Henry C., Jr., and Johanningmeier, Erwin. *Teachers for the Prairie: The University of Illinois and the Schools, 1868-1945.* Urbana: University of Illinois Press, 1972.

535 Johnson, Ronald M. "Captain of Education: An Intellectual Biography of Andrew S. Draper, 1848-1913." Doctoral dissertation, University of Illinois, 1970.

536 Kersey, Harry A., Jr. *John Milton Gregory and the University of Illinois.* Urbana: University of Illinois Press, 1968. [Gregory was First President, 1867-1880.]

537 Larson, Laurence Marcellus. *The Logbook of a Young Immigrant.* Northfield: Norwegian-American History Association, 1939. [Author was Professor of History, 1907-1935.]

538 Nevins, Allan. *Illinois.* New York: Oxford University Press, 1917.

539 Powell, Burt E. *The Movement for Industrial Education and the Establishment of the University of Illinois, 1840-70.* Urbana: University of Illinois Press, 1918.

540 Rodnitzky, Jerome L. "David Kinley: A Paternal President in the Roaring Twenties." *Journal of the Illinois State Historical Society* 66 (Spring 1973): 5-19.

541 Rodnitzky, Jerome L. "Getting the Ear of the State: A Pioneer University Radio Station in the 1920s." *History of Education Quarterly* 8 (1968): 505-509.

542 Rodnitzky, Jerome L. "A History of Public Relations at University of Illinois, 1904-30." Doctoral dissertation, University of Illinois, 1968.

543 Rodnitzky, Jerome L. "President James and His Campaigns for University of Illinois Funds." *Journal of the Illinois State Historical Society* 63 (1970): 69-90. [James was President, 1904-1920.]

544 Slater, Clarence P. *History of the Land Grant Endowment Fund of the University of Illinois.* Urbana: University of Illinois Press, 1940.

545 Solberg, Winton U. "The Conflict Between Religion and Secularism at the University of Illinois, 1867-1894." *American Quarterly* 18 (1966): 183-199.

ILLINOIS

546 Swanson, Richard A. "Edmund J. James, 1855-1925: A 'Conservative-Progressive' in American Education." Doctoral dissertation, University of Illinois, 1966.

547 Tilton, Leon D. History of Growth and Development of Campus of the University of Illinois. Urbana: University of Illinois Press, 1930.

548 Turner, F.H. "Misconceptions Concerning Early History of the University of Illinois." Illinois State Historical Society Transactions 39 (1932): 63-90.

ILLINOIS WESLEYAN UNIVERSITY

549 Watson, Elmo Scott. The Illinois Wesleyan Story, 1850-1950. Bloomington: Illinois Wesleyan University Press, 1950.

ILLINOIS WOMAN'S COLLEGE

550 Harker, Joseph R. Eventide Memories... Jacksonville: A.B. Press, 1931. [Author was President, 1893-1925.]

JUBILEE COLLEGE

551 Chase, Virginius H. "Jubilee College and Its Founder." Journal of the Illinois State Historical Society 40 (1947): 154-167.

552 Shively, Roma Louise. Jubilee--A Pioneer College. Elmwood: Elmwood Gazette, 1935.

KNOX COLLEGE

553 Calkins, Earnest. They Broke the Prairie. New York: Scribner's, 1937.

554 Askew, Thomas A. "The Liberal Arts College Encounters Intellectual Change: A Comparative Study of Education at Knox and Wheaton Colleges, 1837-1925." Doctoral dissertation, Northwestern University, 1969.

555 Bailey, John W. Knox College, by Whom Founded and Endowed. Chicago: Press & Tribune Printing Office, 1860.

556 Gettleman, Marvin E. "College President on the Prairie: John H. Finley and Knox College in the 1890s." History of Education Quarterly 9 (1969): 129-153. [Finley was President, 1892-1899.]

557 Gettleman, Marvin E. "John H. Finley's Illinois Education." *Journal of the Illinois State Historical Society* 62 (1969): 147-169.

558 Lamb, Wallis E. "George Washington Gale, Theologian and Educator." Doctoral dissertation, Syracuse University, 1949. [Gale was Professor of Philosophy and Trustee, 1837-1861.]

559 Simonds, William Edward. "Newton Bateman (1822-1897) State Superintendent of Public Instruction and President of Knox College." *Illinois State Historical Society Transactions* 42 (1935): 141-184. [Bateman was President, 1874-1892.]

560 Webster, Martha F. *Seventy-Five Significant Years: The Story of Knox College, 1837-1912.* Galesburg: Knox College, 1913.

MC KENDREE COLLEGE

561 Farthing, Paul, and Farthing, Chester, eds. *Philosophian History: Chronicles and Biographies of the Philosophian Literary Society of McKendree College.* Lebanon: Published for the Society, 1911.

MONMOUTH COLLEGE

562 Davenport, Francis Garvin. *Monmouth College; The First Hundred Years, 1853-1953.* Cedar Rapids, Ia.: Torch Press, 1953.

563 Beth, Loren P. "Monmouth Literary Societies." *Journal of the Illinois State Historical Society* 43 (1950): 120-136.

564 Davenport, Francis Garvin. "The Pioneers of Monmouth College." *Journal of the Illinois State Historical Society* 46 (1953): 45-59.

NORTH CENTRAL COLLEGE

565 Roberts, Clarence N. *North Central College: A Century of Liberal Education, 1861-1961.* Naperville: North Central College, 1960.

NORTH PARK COLLEGE

566 Carlson, Leland H. *A History of North Park College, Commemorating the Fiftieth Anniversary, 1891-1941.* Chicago: North Park College, 1941.

ILLINOIS

NORTHERN ILLINOIS UNIVERSITY

567 Hayter, Earl W. Northern Illinois University: A Portrait, 1895-1972. DeKalb: Northern Illinois University Press, 1974.

NORTHWESTERN FEMALE COLLEGE

568 Clark, Dwight F. "A Forgotten Evanston Institution: The Northwestern Female College." Journal of the Illinois State Historical Society 35 (1942): 115-132.

NORTHWESTERN UNIVERSITY

569 Ward, Estelle F. The Story of Northwestern University. New York: Dodd, Mead, 1924.

570 Black, Carl Ellsworth, and Black, Bessie McLaughlin. From Pioneer to Scientist; The Life Story of Greene Vardiman Black (1836-1915) "Father of Modern Dentistry," and His Son, Arthur Davenport Black (1870-1937) Late Dean of Northwestern University Dental School. St. Paul, Minn.: Bruce, 1940.

571 Lynch, Edmund C. "Walter Dill Scott: Pioneer Industrial Psychologist." Business History Review 42 (1968): 149-170. [Scott was Professor of Psychology, 1901-1920; President, 1920-1939.]

572 Porter, Jack N. Student Protest and the Technocratic Society: The Case of R.O.T.C. Milwaukee: Zalonka Publications, 1972.

573 Scott, F.D., ed. A Pictorial History of Northwestern University: 1851-1951. Evanston: Northwestern University Press, 1951.

PRINCIPIA COLLEGE

574 Leonard, Edwin S., Jr. As the Sowing: The First Fifty Years of Principia. St. Louis: n.p., 1951.

QUINCY COLLEGE

575 St. Francis Solanus College; Jubilee; A Keepsake for Alumni, Friends, and Students. Quincy: n.p., 1912.

ROCKFORD COLLEGE

576 Cederborg, Hazel Paris. "History of Rockford College." Master's thesis, Wellesley College, 1926.

577 Sill, G.G. *Memorials of Anna Peck Sill, First Principal at Rockford Female Seminary, 1849-1889.* Rockford: Daily Register Electric Print, 1889.

SHURTLEFF COLLEGE

578 Potter, George M. "Shurtleff College Centennial." *Journal of the Illinois State Historical Society* 20 (1927): 258-264.

SOUTHERN ILLINOIS UNIVERSITY

579 Plochmann, George K. *The Ordeal of Southern Illinois University.* Carbondale: Southern Illinois University, 1959.

580 Beyer, Richard L. "The Southern Illinois College." *Journal of the Illinois State Historical Society* 27 (1934): 330-340.

581 Dukes, E.L. "The Southern Collegiate Institute (1891-1916)." *Journal of the Illinois State Historical Society* 38 (1945): 295-318.

582 Lentz, Eli G. *Seventy-Five Years in Retrospect; From Normal School to Teachers College to University.* Carbondale: University Editorial Board, Southern Illinois University, 1955.

WESTERN ILLINOIS UNIVERSITY

583 Hicken, Victor. *The Purple and the Gold; The Story of Western Illinois University.* Macomb: Western Illinois University Foundation, 1970.

WHEATON COLLEGE

584 Willard, W. Wyeth. *Fire on the Prairie: The Story of Wheaton College.* Wheaton: Van Kamper Press, 1950.

585 Blanchard, Frances C. *Life of Charles A. Blanchard, 1848-1925.* New York: F.H. Revell Co., 1932. [C.A. Blanchard was President, 1886-1915.]

586 Keeton, Morris, and Hilberry, Conrad. *Struggle and Promise: A Future for Colleges*. New York: McGraw-Hill, 1969, pp. 17-50.

Indiana

GENERAL REFERENCES

587 Woodburn, James A. *Higher Education in Indiana.* Washington, D.C.: U.S. Bureau of Education, 1891.

588 Hadley, Murray N. "Medical Educational Institutions in Indiana." *Indiana Magazine of History* 27 (1931): 307-315.

589 Heller, Herbert L. "Negro Education in Indiana from 1816-1869." Doctoral dissertation, Indiana University, 1952.

590 Morgan, Clarence M. "The Development of Teacher Training in Indiana Prior to 1900." Doctoral dissertation, Indiana University, 1936.

591 Parker, Paul E. "The Administration of Privately Controlled Colleges and Universities in Indiana." Doctoral dissertation, University of Arizona, 1949.

592 Rahe, Herbert Edgar. "The History of Speech Education in Ten Indiana Colleges, 1820-1938." Doctoral dissertation, University of Wisconsin, 1939.

593 Zerfas, L.G. "Medical Education in Indiana." *Indiana Magazine of History* 30 (1934): 139-148.

INSTITUTIONAL HISTORIES

BALL STATE UNIVERSITY

594 White, Glen. *The Ball State Story: From Normal Institute to University.* Muncie: Ball State University, 1967.

INDIANA

595 Keeton, Morris, and Hilberry, Conrad. <u>Struggle and Promise: A Future for Colleges</u>. New York: McGraw-Hill, 1969, pp. 351-368.

596 Thompson, Wade H. "Historical Development of Student Personnel Services Administration at Ball State University, 1918-1969." Doctoral dissertation, Indiana University, 1971.

BETHEL COLLEGE

597 Beutler, Albert J. "The Founding and History of Bethel College of Indiana." Doctoral dissertation, Michigan State University, 1970.

BUTLER UNIVERSITY

598 Benton, Allen R. "Early Educational Conditions and Founding of a Denominational College (Northwestern Christian University or Butler College)." <u>Indiana Magazine of History</u> 4 (1908): 13-17.

599 Shaw, Henry K. "The Founding of Butler University, 1847-1855." <u>Indiana Magazine of History</u> 58 (1962): 233-264.

CANTERBURY COLLEGE

600 Beeler, Kent B. "Canterbury (Indiana) College, 1946-1951. Its Decline and Demise." Doctoral dissertation, Indiana University, 1969.

CENTRAL NORMAL COLLEGE

601 Beeler, Kent B., and Chamberlain, Philip. "Give a Buck to Save a College: The Demise of Central Normal College." <u>Indiana Magazine of History</u> 67 (1971): 117-127.

DE PAUW UNIVERSITY

602 Manhart, George Born. <u>DePauw Through the Years</u>. Greencastle: DePauw University, 1962.

603 Eiler, Homer. "At DePauw Fifty Years Ago." <u>Indiana Magazine of History</u> 37 (1941): 57-60.

604 McConnell, Francis J. <u>By the Way: An Autobiography</u>. New York: Abingdon-Cokesbury Press, 1952. [McConnell was President.]

605 Sweet, William W. *Indiana Asbury-DePauw University, 1837-1937.* New York: Abingdon-Cokesbury Press, 1937.

EARLHAM COLLEGE

606 Thornburg, Opal. *Earlham: The Story of the College, 1847-1962.* Richmond: Earlham College, 1963.

607 Cottle, Thomas J. "A Learning Place Called Earlham." *Change* 3 (1971): 52-59.

608 Keeton, Morris, and Hilberry, Conrad. *Struggle and Promise: A Future for Colleges.* New York: McGraw-Hill, 1969, pp. 283-306.

ELEUTHERIAN COLLEGE

609 Thompon, William C. "Eleutherian College." *Indiana Magazine of History* 19 (1923): 109-131.

FRANKLIN COLLEGE OF INDIANA

610 Cady, John Frank. *The Centennial History of Franklin College.* Franklin: n.p., 1934.

611 Franklin College of Indiana, Board of Trustees. *First Half Century of Franklin College, 1834-1884.* Cincinnati: Journal and Messenger, 1884.

GOSHEN COLLEGE

612 Umble, John Sylvanus. *Goshen College, 1894-1954: A Venture in Christian Higher Education.* Goshen: Goshen College, 1955.

HANOVER COLLEGE

613 Millis, William A. *The History of Hanover College from 1827 to 1927.* Hanover: Hanover College, 1927.

614 Fisher, Daniel Webster. *A Human Life...* New York: F.H. Revell Co., 1909. [Author was President, 1879-1907.]

INDIANA

615 Moore, Archibald Y. <u>History of Hanover College</u>. Indianapolis: Hollenbeck Press, 1900.

HARTSVILLE COLLEGE

616 Pentzer, O.W. <u>Hartsville College (Indiana), 1850-1897</u>. Columbua: O.W. Pentzer & Son, 1928.

HUNTINGTON COLLEGE

617 Pfister, J. Ralph. <u>Seventy-Five Years--Where Character and Culture Blend</u>. Huntington: Huntington College, 1972.

INDIANA CENTRAL COLLEGE

618 Vance, Russell E., Jr. <u>Fifty Years of Christian Education</u>. Indianapolis: n.p., 1955.

INDIANA CENTRAL MEDICAL COLLEGE

619 Manhart, George B. "The Indiana Central Medical College 1849-1852." <u>Indiana Magazine of History</u> 56 (1960): 105-122.

INDIANA STATE UNIVERSITY

620 Lynch, William O. <u>A History of Indiana State Teachers College: Indiana State Normal School 1870-1929</u>. Terre Haute: Indiana State Teachers College, 1946.

621 Tirey, Ralph N. <u>Exciting, Exacting, and Expansion Years at Indiana State Teachers College, 1934-1953</u>. Terre Haute: Indiana State Teachers College, 1953.

INDIANA UNIVERSITY

622 Clark, Thomas D. <u>Indiana University: Midwestern Pioneer</u>. Bloomington: Indiana University Press, 1970.

623 Banta, David L. "History of the Indiana University." In <u>Indiana University, 1820-1920</u>, pp. 11-113. Bloomington: Indiana University Press, 1921.

624 Beck, Daisy (Woodward). *Once Over Lightly; An Indiana University Story*. Privately Printed, 1962.

625 Carmony, Donald F., ed. "Family Letters of Andrew Wylie, President of Indiana University." *Indiana Magazine of History* 64 (1968): 289-298. [Wylie was President, 1828-1851.]

626 Dickason, David. "David Starr Jordan as a Literary Man." *Indiana Magazine of History* 38 (December 1941): 345-358. [Jordan was President, 1885-1891.]

627 Elmes, Robert J. "Henry Lester Smith, Dean, School of Education, Indiana University, 1916-1946." Doctoral dissertation, Indiana University, 1969.

628 Gering, William M. "David Starr Jordan, Spokesman for Higher Education in Indiana." Doctoral dissertation, Indiana University, 1963.

629 Henwood, Hilda. "Back in the Days 'When' on the I. U. Campus." *Indiana University Alumni Quarterly* 23 (1936): 18-31 and 133-146. [Campus Life, 1897-1901.]

630 Indiana University. *Indiana University, Its History from 1820, When Founded, to 1890, with Biographical Sketches of Its Presidents, Professors and Graduates, and a List of Its Students from 1820-1887*. Indianapolis: W.B. Burford, 1890.

631 Mackay, Vera A. "Intercultural Education: An Historical Narrative and the Role of the Indiana University." Doctoral dissertation, Indiana University, 1954.

632 Matthews, Alfred T. "The Evolution of Student Participation in Policy Formation at Indiana University." Doctoral dissertation, Indiana University, 1967.

633 Myers, Burton D. "A Study of Faculty Appointments at Indiana University, 1824-1937." *Indiana Magazine of History* 40 (1944): 129-155.

634 Nutt, Cyrus. "A Letter of 1863 from Cyrus Nutt to Evan Pugh." *Indiana Magazine of History* 25 (1929): 306-311. [Nutt, President of Indiana; Pugh, President of Penn State University.]

635 Wells, Herman G. "The Early History of Indiana University as Reflected in the Administration of Andrew Wylie, 1829-1851." *Filson Club* 36 (1962): 113-127.

636 Wylie, Theophilus Adam. *Indiana University*. Indianapolis: Indianapolis Journal Co., 1890.

INDIANA

MANCHESTER COLLEGE

637 Bollinger, Russell V., et al. The First Seventy-Five Years. Elgin, Ill.: Brethren Press, 1964.

MARIAN COLLEGE

638 Whalen, Sister Mary Giles, O.S.F. "Marian College, Indianapolis, Indiana: The First Quarter Century, 1937-1962." Doctoral dissertation, University of Cincinnati, 1965.

NOTRE DAME, UNIVERSITY OF

639 Hope, Arthur J. Notre Dame: One Hundred Years. Notre Dame: University Press, 1943.

640 Egan, Maurice Francis. Recollections of a Happy Life. New York: Doran, 1924. [Author was Professor of English, 1887-1895.]

641 Lyons, Joseph A., comp. Silver Jubilee of the University of Notre Dame, June 23rd, 1869... Chicago: E.B. Myers, 1869.

642 Moore, Philip S. A Century of Law at Notre Dame. Notre Dame: University Press, 1970.

643 Notre Dame, University of. A Brief History of the University of Notre Dame du Lac, Indiana from 1842 to 1892. Chicago: Werner, 1895.

644 Notre Dame, University of. One Hundred Twenty-Fifth Anniversary; University of Notre Dame, 1842-1967. Notre Dame: University Press, 1967.

645 Rockne, Knute K. The Autobiography of Knute K. Rockne. New York: Bobbs-Merrill Co., 1931. [Rockne was Football Coach, 1918-1931.]

646 Sullivan, Richard. Notre Dame. New York: Holt, 1951.

647 Wack, John Theodore. "The University of Notre Dame du Lac: Foundation, 1842-1857." Doctoral dissertation, University of Notre Dame, 1966.

PURDUE UNIVERSITY

648 Hepburn, William. Purdue University--Fifty Years of Progress. Indianapolis: Hollenbeck Press, 1925.

649 Anderson, Kenneth C. "Biography of Emerson White." Doctoral dissertation, Western Reserve University, 1952. [White was President, 1876-1883.]

650 Burrin, Frank Dleiser. "Edward Charles Elliott, Educator." Doctoral dissertation, Purdue University, 1956. [Elliott was President, 1921-1945.]

651 Garman, Harry O. "A Student from a Pioneer Family at Purdue." Indiana Magazine of History 36 (1940): 217-229.

652 Johnston, Thomas R., and Hand, Helen. The Trustees and the Officers of Purdue University, 1865-1940. Lafayette: Purdue University, 1940.

653 Knoll, H.B. A Record of the University in the War Years, 1941-1945. Lafayette: n.p., 1947.

654 Purdue University. Winthrop E. Stone, 1862-1921. Indianapolis: Levey Printing Co., 1922. [Stone was President, 1900-1921.]

655 Wiley, Harvey Washington. An Autobiography. Indianapolis: Bobbs-Merrill, 1930. [Author was Professor of Chemistry, 1874-1883.]

ROSE-HULMAN INSTITUTE OF TECHNOLOGY

656 Bloxsome, John L. Rose: The First One Hundred Years. Terre Haute: Rose-Hulman Institute of Technology, 1973.

SAINT FRANCIS COLLEGE

657 Scheetz, Mary J. "Service Through Scholarship: A History of St. Francis College (Fort Wayne, Indiana)." Doctoral dissertation, University of Michigan, 1970.

SAINT MARY-OF-THE-WOODS COLLEGE

658 Brown, Mary Borromeo. History of the Sisters of Providence of Saint Mary-of-the-Woods. New York: Benziger Bros., 1949.

659 O'Neill, Margaret Agnes. "History of Saint Mary-of-the-Woods College." Master's thesis, Indiana State Teachers College, 1940.

SMITHSON COLLEGE

660 Tidrick, Helen L. "Smithson College Circular." Indiana Magazine of History 53 (1957): 69-88.

INDIANA

TAYLOR UNIVERSITY

661 Ringenberg, William C. *Taylor University: The First One Hundred Twenty-Five Years*. Grand Rapids, Mich.: Eerdmans, 1973.

VALPARAISO UNIVERSITY

662 Strietelmeier, John. *Valparaiso's First Century, a Centennial History of Valparaiso University*. Valparaiso: The University, 1959.

VINCENNES UNIVERSITY

663 Burnett, Howard K. "Early History of Vincennes University." *Indiana Magazine of History* 29 (1933): 114-121.

664 Constantine, Robert. "Minutes of the Board of Trustees for Vincennes University, 1801-1807, 1807-1811, 1812-1824." *Indiana Magazine of History* 54 (1958): 313-364; 55 (1959): 247-294; 57 (1961): 311-368.

665 Mooney, Chase C. "From Old Vincennes, 1815." *Indiana Magazine of History* 57 (1961): 141-155.

WABASH COLLEGE

666 Osborne, James I. *Wabash College, 1832-1932*. Crawfordsville: R.E. Banta, 1932.

667 Lind, L.R. "Early Literary Societies at Wabash College." *Indiana Magazine of History* 42 (1946): 173-176.

Iowa

GENERAL REFERENCES

668 Parker, Leonard. *Higher Education in Iowa*. Washington, D.C.: U.S. Bureau of Education, 1893.

669 Darling, Elmer C. "Curricular Trends in Higher Education in Iowa Since 1900." Doctoral dissertation, Iowa State University, 1935.

670 Hart, Irving H. "State Support of Higher Education in Iowa." *Iowa Journal of History* 55 (1957): 147-167.

671 Macbride, Thomas H. "The Colleges of the Pioneers." *Palimpsest* 16 (1935): 174-188.

672 Peterson, William J. *The Story of Iowa*. New York: Lewis, 1952.

673 Rutland, Robert. "College Football in Iowa." *Palimpsest* 34 (1953): 401-432.

674 Swisher, Jacob A. "The Iowa Academy of Science." *Iowa Journal of History* 29 (1931): 315-374.

675 U.S. Commissioner of Education. *State Higher Educational Institutions in Iowa*. Washington, D.C.: U.S. Bureau of Education, 1916.

INSTITUTIONAL HISTORIES

CENTRAL COLLEGE

676 Thostenson, Josephine E. *One Hundred Years of Service; A History of Central 1853-1953*. Pella: Central College, 1953.

COE COLLEGE

677 Eriksson, Erik M. *Coe Collegiate Institute and Its Founders, 1875-1881.* Cedar Rapids: Coe College, 1930.

COLUMBIA COLLEGE

678 Hoffman, M.M. "The Oldest College in Iowa." *Iowa Catholic Historical Review* 8 (1935): 3-14.

CORNELL COLLEGE

679 King, William F. *Reminiscences.* New York: Abington Press, 1915. [Author was President, 1865-1900.]

DES MOINES UNIVERSITY

680 Clark, Dan E. "John A. Nash and the Early History of Des Moines College." *Iowa Journal of History* 8 (July 1915): 392-415.

681 May, George S. "Des Moines University and Dr. T.T. Shields." *Iowa Journal of History* 54 (1956): 193-232.

DRAKE UNIVERSITY

682 Ritchey, Charles J. *Drake University Through Seventy-Five Years, 1881-1956.* Des Moines: Drake University, 1956.

683 Blanchard, Charles. *History of Drake University.* Des Moines: Drake University, 1931.

684 Herriott, F.I. "Norman Dunshee, Professor of Ancient Languages, Drake University." *Annuals of Iowa,* 3d series, 20 (1936): 163-206, 253-296.

685 Smith, Ferdinand J. "History of the Drake University College of Medicine." *Iowa State Medical Society Journal* 26 (1936): 165-167, 225-227, 271-274, 322-327, 436-438.

DUBUQUE, UNIVERSITY OF

686 Steffens, Cornellius M. *Adventure in Money Raising: An Outline of Presidential Duties and Experiences.* New York: Macmillan, 1930.

GRACELAND COLLEGE

687 Edwards, Paul M. *The Hilltop Where; An Informal History of Graceland College.* Lamoni: Venture Foundation, 1972.

GRINNELL COLLEGE

688 Nollen, John Scholte. *Grinnell College.* Iowa City: State Historical Society of Iowa, 1953.

689 Beatty, Shelton Lee. "A Curricular History of Grinnell College, 1848-1931." Doctoral dissertation, Stanford University, 1955.

690 Gates, Idabel S. *The Life of George Augustus Gates.* Boston: Pilgrim Press, 1915. [Gates was President, 1887-1900.]

691 Noyes, Katherine M., ed. *Jesse Macy, An Autobiography.* Springfield, Ill.: C.C. Thomas, 1933. [Macy was Professor of Political Science, 1895-1912.]

GRISWOLD COLLEGE

692 Chitty, Arthur Ben. "Griswold College, 1859-1897: Davenport, Iowa." *Historical Magazine of the Protestant Episcopal Church* 37 (1968): 73-76.

IOWA COLLEGE

693 Aurner, Clarence R. "The Founding of Iowa College." *Palimpsest* 25 (1944): 65-77.

694 Hill, James L. "Iowa College in the War." *Iowa Historical Record* 15 (1899): 408-419.

695 Parker, Leonard F. "The Founder of Iowa College." *Iowa Historical Record* 14 (1898): 360-375.

IOWA STATE UNIVERSITY OF SCIENCE AND TECHNOLOGY

696 Ross, Earle D. *The Land Grant Idea of Iowa State College: A Centennial Trial Balance, 1858-1958.* Ames: Iowa State College Press, 1958.

697 Collins, Robert M. "History of Agronomy at the Iowa State College." Doctoral dissertation, Iowa State College, 1954.

698 Hilton, Robert T. *Profiles of Iowa State University History*. Ames: Iowa State College Press, 1958.

699 Horack, Frank H. "A Brief History of the Political Science Club of Iowa State University, 1896-1906." *Iowa Journal of History* 5 (1907): 213-233.

700 Iowa State University of Science and Technology. *An Historical Sketch...Published for the Semi-Centennial Celebration, June 6-7, 1920*. Ames: Iowa State College Press, 1920.

701 Ross, Earle D. *A History of the Iowa State College of Agriculture and Mechanic Arts*. Ames: Iowa State College Press, 1942.

IOWA, UNIVERSITY OF

702 Mahan, Bruce E. "University of Iowa." *Palimpsest* 52, No.2 (February 1971), A special issue. Iowa City: State Historical Society, 1971.

703 Bach, M. *Of Faith and Learning*. Iowa City: School of Religion, State University of Iowa, 1952.

704 Barrett, Norbert C. "History of the State University of Iowa, The College of Engineering." Doctoral dissertation, University of Iowa, 1945.

705 Carstensen, Vernon R. "The State University of Iowa: The Collegiate Department from the Beginning to 1878." Doctoral dissertation, Iowa State University, 1935.

706 Carstensen, Vernon R. "The University as Head of the Iowa Public School System." *Iowa Journal of History* 53 (1955): 213-246.

707 Cowperthwaite, Lowery LeRoy. "Forensics at the State University." *Iowa Journal of History* 46 (1948): 266-296.

708 Crary, Ryland W. "History of the State University of Iowa, The Liberal Arts College in the Gilmore and Hancher Administrations." Doctoral dissertation, University of Iowa, 1946.

709 Davies, Frederick G. "History of the State University of Iowa: The College of Liberal Arts 1900-1916." Doctoral dissertation, University of Iowa, 1948.

710 Doty, Franklin A. "History of the State University of Iowa: The College of Liberal Arts 1900-1916." Doctoral dissertation, University of Iowa, 1947.

711 Fogdall, Vergil S. "History of the State University of Iowa: The Governing Boards, 1847-1947." Doctoral dissertation, University of Iowa, 1948.

712 Howard, Donald F. "History of the State University of Iowa, The Graduate College." Doctoral dissertation, University of Iowa, 1947.

713 Iowa, University of. *Centennial Memoirs*. 2 vols. Iowa City: University of Iowa Press, 1947.

714 Johnson, Ellen E. "A History of the State University of Iowa: The Administration of President MacLean." Master's thesis, State University of Iowa, 1946. [MacLean was President, 1899-1911.]

715 Patrick, George T.W. "Founding the Psychological Laboratory of the State University of Iowa: A Historical Sketch." *Iowa Journal of History* 30 (1932): 404-416.

716 Patrick, George T.W. *George Thomas White Patrick: An Autobiography*. Iowa City: University of Iowa Press, 1947. [Author was Professor of Philosophy, 1887-1928.]

717 Pickard, J.L. "Historical Sketch of the State University of Iowa." *Annals of Iowa* 4 (1899): 1-66.

718 Rich, Ellen M. "State University of Iowa and the Civil War." *Iowa Historical Record* 15 (1899): 395-408.

719 Rockwood, Alan C. "A History of the Military Department of the State University of Iowa." *Iowa Journal of History* 21 (1923): 183-321.

720 Smith, Ferdinand J. "The Transition from Franklin Medical School to the Keokuk College of Medicine of the State University of Iowa." *Iowa State Medical Society Journal* 26 (1936): 595-597, 656-662, 707-709.

721 Thornton, Harrison J. "Coeducation at the State University of Iowa." *Iowa Journal of History* 44 (1947): 380-412.

722 Thornton, Harrison J. "Locating the State University of Iowa." *Iowa Journal of History* 47 (1949): 50-62.

723 Thornton, Harrison J. "A State University Is Born." *Palimpsest* 28 (1947): 33-45.

724 Thornton, Harrison J. "The State University of Iowa, and the Civil War." *Annals of Iowa* 30 (1950): 198-209.

725 Wanerus, Theodore H. *A History of the Zetagathian Society of the State University of Iowa*. Iowa City: University of Iowa Press, 1911.

IOWA

726 Westerberg, Virginia May. "A History of the University Elementary School, State University of Iowa, 1915-1958." Doctoral dissertation, State University of Iowa, 1959.

IOWA WESLEYAN COLLEGE

727 Haselmayer, Louis A. History and Alumni Directory of Iowa Wesleyan College, 1842-1967. Mt. Pleasant: Iowa Wesleyan College, 1967.

728 Haselmayer, Louis A. "Das Deutsche Kollegium: Wesleyan's Teutonic Past." Annals of Iowa 35 (Winter 1960): 206-215.

729 Kennedy, Charles J. History and Alumni Record of Iowa Wesleyan College, 1842-1942. Mt. Pleasant: Iowa Wesleyan College, 1942.

730 Wilson, Ben Hur. "Iowa Wesleyan College." Palimpsest 11 (1930): 432-445.

LORAS COLLEGE

731 Hoffmann, Mathias M. The Story of Loras College, 1839-1939; The Oldest College in Iowa. Dubuque: Loras College Press, 1939.

LUTHER COLLEGE

732 Nelson, David T. Luther College, 1861-1961. Decorah: Luther College Press, 1961.

733 Larsen, Karen. Laur, Larsen, Pioneer College President. Northfield, Minn.: Norwegian-American Historical Association, 1936.

734 Luther College Faculty. Luther College Through Sixty Years, 1861-1921. Minneapolis: Augsburg Publishing House, 1922.

735 Nelson, David T. "Luther College." Palimpsest 42 (1961): 321-384.

NORTH IOWA AREA COMMUNITY COLLEGE

736 Carlson, Gretchen. "Mason City Junior College." Palimpsest 11 (1930): 462-470.

NORTHERN IOWA, UNIVERSITY OF

737 Hart, Irving H. The First Seventy-Five Years. Cedar Falls: Iowa State Teachers College, 1951.

738 Comment by the Editor: "Iowa State Normal School." Palimpsest 13 (1932): 1-40.

739 Disque, Ned. "Iowa State College, 1858-1958." Palimpsest 39 (1958): 361-425.

740 Wright, David Sands. Fifty Years at the Teachers College; Personal and Historical Reminiscences. Cedar Falls: Iowa State Teachers College, 1926.

NORTHWESTERN COLLEGE

741 Hubers, Dale. "A History of the Northwestern Classical Academy 1882-1957." Master's thesis, University of South Dakota, 1957.

742 McDonald, Robert L. "The Struggle for Education in Northwest Iowa: University of the Northwest, 1889-1895." American Iowa 39 (1969): 481-496.

PARSONS COLLEGE

743 Koerner, James D. The Parsons College Bubble: A Tale of Higher Education in America. New York: Basic Books, 1971.

744 Hall, John Oliver. Parsons College: Nine Years of Change 1955-1964. Pittsburgh: University of Pittsburgh Press, 1966.

745 Millsap, Kenneth. "Parsons College." Palimpsest 31 (1950): 281-328.

746 Parsons, Willis Edwards. Fifty Years of Parsons College, 1875-1925. Fairfield: Parsons College, 1925.

SIMPSON COLLEGE

747 Jackson, Ruth M. The History of Simpson College, 1860-1910. Unpublished manuscript, n.d.

IOWA

UPPER IOWA COLLEGE

748 Alderson, M.H. *Upper Iowa University*. Iowa City: Iowa Historical Society, 1965.

749 Engel, Robert E. "Non-Sectarianism and the Relationship of the Methodist Church in Iowa to Upper Iowa College and Iowa Wesleyan College." Doctoral dissertation, University of Iowa, 1969.

WARTBURG COLLEGE

750 Ottersberg, Gerhard. *Wartburg College, 1852-1952: A Centennial History*. Waverly: Waverly Publishing Co., 1952.

WESTERN COLLEGE

751 John, Lewis F. *The Life of Ezekial Boring Kephart*. Dayton, Ohio: United Brethren Publishing House, 1907. [Kephart was President, 1868-1881.]

WESTMAR COLLEGE

752 Kempers, Garret. *A History of Westmar College*. Lakeland, Fla.: n.p., 1965.

WHITTIER COLLEGE

753 Hawley, Charles A. "Correspondence Between John Greenlief Whittier and Iowa." *Iowa Journal of History* 35 (1937): 115-141.

WILLIAM PENN COLLEGE

754 Watson, Sheppard Arthur. *Penn College: A Product and a Producer*. Oskaloosa: William Penn College, 1971.

755 Moore, George H. "A History of the Curriculum and Instruction of William Penn College, 1873-1954." Doctoral dissertation, University of Iowa, 1955.

WITTEMBERG MANUAL LABOR COLLEGE

756 Kerr, Robert Y. "The Wittemberg Manual Labor College."
     Iowa Journal of History 24 (1926): 290-304.

Kansas

GENERAL REFERENCES

757 Blackmar, Frank W. _Higher Education in Kansas_. Washington, D.C.: U.S. Bureau of Education, 1900.

758 Connelley, William. _A Standard History of Kansas and Kansans_. New York: Lewis, 1918.

759 Evans, Harold C. "College Football in Kansas." _Kansas Historical Quarterly_ 9 (1940): 285-311.

760 Evans, Harold C. "Some Notes on College Basketball." _Kansas Historical Quarterly_ 11 (1942): 199-215.

INSTITUTIONAL HISTORIES

BAKER UNIVERSITY

761 Ebright, Homer Kingsley. _The History of Baker University_. Baldwin: n.p., 1951.

BETHEL COLLEGE

762 Wedel, P.J. _The Story of Bethel College_. North Newton: Mennonite Press, 1954.

763 Kliewer, John W. _Memories..._ North Newton: Bethel College, 1943.

COOPER MEMORIAL

764 Porter, Kenneth W., ed. "College Days at Cooper Memorial." *Kansas Historical Quarterly* 26 (1960): 383-409.

FORT HAYS KANSAS STATE COLLEGE

765 Wooster, Lyman Dwight. *A History of Fort Hays Kansas State College, 1902-1961*. Hays: Fort Hays Kansas State College, 1961.

FRIENDS UNIVERSITY

766 Reeves, Juliet. *Friends University: The Growth of an Idea*. Wichita: Wichita Eagle, 1948.

KANSAS STATE TEACHERS COLLEGE

767 Dunham, E. Alden. *Colleges of the Forgotten Americans*. New York: McGraw-Hill, 1969.

768 *A History of the State Normal School of Kansas for the First Twenty-Five Years*. Topeka: Kansas Publishing House, 1889.

769 Taylor, Albert Reynolds. *Autobiography of Albert Reynolds Taylor*. Decatur: Review Printing and Stationery Co., 1929. [Author was President, 1882-1901.]

770 Willard, J.T. "Bluemont Central College, the Forerunner of Kansas State College." *Kansas Historical Quarterly* 13 (1945): 323-357.

KANSAS STATE UNIVERSITY OF AGRICULTURE AND APPLIED SCIENCE

771 Willard, Julius Terrass. *History of the Kansas State College of Agriculture and Applied Science*. Manhattan: Kansas State College Press, 1940.

772 Correll, Charles M. "The First Century of Kansas State University." *Kansas Historical Quarterly* 28 (1962): 409-444.

773 Fairchild, George T. "Populism in a State Educational Institution, the Kansas State Agricultural College." *American Journal of Sociology* 3 (1897): 392-404.

KANSAS

774 Katz, Robert. "A Movement West." In The New Professors, edited by Robert O. Bowen, pp. 38-53. New York: Holt, Rinehart, and Winston, 1960. [Katz was Professor of Physics.]

KANSAS, UNIVERSITY OF

775 Griffin, Clifford S. The University of Kansas: A History. Lawrence: University Press of Kansas, 1973.

776 Griffin, Clifford S. "The University of Kansas and the Sack of Lawrence: A Problem of Intellectual Honesty." Kansas Historical Quarterly 34 (1968): 409-426.

777 Griffin, Clifford S. "The University of Kansas and the Years of Frustration, 1854-1864." Kansas Historical Quarterly 32 (Spring 1966): 1-32.

778 Kansas, University of, Department of Chemistry. History of the Chemistry Department of the University of Kansas. Topeka: Kansas State Printer, 1925.

779 Sterling, Wilson, ed. Quarter Centennial History of the University of Kansas, 1866-1891. Topeka: Crane, 1891.

780 Taft, Robert. The Years on Mount Oread. Lawrence: University of Kansas Press, 1955.

OTTAWA UNIVERSITY

781 Haworth, B. Smith. Ottawa University: Its History and Its Spirit. Lawrence: Allen Press, 1957.

782 Le Page, Samuel Maynard. Short History of Ottawa University. Ottawa: n.p., 1929.

TABOR COLLEGE

783 Janzen, Abraham Ewell. A History of Tabor College. Hillsboro: Mennonite Brethren Publishing House, 1958.

784 Farguhar, Catharine G.B. "Tabor and Tabor College." Iowa Journal of History 41 (1943): 337-393.

785 Schmidt, William J. "History of Tabor College." Master's thesis, University of Wichita, 1961.

WASHBURN UNIVERSITY OF TOPEKA

786 Hickman, Russell K. "Lincoln College--Forerunner of Washburn Municipal University." Pt I: "Founding a Pioneer Congregational College." Pt II: "Later History and Change of Names." Kansas Historical Quarterly 18 (1950): 20-54, 164-204.

Kentucky

GENERAL REFERENCES

787 Lewis, Alvan F. History of Higher Education in Kentucky. Washington, D.C.: U.S. Bureau of Education, 1899.

788 Alston, Jerry G. "The Role of the State Legislature in Public Higher Education in Kentucky, 1950-1968." Doctoral dissertation, Southern Illinois University, 1970.

789 Godbey, Edsel Taylor. "Early Kentucky Governors and Education." Doctoral dissertation, University of Kentucky, 1959.

790 Howard, Boyd Davis. "The Origins of Higher Education in the State of Kentucky." Doctoral dissertation, University of Cincinnati, 1940.

791 McMullen, Hayes. "College Libraries in Ante-Bellum Kentucky." Regional Kentucky State Historical Society 60 (1962): 106-133.

792 Smith, Travis E. The Rise of Teacher Training in Kentucky. Nashville, Tenn.: George Peabody College for Teachers, 1932.

793 Venable, Tom C. "A History of Negro Education in Kentucky." Doctoral dissertation, George Peabody University, 1953.

794 Wallis, Frederick, ed. A Sesquicentennial History of Kentucky. Hopkinsville: Historical Record Association, 1942.

INSTITUTIONAL HISTORIES

ASBURY COLLEGE

795 Hughes, John Wesley. The Autobiography of John Wesley Hughes, D.D. Louisville: Pentecostal Publishing Co., 1923. [Hughes was Founder.]

AUGUSTA COLLEGE

796 Rankin, Walter H. "Money for Minerals But Not a Cent for Athletics." Filson Club Historical Quarterly 34 (April 1960): 136-139.

BEREA COLLEGE

797 Peck, Elisabeth S. Berea's First Century. Lexington: University of Kentucky Press, 1955.

798 Embree, Edwin R. "A Kentucky Crusader." American Mercury 24 (1931): 98-107.

799 Fee, John Gregg. Autobiography of John G. Fee, Berea, Kentucky. Chicago: National Christian Association, 1891. [Author was Founder.]

800 Frost, William Goodell. For the Mountains; An Autobiography. New York: F.H. Revell Co., 1937. [Author was President, 1892-1920.]

801 Hall, Betty Jean, and Heckman, Richard Allen. "Berea College and the Day Law." Register of the Kentucky Historical Society 66 (1968): 35-52.

802 Hutchins, Francis S. Berea College. New York: Newcomen Society in North America, 1963.

803 Keeton, Morris, and Hilberry, Conrad. Struggle and Promise: A Future for Colleges. New York: McGraw-Hill, 1969, pp. 51-79.

804 Morgan, Charles. The Fruit of This Tree. Berea: Berea College, 1946.

805 Rogers, John A.R. The Birth of Berea College. Philadelphia: H.T. Coates & Co., 1903.

CENTRAL UNIVERSITY

806 Dorris, J.T. "Central University, Richmond, Kentucky." Register of the Kentucky State Historical Society 32 (1934): 91-124.

807 Engle, Fred A., Jr. "Central University of Richmond, Kentucky." Register of the Kentucky Historical Society 66 (1968): 279-304.

KENTUCKY

CENTRE COLLEGE

808 McMurty, R. Gerald. "Centre College, John Todd Stuart and Abraham Lincoln." Filson Club Historical Quarterly 33 (1959): 117-124.

809 Snider, Norman L. "Centre College and the Presbyterians: Corporation and Partnership." Register of the Kentucky Historical Society 67 (1969): 103-118.

CUMBERLAND COLLEGE

810 Hall, Ida Janie. "A History of Cumberland College." Doctoral dissertation, University of Tennessee, 1962.

DANVILLE THEOLOGICAL SEMINARY

811 Vaughan, William Hutchinson. Robert Jefferson Breckinridge (1800-1871) as an Educational Administrator. Nashville, Tenn.: George Peabody University, 1937.

EASTERN KENTUCKY UNIVERSITY

812 Dorris, Jonathon T., ed. Three Decades of Progress: Eastern Kentucky State Teachers College, 1906-1936. Richmond: Eastern Kentucky State Teachers College, 1936.

813 Martin, Robert. "Eastern Kentucky State College--Retrospect and Prospect." Filson Club Historical Quarterly 39 (October 1965): 281-286.

GEORGETOWN COLLEGE

814 Daley, John M. "Georgetown College: The First Fifty Years." Doctoral dissertation, Georgetown University, 1953.

815 Huddle, Orlando Earhardt. "A History of Georgetown College." Master's thesis, University of Kentucky, 1930.

816 Meyer, Leland W. Georgetown College, Its Background and a Chapter in Its Early History; A Contribution to the Centennial Anniversary of Georgetown College, Kentucky. Georgetown: Western Recorder, 1929.

817 Snyder, Robert. Georgetown College: A History. Forthcoming.

KENTUCKY, UNIVERSITY OF

818 Talbert, Charles Gano. *The University of Kentucky*. Lexington: University of Kentucky Press, 1965.

819 Ellis, William E. "Frank L. McVey: His Defense of Academic Freedom." *Register of the Kentucky Historical Society* 67 (1969): 37-54.

820 Hopkins, James F. The University of Kentucky: Origins and Early Years. Lexington: University of Kentucky Press, 1951.

821 Irvin, Helen D. *Hail Kentucky: A Pictorial History of the University of Kentucky*. Lexington: University of Kentucky Press, 1965.

822 Murrell, Glen. "The Merger of Paducah Junior College with the University of Kentucky." *Filson Club Historical Quarterly* 44 (1970): 5-18, 179-187, 293-301, 367-377.

823 Pollitt, Mabel Hardy. *A Biography of James Kennedy Patterson*. Louisville: Press, Westerfield-Bonte, 1925. [Patterson was President, 1869-1910.]

824 Pryor, Joseph William. *Doctor Pryor, An Autobiography*. Cynthia: Hobson Press, 1943. [Author was Professor of Medicine.]

825 Pyles, Henry Milton. "The Life and Work of John Bryan Bowman." Doctoral dissertation, University of Kentucky, 1945. [Bowman was Trustee, 1865-1878.]

LOUISVILLE, UNIVERSITY OF

826 Federal Writers' Project, Kentucky. *A Centennial History of the University of Louisville, Written by Kentucky Writers' Project of the Work Projects Administration*. Louisville: University of Louisville, 1939.

827 Anderson, John Q. "Henry Clay Lewis, Louisville Medical Student, 1844-1846." *Filson Club Historical Quarterly* 32 (January 1958): 30-37.

828 Hammon, Stratton. "'School of Architecture,' 1914 to 1926, University of Louisville." *Filson Club Historical Quarterly* 42 (1968): 125-131.

829 Houne, E.F. "History of Louisville Medical Institute and Establishment of the University of Louisville and Its School of Medicine, 1833-46." *Filson Club Historical Quarterly* 7 (1933): 133-147.

KENTUCKY

830 Mallalieu, William C. "Origins of the University of Louisville." Filson Club Historical Quarterly 12 (1938): 24-41.

831 Miller, Neville. "Justice Brandeis and the University of Louisville School of Law." Filson Club Historical Quarterly 34 (1960): 156-159.

MOREHEAD STATE UNIVERSITY

832 Rose, Harry E. "The Historical Development of a State College: Morehead Kentucky State College, 1887-1964." Doctoral dissertation, University of Cincinnati, 1965.

OGDEN COLLEGE

833 Johnson, Jesse, and Harrison, Lowell. "Ogden College: A Brief History." Register of the Kentucky Historical Society 68 (1970): 189-220.

PADUCAH JUNIOR COLLEGE

834 Murrell, Glen. "The Desegregation of Paducah Junior College." Register of the Kentucky Historical Society 67 (1969): 63-79.

PIKEVILLE COLLEGE

835 Page, A.A. "Pikeville College." Filson Club Historical Quarterly 31 (1957): 23-27.

SAINT THOMAS COLLEGE

836 Pitt, Felix N. "Two Early Catholic Colleges in Kentucky: Saint Thomas and Gethsemani." Filson Club Historical Quarterly 38 (April 1964): 133-148.

THOMAS MORE COLLEGE

837 Saelinger, M. Irmina. Retrospect and Vista: The First Fifty Years of Thomas More College. Covington: Thomas More College, 1971.

838 Hanna, Thomas Henry. "The History and Status of Villa Madonna College, 1921-1961." Doctoral dissertation, University of Cincinnati, 1962.

TRANSYLVANIA UNIVERSITY

839 Jennings, Walter W. *Transylvania: Pioneer University of the West*. New York: Pageant, 1955.

840 Adams, James, and Hoberman, Arnold. "Joseph Buchanan, 1785-1829: Pioneer American Psychologist." *Journal of the History of the Behavioral Sciences* 5 (1969): 340-348.

841 Anderson, Annie Stuart. "Transylvania Seminary's First Site and Some Circumstances of Its Beginnings." *Register of the Kentucky Historical Society* 33 (1935): 356-367.

842 Baker, Henry G. "Transylvania: A History of the Pioneer University of the West 1780-1865." Doctoral dissertation, University of Cincinnati, 1949.

843 Caldwell, Charles. *Autobiography of Charles Caldwell, M.D.* Philadelphia: J. B. Lippincott, 1855. [Author was Director of Medical School, 1819-1837.]

844 Dupre, A. Hunter. "Transylvania University and Rafinesque, 1819-1825." *Filson Club Historical Quarterly* 35 (April 1961): 110-121.

845 Eaton, Clement. "A Law Student at Transylvania University in 1810-1812." *Filson Club Historical Quarterly* 31 (1957): 267-273.

846 Henkle, Moses M. *Life of Bascom*. Nashville, Tenn.: E. Stevenson, 1856. [Henry Bidleman Bascom was President, 1842-1849.]

847 Kerr, Charles. "Transylvania University's Law Department." *Americana* 31 (1937): 7-44.

848 Lunger, Irvin E. "Transylvania College: Its History and Its Future." *Register of the Kentucky State Historical Society* 56 (1958): 309-318.

849 Miller, James L., Jr. "Transylvania University as the Nation Saw It, 1818-1828." *Filson Club Historical Quarterly* 34 (1960): 305-318.

850 Norton, Elizabeth. "The Old Library of Transylvania College." *Filson Club Historical Quarterly* 1 (1927): 123-133.

851 Smith, Z.F. "A Kentucky Ideal a Century Ago, Transylvania University." *Register of the Kentucky State Historical Society* 6 (1908): 17-21.

KENTUCKY

UNION COLLEGE

852 Bradley, Erwin S. <u>Union College, 1879-1954</u>. Barbourville: Union College, 1954.

WESTERN KENTUCKY UNIVERSITY

853 Cornette, James P. "A History of the Western Kentucky State Teachers College." Doctoral dissertation, George Peabody University, 1939.

Louisiana

GENERAL REFERENCES

854   Beasley, Leon Odum. "A History of Education in Louisiana During the Reconstruction Period, 1862-1877." Doctoral dissertation, Louisiana State University, 1957.

855   Jones, John A. "The Development of the Professional Education of White Teachers in Louisiana." Doctoral dissertation, Louisiana State University, 1948.

856   Marshall, David Coughlin. "A History of the Higher Education of Negroes in the State of Louisiana." Doctoral dissertation, Louisiana State University, 1957.

857   Terrebonne, Linus P. A Study of Higher Education Under Control of the State Board of Education. Baton Rouge: n.p., 1954.

INSTITUTIONAL HISTORIES

CENTENARY COLLEGE OF LOUISIANA

858   Nelson, William H. A Burning Torch and Flaming Fire: The Story of Centenary College of Louisiana. Nashville, Tenn.: Methodist Publishing House, 1931.

DILLARD UNIVERSITY

859   New Orleans University. Seventy Years of Service, New Orleans University. New Orleans: Faculty of New Orleans University, 1937.

LOUISIANA

LOUISIANA STATE UNIVERSITY

860 Bedsole, Vergil L., and Richard, Oscar, eds. Louisiana State University; A Pictorial Record of the First Hundred Years. Baton Rouge: Louisiana State University Press, 1959.

861 Barnidge, James L. "George Mason Graham: The Father of Louisiana State University." Louisiana History 10 (1969): 225-240.

862 Fleming, Walter L. Louisiana State University 1860-1896. Baton Rouge: Louisiana State University Press, 1936.

863 Postell, William Dosite. "The Special School of Medicine of the Louisiana State Seminary of Learning." Surgery, Gynecology, and Obstetrics 70 (1940): 980-982.

864 Wilkerson, Marcus M. Thomas Duckett Boyd; The Story of a Southern Educator. Baton Rouge: Louisiana State University Press, 1935. [Boyd was President, 1896-1927.]

SOUTHEASTERN LOUISIANA UNIVERSITY

865 Ancelet, Leroy. "A History of Southeastern Louisiana College." Doctoral dissertation, Louisiana State University, 1971.

TULANE UNIVERSITY

866 Dyer, John P. Tulane: The Biography of a University, 1834-1965. New York: Harper, 1966.

867 Dixon, Brandt Van Blarcom. A Brief History of H. Sophie Newcomb Memorial College, 1887-1919. New Orleans: Hauser, 1928.

Maine

GENERAL REFERENCES

868   Hall, Edward W.   <u>History of Higher Education in Maine</u>.
      Washington, D.C.: U.S. Bureau of Education, 1903.

869   Maine, University of.   <u>Survey of Higher Education in Maine</u>.
      Orono: n.p., 1932.

870   Sammis, George F.   "A History of the Maine Normal Schools."
      Doctoral dissertation, University of Connecticut, 1970.

INSTITUTIONAL HISTORIES

BANGOR THEOLOGICAL SEMINARY

871   Cook, Walter Leonard.   <u>Bangor Theological Seminary, A Sesqui-
      centennial History</u>.   Orono: University of Maine Press, 1971.

872   Clark, Calvin Montague.   <u>History of Bangor Theological
      Seminary</u>.   Boston: Pilgrim Press, 1916.

BATES COLLEGE

873   Anthony, Alfred Williams.   <u>Bates College and Its Background: A
      Review of Origins and Causes</u>.   Philadelphia: Judson Press,
      1936.

874   Chase, George M.   <u>George C. Chase, a Biography</u>.   Boston: Houghton
      Mifflin, 1924.   [Chase was President, 1894-1919.]

MAINE

BOWDOIN COLLEGE

875   Hatch, Louis Clinton. The History of Bowdoin College. Portland: Loring, Short & Harmon, 1927.

876   Brown, Herbert Ross. Sills of Bowdoin. New York: Columbia University Press, 1964. [Kenneth Sills was Professor of Latin, 1906-1918, and President, 1918-1952.]

877   Burnett, Charles T. Hyde of Bowdoin. Boston: Houghton Mifflin, 1931. [Hyde was President, 1885-1917.]

878   Cleaveland, Nehemiah, and Packard, Alpheus Spring. History of Bowdoin College, with Biographical Sketches of Its Graduates 1806-1879. Boston: J.R. Osgood & Co., 1882.

879   Elliott, G.R. "President Hyde and the American College." American Review 2 (1933): 1-26, 143-169.

880   Harker, John S. "The Life and Contributions of Calvin Ellis Stowe." Doctoral dissertation, University of Pittsburgh, 1951. [Stowe was Professor of Religion.]

881   Hoeltje, Hubert H. "Hawthorne as a Senior at Bowdoin." Essex Institute Historical Collections 94 (July 1958): 205-228.

882   Johnson, Paul O. "Bowdoin Under Hyde; The Mission and Policies of a Small Liberal Arts College: 1885-1917." Doctoral dissertation, Yale University, 1953.

883   Park, Edwards Amasa. The Life and Character of Leonard Woods. Andover: W.F. Draper, 1880. [Woods was President, 1839-1866.]

884   Tapley, Harriet. "Hawthorne's 'Pot-8-O' Club at Bowdoin College." Essex Institutional History Collection 67 (1931): 225-231.

885   Walett, Francis G. "James Bowdoin and the Massachusetts Council." Doctoral dissertation, Boston University, 1948.

COLBY COLLEGE

886   Marriner, Ernest Cummings. The History of Colby College. Waterville: Colby College Press, 1963.

887   Soule, Bertha L. Colby's President Roberts. Waterville: Colby College, 1943.

888 Whittemore, Edwin Carey. *Colby College, 1820-1925; An Account of Its Beginnings, Progress and Service*. Waterville: Trustees of Colby College, 1927.

MAINE, UNIVERSITY OF

889 Fernald, Merritt C. *History of Maine State College and the University of Maine*. Orono: University of Maine, 1916.

MAINE, UNIVERSITY OF, AT FARMINGTON

890 Purington, George C. *History of the State Normal School, Farmington, Maine*. Farmington: Knowlton, McLeary, 1889.

Maryland

GENERAL REFERENCES

891 Steiner, Bernard C. *History of Education in Maryland.* Washington, D.C.: U.S. Government Printing Office, 1894.

892 Cain, Mrs. Mary C. "The Historical Development of State Normal Schools for White Teachers in Maryland." Doctoral dissertation, Columbia University, 1941.

893 Lockard, G.C. "Early Medical Education in Baltimore." *Bulletin of the School of Medicine of the University of Maryland* 23 (1939): 128-137.

INSTITUTIONAL HISTORIES

BALTIMORE COLLEGE OF DENTAL SURGERY

894 Lewis, Carl P., Jr. "The Baltimore College of Dental Surgery and the Birth of Professional Dentistry." *Maryland Historical Magazine* 59 (September 1964): 268-285.

GOUCHER COLLEGE

895 Knipp, Anna (Heubeck), and Thomas, Thaddeus P. *The History of Goucher College.* Baltimore: Goucher College, 1938.

896 Lord, Eleanor. *Stars over the Schoolhouse: The Evolution of a College Dean.* New York: Smith, 1938.

JOHNS HOPKINS UNIVERSITY

897 Hawkins, Hugh. *Pioneer: A History of the Johns Hopkins University, 1874-1889*. Ithaca, N.Y.: Cornell University Press, 1960.

898 Barker, Lewellys Franklin. "The Early Days of the Johns Hopkins Hospital." *Maryland Historical Magazine* 38 (1943): 1-18.

899 Barker, Lewellys Franklin. *Time and the Physician...* New York: Putnam, 1942. [Author was Professor of Medicine, 1894-1900 and 1905-1913.]

900 Chesney, Alan M. *The Johns Hopkins Hospital and the Johns Hopkins School of Medicine*. Baltimore: Johns Hopkins University Press, 1943.

901 Connor, George. "Basil Lanneau Gildersleeve, Scholar and Humanist, 1881-1924." Doctoral dissertation, University of Wisconsin, 1960. [Gildersleeve was Professor of Ancient Languages.]

902 Corson, Louis D. "University Problems as Described in the Personal Correspondence Among D.C. Gilman, A.D. White and C.W. Eliot." Doctoral dissertation, Stanford University, 1951.

903 Dykhuizen, George. "John Dewey at Johns Hopkins, 1882-1884." *Journal of the History of Ideas* 22 (March 1961): 103-116.

904 Fisch, Max H., and Cope, Jackson I. "Peirce at the Johns Hopkins University." In *Studies in the Philosophy of Charles Sanders Peirce*, edited by Philip D. Weiner and Frederick H. Young, pp. 277-311. Cambridge: Harvard University Press, 1952.

905 Flexner, Abraham. *Abraham Flexner: An Autobiography*. New York: Simon, 1960. [Flexner was Graduate Student.]

906 Flexner, Abraham. *Daniel Coit Gilman: Creator of the American Type of University*. New York: Harcourt, Brace, 1946. [Gilman was First President, 1876-1901.]

907 Flexner, Abraham. *I Remember...* New York: Simon & Schuster, 1940.

908 French, John C. *A History of the University Founded by Johns Hopkins*. Baltimore: Johns Hopkins University Press, 1946.

909 Gass, W. Conrad. "Herbert Baxter Adams and the Development of Historical Instruction in American Colleges and Universities." Doctoral dissertation, Duke University, 1962.

MARYLAND

910 Getman, Frederick. *The Life of Ira Remson*. Easton, Pa.: Journal of Chemical Education, 1940. [Remson was President, 1902-1913.]

911 Gilman, Daniel Cort. *The Launching of the University*. New York: Dodd, Mead, 1906.

912 Hawkins, Hugh D. "George William Brown and His Influence on the Johns Hopkins University." *Maryland Historical Magazine* 52 (September 1957): 173-186. [Brown was one of first Trustees.]

913 Holt, W.S. "Henry Adams and The Johns Hopkins University." *New England Quarterly* 11 (1938): 632-638.

914 Malone, Kemp. "Historical Sketch of the English Department of the Johns Hopkins University." *Johns Hopkins Alumni Quarterly* 15 (1920): 116-128.

915 Oliver, John Rathbone. *Foursquare*. New York: Macmillan, 1929. [Author was Professor of Psychiatry, 1930-1943.]

916 Penniman, George D. "The Beginnings of Hopkins Athletics." *Johns Hopkins Alumni Magazine* 27 (1939): 101-106.

917 Ryan, W. Carson. *Studies in Early Graduate Education: Johns Hopkins University, Clark University, and the University of Chicago*. New York: Carnegie Foundation for the Advancement of Teaching, 1939.

918 Whitehead, J.B. "The School of Engineering, 1912-1937." *Johns Hopkins Alumni Magazine* 25 (1937): 323-337.

LOYOLA COLLEGE

919 Varga, Nicholas. "Ninety-Five Pioneers: The First Students Enrolled at Loyola College, 1852-53." *Maryland Historical Magazine* 66 (1971): 181-193.

MARYLAND, UNIVERSITY OF

920 Callcott, George H. *A History of the University of Maryland*. Baltimore: Maryland Historical Society, 1966.

921 Cordell, Eugene F. *The University of Maryland, 1807-1907*. 2 vols. New York: Lewis, 1907.

922 Hallowell, Benjamin. *Autobiography of Benjamin Hallowell*. Philadelphia: Philadelphia Friends Book Association, 1883. [Author was First President.]

923 Thompson, Raymond K. "History of the University of Maryland." Phi Chi Quarterly 36 (1939): 529-536.

MOUNT SAINT MARY'S COLLEGE

924 McSweeney, Edward Francis Xavier. The Story of the Mountain. 2 vols. Emmitsburg: Weekly Chronicle, 1911.

NOTRE DAME OF MARYLAND, COLLEGE OF

925 Cameron, Mary David. The College of Notre Dame of Maryland: 1895-1945. New York: D.X. McMullen, 1947.

SAINT JOHN'S COLLEGE

926 St. John's College. The St. John's Program. Annapolis: St. John's College Press, 1955.

927 Brown, Anne W. "The Phoenix: A History of the St. John's College Library." Maryland Historical Magazine 65 (1970): 413-429.

928 Grant, Gerald, and Riesman, David. "St. John's and the Great Books." Change 6 (May 1974): 28-36.

929 St. John's College. 1789-1889. Baltimore: Boyle, 1890.

930 U.S. Congress., Senate Committee on Naval Affairs. Acquisition of St. John's College for Expansion of the U.S. Naval Academy: Hearing, 79th Cong., 1st session, 1945.

SALISBURY STATE COLLEGE

931 Purnell, Henrietta S., and Blackwell, Jefferson Davis. The State Teachers College at Salisbury, Maryland. Salisbury: State Teachers College, 1954.

TOWSON STATE COLLEGE

932 A Committee of the Alumni. Seventy-Five Years of Teacher Education. Towson: The Alumni Association, 1941.

UNITED STATES NAVAL ACADEMY

933 Karsten, Peter. *The Naval Aristocracy: The Golden Age of Annapolis and the Emergence of Modern American Navalism*. New York: Free Press, 1972.

934 Burr, Henry L. "Education in the Early Navy." Doctoral dissertation, Temple University, 1939.

935 Chiles, Rosa, ed. *Letters of Alfred T. Mahan to Samuel A. Ashe, 1858-59*. Durham: Duke University Press, 1931. [Mahan was Student.]

936 Norris, Walter B. *Annapolis: Its Colonial and Naval Story*. New York: Crowell, 1925.

937 Puleston, William D. *Annapolis: Gangway to the Quarterdeck*. New York: Appleton-Century-Crofts, 1942.

938 Rilling, Alexander. "The First Fifty Years of Graduate Education in the U.S. Navy, 1909-1959." Doctoral dissertation, University of Southern California, 1972.

939 Soley, James R. *A Historical Sketch of the U.S. Naval Academy*. Washington, D.C.: U.S. Government Printing Office, 1876.

WOODSTOCK COLLEGE

940 Ryan, Rev. Edmund Granville, S.J. "An Academic History of Woodstock College in Maryland, 1869-1944: The First Jesuit Seminary in North America." Doctoral dissertation, Catholic University of America, 1963.

Massachusetts

GENERAL REFERENCES

941 Bush, George G. History of Higher Education in Massachusetts. Washington, D.C.: U.S. Bureau of Education, 1891.

942 Albree, John. Charles Brooks and His Work for the Normal Schools. Medford: J.C. Miller, 1907.

943 Dunlea, Thomas A. "Agricultural Education in Massachusetts, 1792-1867." Doctoral dissertation, University of Chicago, 1953.

944 Lefavour, Henry. "The Proposed College in Hampshire County in 1762." Massachusetts Historical Society Proceedings 66 (1942): 53-79.

945 Mangun, Vernon L. The American Normal School, Its Rise and Development in Massachusetts. Baltimore: Warwick & York, Inc., 1928.

INSTITUTIONAL HISTORIES

AMERICAN INTERNATIONAL COLLEGE

946 A History of American International College. Springfield: American International College, 1960.

947 Stryker, Rev. Garrett Voorhees, D.D. A Brief History of the American International College. Springfield: American International College, 1945.

MASSACHUSETTS

AMHERST COLLEGE

948 LeDuc, Thomas. Piety and Intellect at Amherst College, 1865-1912. New York: Columbia University Press, 1946.

949 Peterson, George E. The New England College in the Age of the University. Amherst: Amherst College Press, 1964.

950 Andrews, Charles A. "The Amherst Gift Record." Amherst Graduate Quarterly 24 (1935): 281-286.

951 Canfield, F. Curtis. The Seed and the Sowers, A Series of Chapel Talks on the History of Amherst College and a Play About Its Founding. Amherst: Amherst College Press, 1955.

952 Cutting, George R. Student Life at Amherst College: Its Organizations, Their Membership and History. Amherst: Amherst College Press, 1871. [Very useful contemporary account by a student.]

953 French, Howard D. "Music at Amherst." Amherst Graduate Quarterly 25 (1935): 1-9.

954 Fuess, Claude Moore. The Amherst Memorial Volume, A Record of the Contribution Made by Amherst College and Amherst Men in the World War, 1914-1918. Amherst: Amherst College Press, 1926.

955 Fuess, Claude Moore. Amherst, the Story of a New England College. Boston: Little, Brown, 1935.

956 Hammond, William G. Remembrance of Amherst: An Undergraduate's Diary, 1846-1848. New York: Columbia University Press, 1946.

957 Hitchcock, Edward. Reminiscences of Amherst College, Historical, Scientific, Biographical, and Autobiographical. Northampton: Bridgman & Childs, 1863. [Author was Professor of Natural History, 1825-1845, and President, 1845-1854.]

958 Johnson, Burges. Campus Versus Classroom. New York: I. Washburn, Inc., 1946. [About student life in 1890s.]

959 Kennedy, Gail, ed. Education at Amherst, the New Program. New York: Harper, 1955.

960 King, Stanley. The Consecrated Eminence: A History of the Development of the Physical Campus. Amherst: Amherst College Press, 1951.

961 King, Stanley. A History of the Endowment of Amherst College. Amherst: Amherst College Press, 1950.

962 Nichols, Martha. The Preparation of Stewart Burton Nichols: His Life and Letters, 1900-1925. New York: Grafton Press, 1928. [Pp. 40-82 on student life.]

963 Riley, Herbert E., ed. An Amherst Book: A Collection of Stories, Poems, Songs, Sketches and Historical Articles by Alumni and Undergraduates of Amherst College. New York: Republic Press, 1896.

964 Tyler, William Seymour. Autobiography of William Seymour Tyler. Privately printed, 1912. [Author was Professor of Classics, 1836-1892.]

965 Tyler, William Seymour. History of Amherst College During Its First Half Century, 1821-1871. Springfield: Clark W. Bryan, 1873.

ANNA MARIA COLLEGE FOR WOMEN

966 Madden, Catherine Christmas. Anna Maria College 1946-1971. Forthcoming.

BOSTON COLLEGE

967 Frost, John Edward. The Crowned Hilltop: Boston College in Its Hundredth Year. New York: Hawthorne Press, 1962.

968 Dunigan, David R. A History of Boston College. Milwaukee: Bruce, 1947.

BOSTON UNIVERSITY

969 Center, Harry B. "History of Boston University News." Bostonia 9 (1935): 13-14, 23.

970 Forbes, Abner, and Green, J.W. The Rich Men of Massachusetts. Boston: Fetridge, 1851. [Includes Jacob Sleeper, a Founder.]

971 Geddes, James, Jr. Memories of a College Professor. Edited by Samuel W. Waxman. Boston: Boston University Press, 1945. [Geddes was Professor of Modern Languages.]

972 Marsh, Daniel L. "William Edwards Huntington, The 'Dear, Dear Dean' Who Became President." Bostonia 9 (1935): 3-11, 32-33. [Marsh was President, 1903-1911.]

973 Speare, Edward R. Interesting Happenings in Boston University's History, 1839-1951. Boston: Boston University Press, 1957.

MASSACHUSETTS

974 Taylor, Joseph Richard. "Lemuel Herbert Murlin, 1861-1935." Bostonia 9 (1935): 3-5, 20. [Murlin was President, 1911-1925.]

975 Warren, William F. The Origin and Progress of Boston University. Boston: University Offices, 1893.

BRANDEIS UNIVERSITY

976 Goldstein, I. Brandeis University. New York: Bloch, 1951.

BRIDGEWATER STATE COLLEGE

977 Bridgewater State College Alpha Board. As We Were 1840-1940. Bridgewater: Bridgewater State College, 1940.

978 Boyden, Arthur Clarke. Albert Gordon Boyden and the Bridgewater State Normal School. Bridgewater: Arthur H. Willis, 1919. [Author was President, 1906-1915.]

979 Boyden, Arthur Clarke. The History of Bridgewater Normal School. Bridgewater: Alumni Association, 1933.

980 Bridgewater State College Alumni Association. Seventy-Fifth Anniversary of the State Normal School. Bridgewater: Arthur H. Willis, 1915.

CLARK UNIVERSITY

981 Atwood, Wallace W. The First Fifty Years: An Administrative Report. Worcester: Clark University, 1937.

982 Barnes, Henry E. "Clark University: An Adventure in American Educational History." American Review 3 (1925): 271-288.

983 Hall, Granville Stanley. Life and Confessions of a Psychologist. New York: Appleton, 1923. [Author was First President, 1888-1919.]

984 McPheeters, Alphonso A. "The Origin and Development of Clark University and Gammon Theological Seminary 1869-1944." Doctoral dissertation, University of Cincinnati, 1944.

985 Murchison, Carl A. "Recollections of a Magic Decade at Clark." Journal of General Psychology 61 (1959): 3-12. [Author was Professor of Psychology, 1925-1935.]

986 Ross, Dorothy. *G. Stanley Hall; The Psychologist as a Prophet.*
Chicago: University of Chicago Press, 1972.

EASTERN NAZARENE COLLEGE

987 Cameron, James Reese. *Eastern Nazarene College: The First Fifty Years 1900-1950.* Kansas City, Mo.: Nazarene Publishing House, 1968.

FRAMINGHAM STATE COLLEGE

988 Peirce, Cyrus. *The First State Normal School in America: The Journals of Cyrus Peirce and Mary Swift.* Cambridge: Harvard University Press, 1926. [Author was First President, 1839-1849.]

HAMPSHIRE COLLEGE

989 Patterson, Franklin, and Longsworth, Charles R. *The Making of a College.* Cambridge: Massachusetts Institute of Technology Press, 1966.

HARVARD UNIVERSITY

990 Morison, Samuel E. *Three Centuries of Harvard, 1636-1936.*
Cambridge: Harvard University Press, 1936.

991 Adams, Henry. *The Education of Henry Adams.* Boston: Houghton Mifflin, 1918. [Author was Student and Professor of History.]

992 Adams, J. Donald. *Copey of Harvard: A Biography of Charles Townsend Copeland.* Cambridge: Harvard University Press, 1960.
[Copeland was Professor of English, 1893-1940.]

993 Allen, Gay Wilson. *William James: A Biography.* New York: Viking, 1967. [James was Professor of Psychology, 1885-1910.]

994 Archibald, Raymond C. *Benjamin Peirce, 1809-1880.* Oberlin: The Mathematical Association of America, 1925. [Peirce was Professor of Mathematics and Astronomy.]

995 Arnold, J.H. "The Harvard Law Library." *Harvard Graduate Magazine* 16 (1907): 230-241.

996 Atkinson, Brooks, ed. *College in a Yard: Minutes by Thirty-Nine Harvard Men.* Cambridge: Harvard University Press, 1957.

997 Bail, H.V. "The Death of Football and the Riot of 1860." *Harvard Alumni Bulletin* 36 (1933): 36-46.

998 Bail, H.V. "Harvard Fiction: Some Critical and Bibliographical Notes." *Proceedings of the American Antiquarian Society* 68 (1958): 211-347.

999 Batchelder, Samuel F. *Bits of Harvard History.* Cambridge: Harvard University Press, 1924.

1000 Bealle, Morris A. *The History of Football at Harvard 1874-1948.* Washington, D.C.: Columbia Publishing Co., 1948.

1001 Bentinck-Smith, William. *The Harvard Book: Selections from Three Centuries.* Cambridge: Harvard University Press, 1953.

1002 Bernardin, Charles W. "John Dos Passos' Harvard Years." *New England Quarterly* 27 (1954): 3-26.

1003 Bevis, A.M. *Diets and Riots, An Interpretation of the History of Harvard University.* Boston: Marshall Jones Co., 1936.

1004 Billington, Ray A. *Frederick Jackson Turner: Historian, Scholar, Teacher.* New York: Oxford University Press, 1973. [Turner was Professor of History, 1910-1924.]

1005 Bliss, Allen D. "Men and Machines in Early Harvard Science." *Journal of Chemical Education* 17 (1940): 353-360.

1006 Bolles, Frank. *Students' Expenses. A Collection of Letters from Undergraduates, Graduates, and Professional School Students, Describing in Detail Their Necessary Expenses at Harvard University.* Cambridge: Boston Heliotype Printing Co., 1893.

1007 Boring, Edwin G. *Psychologist at Large. An Autobiography and Selected Essays.* New York: Basic Books, 1961. [Author was Professor of Psychology, 1922-1968.]

1008 Brewster, Edwin Tenney. *Life and Letters of Josiah Dwight Whitney.* Boston: Houghton Mifflin, 1909. [Whitney was Professor of Geology, 1865-1896.]

1009 Brown, Francis H. "Harvard University in the War of 1861-65." *Harvard Graduate Magazine* 10 (1901-1902): 402-413.

1010 Brown, Rollo. *Dean Briggs.* New York: Harper, 1926. [LeBarron Russell Briggs was Dean of the College, 1878-1925.]

1011 Buck, Paul, ed. *Social Sciences at Harvard, 1860-1920.* Cambridge: Harvard University Press, 1965.

1012 Cadbury, Henry J. "What Happened to John Harvard's Books?" Harvard Alumni Bulletin 41 (1938): 241-248.

1013 Carver, Thomas Nixon. Recollections of an Unplanned Life. Los Angeles: Ritchie, 1949. [Author was Professor of Politics, 1902-1950.]

1014 Chaplin, Jeremiah. The Life of Henry Dunster. Boston: J.R. Osgood, 1872. [Dunster was President, 1640-1654.]

1015 Church, Robert L. "The Development of the Social Sciences as Academic Discipline at Harvard University, 1869-1900." Doctoral dissertation, Harvard University, 1966.

1016 Conant, James Bryant. My Several Lives. New York: Harper and Row, 1970. [Author was Professor of Chemistry, President, 1933-1953.]

1017 Cooke, George W. John Sullivan Dwight, Brook Farmer, Editor, and Critic of Music. Boston: Small & Maynard, 1898. [Dwight was Director of Music, 1855-1893.]

1018 Cooper, L. Louis Agassiz as a Teacher. Rev. ed. Ithaca, N.Y.: Comstock, 1945. [Agassiz was Professor of Biology, 1848-1873.]

1019 Copeland, Melvin T. And Mark an Era: The Story of the Harvard Business School. Boston: Little, Brown, 1958.

1020 Curtis, Charles P. "Learning and Liquor at Harvard, 1792-1846!" Massachusetts Historical Society Proceedings 70 (1957): 56-64. Also in New England Quarterly 25 (September 1952): 344-353.

1021 DuBois, W.E.B. "A Negro Student at Harvard." Massachusetts Review 1 (1960): 439-458.

1022 Dunn, Edward T. "Tutor Henry Flynt of Harvard College, 1725-1760." Doctoral dissertation, University of Rochester, 1968.

1023 Dupree, A. Hunter. Asa Gray, 1810-1888. Cambridge: Harvard University Press, 1959. [Gray was Professor of Biology, 1842-1873.]

1024 Fessenden, Franklin G. "The Re-Birth of the Harvard Law School." Harvard Law Review 33 (1920): 493-517.

1025 Foster, F. Apthorp. "The Burning of Harvard Hall, 1764, and its Consequences." Publications of the Colonial Society of Massachusetts 14 (1913): 2-43.

1026 Foster, Margery Somers. "Out of Small Beginnings..." Cambridge: Harvard University Press, 1962.

1027 Frankfurter, Felix. Reminiscences. Garden City: Doubleday, 1962. [Author was Professor of Law, 1914-1939.]

1028 Goff, John S. "The Education of Robert Todd Lincoln." Journal of the Illinois State Historical Society 53 (1959): 341-360.

1029 Hanus, Paul Henry. Adventuring in Education. Cambridge: Harvard University Press, 1937. [Author was First Professor of Education, 1901-1921.]

1030 Hapgood, Richard L. History of the Harvard Dental School. Boston: Harvard University Dental School, 1930.

1031 Harrington, Thomas Francis. The Harvard Medical School; A History, Narrative and Documentary, 1782-1905. 3 vols. New York: Lewis, 1905.

1032 Harris, Seymour. Economics of Harvard. New York: McGraw-Hill, 1970.

1033 Hart, Albert Bushnell. "The University: Ten Years of Harvard." Harvard Graduate Magazine 11 (1902-1903): 58-69.

1034 Hawkins, Hugh. Between Harvard and America; The Educational Leadership of Charles W. Eliot. New York: Oxford University Press, 1972. [Eliot was President, 1869-1909.]

1035 Hill, Robert W. "Virginian at Harvard, 1819-1823: Edward T. Tayloe's College Expenses." Virginia Magazine of History and Biography 52 (1944): 262-266.

1036 Howe, Daniel Walker. "The Unitarian Conscience: Harvard Moral Philosophy and the Second Great Awakening, 1805-67." Doctoral dissertation, University of California, 1967.

1037 Hudson, Winthrop S. "The Morison Myth Concerning the Founding of Harvard College." Church History 8 (1939): 148-159.

1038 James, Henry. Charles W. Eliot, President of Harvard University, 1869-1919. 2 vols. Boston: Houghton Mifflin, 1930.

1039 Jones, Bessie, and Boyd, Lyle. The Harvard College Observatory, 1839-1919. Cambridge: Harvard University Press, 1970.

1040 Kahn, E.J. Harvard Through Change and Through Storm. New York: Norton, 1970. [Reminiscences of an alumnus.]

1041 Kaledin, Arthur. "The Mind of John Leverett." Doctoral dissertation, Harvard University, 1965. [Leverett was President, 1708-1724.]

1042 Keppel, Frederick P. "President Lowell and His Influence." Atlantic Monthly 151 (1933): 753-763. [Lowell was President, 1909-1933.]

1043 Koelsch, William A. "The Enlargement of a World: Harvard Students and Geographical Experiences, 1840-1861." Doctoral dissertation, University of Chicago, 1966.

1044 Krick, Jerald R. "Harvard Volunteers: A History of Undergraduate Volunteer Social Service Work at Harvard." Doctoral dissertation, Boston University, 1970.

1045 Land, William Goodfellow. *Thomas Hill: Twentieth President of Harvard*. Cambridge: Harvard University Press, 1933. [Hill was President, 1862-1868.]

1046 Lane, William C. "Building Massachusetts Hall, 1717-1720." *Colonial Society of Massachusetts Transactions* 24 (1920): 81-110.

1047 Lane, William C. "The Rebellion of 1766 in Harvard College." *Colonial Society of Massachusetts Transactions* 10 (1907): 33-59.

1048 Lewis, Frederick T. "The Hollis Family and Harvard." *Harvard Graduate Magazine* 42 (1933): 107-120. [About philanthropy for colonial Harvard.]

1049 Long, O.W. *Frederick Henry Hedge: A Cosmopolitan Scholar*. Portland, Me.: Southworth-Anthoensen Press, 1940. [Hedge was Professor of German Literature and Church History, 1857-1876.]

1050 Lovett, Robert W. "The Undergraduate and the Harvard Library, 1877-1937." *Harvard Library Bulletin* 1 (1947): 221-237.

1051 Lowell, A. Lawrence. "The Harvard House Plan." *Association of American Colleges Bulletin* 17 (1931): 89-96.

1052 Lurie, Edward. *Louis Agassiz: A Life in Science*. Chicago: University of Chicago Press, 1960.

1053 Lyttle, Charles. "A Sketch of the Theological Development of Harvard University, 1636-1805." *Church History* 5 (1936): 301-329.

1054 Mackintosh, Henry S. "Vital Statistics of Harvard College Graduates, 1830-1904." *Harvard Graduate Magazine* 15 (1907): 568-578.

1055 Manchester, Frederick, and Shepard, Odell, eds. *Irving Babbitt: Man and Teacher*. New York: G.P. Putnam's, 1941. [Babbitt was Professor of English, 1894-1933.]

1056 Marcou, Jules. *Life, Letters, and Works of Louis Agassiz*. 2 vols. New York: Macmillan, 1895.

1057 Mason, Daniel G. "At Harvard in the Nineties." *New England Quarterly* 9 (1936): 43-70.

1058 Matthews, Albert. "Comenius and Harvard College." *Publications of the Colonial Society of Massachusetts* 21 (1920): 146-190.

1059   Matthews, Albert. "The Harvard College Charter of 1672." Publications of the Colonial Society of Massachusetts 21 (1920): 363-402.

1060   Matthews, Albert. "A Note on 'Placing' at Harvard College." Publications of the Colonial Society of Massachusetts 25 (1924): 420-427.

1061   Matthews, Albert. "Teaching of French at Harvard College Before 1750." Publications of the Colonial Society of Massachusetts 17 (1914): 216-232.

1062   Meyer, Isidore S. "Hebrew at Harvard (1636-1760). A Resume of the Information in Recent Publications." American Jewish Historical Society Publication 35 (1939): 145-170.

1063   Morison, Samuel E., ed. The Development of Harvard University Since the Inauguration of President Eliot, 1869-1929. Cambridge: Harvard University Press, 1930.

1064   Morison, Samuel E. The Founding of Harvard College. Cambridge: Harvard University Press, 1935.

1065   Morison, Samuel E. "The Great Rebellion in Harvard College and the Resignation of President Kirkland." Colonial Society of Massachusetts Transactions 27 (1927-30): 54-112.

1066   Morison, Samuel E. Harvard College in the Seventeenth Century. 2 vols. Cambridge: Harvard University Press, 1936.

1067   Morison, Samuel E. "The Harvard Presidency." New England Quarterly 31 (1958): 435-446.

1068   Morison, Samuel E. "Precedence at Harvard College in the Seventeenth Century." American Antiquarian Society Proceedings n.s. 42 (1933): 371-431.

1069   Morse, J.T. "Recollections of Boston and Harvard Before the Civil War." Massachusetts Historical Society Proceedings 65 (1940): 150-163.

1070   Muensterberg, Margaret. Hugo Muensterberg: His Life and Work. New York: D. Appleton, 1922. [Muensterberg was Professor, 1892-1916.]

1071   Noble, John. "Harvard College Lotteries." Publications of the Colonial Society of Massachusetts 27 (1932): 162-186.

1072   Norton, Arthur O. "Harvard Text-Books and Reference Books of the Seventeenth Century." Publications of the Colonial Society of Massachusetts 28 (1935): 361-438.

1073   Painter, Nell. "Jim Crow at Harvard: 1923." New England Quarterly 44 (1971): 627-634.

1074 Panchard, Frances L. "George Herbert Palmer." Doctoral dissertation, New York University, 1935. [Palmer was Professor of Philosophy, 1889-1913.]

1075 Peabody, Andrew P. Harvard Reminiscences. Boston: Tecknor & Co., 1888. [Author was Professor of Religion, 1860-1881.]

1076 Perry, Bliss. And Gladly Teach: Reminiscences. Boston: Houghton Mifflin, 1935. [Author was Professor of Literature, 1893-1900.]

1077 Phelps, R.H. "One Hundred and Fifty Years of Phi Beta Kappa at Harvard." American Scholar 1 (1932): 58-64.

1078 Powell, Arthur G. "The Study of Education at Harvard University, 1870-1920." Doctoral dissertation, Harvard University, 1969.

1079 Price, Robert P. "Academic Government at Harvard College, 1636-1723." Doctoral dissertation, University of Michigan, 1969.

1080 Quincy, Josiah. The History of Harvard University. 2 vols. Cambridge: J. Owen, 1840.

1081 Rand, Benjamin. "Philosophical Instruction in Harvard University from 1636-1900." Harvard Graduate Magazine 37 (1928): 29-47, 188-200, 296-311.

1082 Rand, Edward K. "Liberal Education in the 17th Century at Harvard." New England Quarterly 6 (1933): 525-551.

1083 Reznek, Samuel. "The European Education of an American Chemist and Its Influence on Nineteenth Century America: Eben N. Horsford." Technology and Culture 11 (1970): 366-388. [Horsford was Professor of Chemistry, 1847-1863.]

1084 Roelker, William Greene. "Boating at Harvard, 1863-1866." Harvard Alumni Bulletin 41 (1939): 1101-1103.

1085 Santayana, George. Middle Span. New York: Scribner's, 1945. [Author was Professor of Philosophy, 1889-1911.]

1086 Schofield, William. "C.C. Langdell." American Law Register 55 (1907): 273-296. [Langdell was Dean of Law School, 1870-1906.]

1087 Seybolt, Robert F. "Student Libraries at Harvard, 1763-1764." Publications of the Colonial Society of Massachusetts 28 (1935): 449-461.

1088 Shaler, N.S. "The Problem of Discipline in Higher Education." Atlantic Monthly 64 (1889): 24.

1089 Shay, John E. "Residence Halls in the Age of the University: Their Development at Harvard and Michigan, 1850-1930." Doctoral dissertation, University of Michigan, 1964.

MASSACHUSETTS

1090 Sibley, J.L., and Shipton, Clifford K. Biographical Sketches of Graduates of Harvard University. 8 vols. Cambridge: Harvard University Press, 1873-1952.

1091 Spalding, Walter Raymond. Music at Harvard. New York: Coward-McCann, 1935.

1092 Sutherland, Arthur E. The Law at Harvard: A History of Ideas and Men, 1817-1967. Cambridge: Harvard University Press, 1967.

1093 Thomson, Elizabeth H. Harvey Cushing: Surgeon, Author, Artist. New York: Schuman, 1950. [Cushing was Professor of Surgery, 1912-1932.]

1094 Ticknor, George. Life, Letters and Journals of George Ticknor. 2 vols. Boston: J.R. Osgood, 1877. [Ticknor was Professor of Romance Languages, 1819-1833.]

1095 Tuttle, William M., Jr. "James Bryant Conant: The Scientist in Public Affairs, 1917-1957." Doctoral dissertation, University of Wisconsin, 1967.

1096 Tyack, David. George Ticknor and the Boston Brahmins. Cambridge: Harvard University Press, 1967.

1097 Warren, Charles. History of the Harvard Law School and of Early Legal Conditions in America. 3 vols. New York: Lewis, 1908.

1098 Wert, Robert J. "The Impact of Three Nineteenth Century Reorganizations upon Harvard University." Doctoral dissertation, Stanford University, 1952.

1099 Williams, George Huntston. The Harvard Divinity School: Its Place in Harvard University and the American Culture. Boston: Beacon Press, 1954.

1100 Williston, Samuel. Life and Law, An Autobiography. Boston: Little, Brown, 1941. [Author was Professor of Law, 1895-1908.]

1101 Yeomans, Henry A. Abbott Lawrence Lowell: 1856-1943. Cambridge: Harvard University Press, 1948. [Lowell was President, 1909-1933.]

1102 Young, Edward J. "Subjects for a Master's Degree in Harvard College from 1655-1791." Massachusetts Historical Society Proceedings 18 (1881): 119-151.

HOLY CROSS, COLLEGE OF THE

1103 Meagher, Walter J., and Grattan, William J. The Spires of Fenwick: The History of the College of Holy Cross 1843-1963. New York: Vantage, 1966.

1104 Meagher, Walter J. "A History of Holy Cross, 1843-1901." Doctoral dissertation, Fordham University, 1944.

LASELL JUNIOR COLLEGE

1105 Spooner, Ruth Hopkins. Lasell's First Century, 1851-1951. Boston: Rand Avery--Gordon Taylor, 1951.

LOWELL INSTITUTE

1106 Weeks, Edward. The Lowells and Their Institute. Boston: Little, Brown, 1966.

1107 Park, Charles F. A History of Lowell Institute School, 1903-1928. Cambridge: Harvard University Press, 1931.

1108 Rossiter, Margaret. "Benjamin Silliman and the Lowell Institute: The Popularization of Science in Nineteenth Century America." New England Quarterly 44 (1971): 602-626.

MASSACHUSETTS GENERAL HOSPITAL

1109 Parsons, Sara E. History of Massachusetts General Hospital Training School for Nurses. Boston: Whitcomb & Barrows, 1922.

MASSACHUSETTS INSTITUTE OF TECHNOLOGY

1110 Prescott, Samuel. When M.I.T. Was "Boston Tech", 1861-1916. Cambridge: Technology Press, 1954.

1111 Burchard, John E. Q.E.D.; M.I.T. in World War II. New York: Wiley, 1948.

1112 Costantino, Nicholas V. "Education in the Industrial Republic: An Interpretive Study of Francis Amasa Walker's Philosophy of Education." Doctoral dissertation, University of Florida, 1967. [Walker was President, 1881-1897.]

MASSACHUSETTS

1113 Cross, Charles B. "Early History of the Alumni Association of M.I.T." Technical Review 22 (1920): 532-559.

1114 Flexner, Abraham. Henry S. Pritchett. New York: Columbia University Press, 1943. [Pritchett was President, 1900-1905.]

1115 Hunt, Caroline L. The Life of Ellen H. Richards. Boston: Whitcomb and Barrows, 1912. [Richards was Professor of Home Economics, 1884-1911.]

1116 Jordan, Edwin Oakes, Whipple, G.C., and Winslow, C.E.A. A Pioneer of Public Health, William Thompson Sedgwick. New Haven: Yale University Press, 1924. [Sedgwick was Professor of Biology, 1883-1921.]

1117 Munroe, James P. A Life of Francis Amasa Walker. New York: Holt, 1923.

1118 Munroe, James P. "The Massachusetts Institute of Technology." New England Magazine 27 (1902): 131-158.

1119 Pierce, Myron E. "The Institute of Technology and the Commonwealth of Massachusetts." Technical Review 5 (1903): 156-180.

1120 Richards, Robert H. Robert Hallowell Richards--His Mark. Boston: Little, Brown, 1936. [Richards was Professor of Metallurgy, 1873-1930.]

1121 Rogers, Emma, and Sedgwick, William T., eds. Life and Letters of William Barton Rogers. 2 vols. Boston: n.p., 1896. [Rogers was First President, 1862-1870 and 1878-1882.]

1122 Wiener, N. Ex-Prodigy: My Childhood and Youth. New York: Simon and Schuster, 1953. [Author was Professor of Mathematics.]

MASSACHUSETTS, UNIVERSITY OF

1123 Cary, Harold W. The University of Massachusetts: A History of One Hundred Years. Amherst: University of Massachusetts Press, 1968.

1124 Bowker, William Henry. A Tribute to Levi Stockbridge. Amherst?, 1904.

1125 Rand, Frank P. Yesterdays at Massachusetts State College, 1863-1933. Amherst: University of Massachusetts Press, 1933.

1126 Stebbins, Calvin. Henry Hill Goodell. Cambridge: Riverside Press, 1911. [Goodell was President, 1886-1905.]

MOUNT HOLYOKE COLLEGE

1127   Cole, Arthur C. A Hundred Years of Mount Holyoke College; The Evolution of an Educational Ideal. New Haven: Yale University Press, 1940.

1128   Gilchrist, Beth Bradford. The Life of Mary Lyon. Boston: Houghton Mifflin, 1910. [Lyon was First President.]

1129   Lansing, Marion, ed. Mary Lyon Through Her Letters. Boston: Books, Inc., 1937.

1130   McCurdy, Persis H. "History of Physical Training at Mt. Holyoke College." American Physical Education Review 14 (1909): 138-151.

1131   Marks, Jeannette Augustus, ed. Life and Letters of Mary Emma Woolley (1863-1947). Washington, D.C.: Public Affairs Press, 1955. [Woolley was President, 1901-1936.]

1132   Nutting, Mary O. Historical Sketch of Mount Holyoke Seminary. Washington, D.C.: U.S. Bureau of Education, 1876.

1133   Stow, Sarah D. History of Mount Holyoke Seminary During Its First Half Century, 1837-87. Springfield: n.p., 1887.

1134   Warner, Frances L. On a New England Campus. Boston: Houghton Mifflin, 1937.

NORTHEASTERN UNIVERSITY

1135   Marston, Everett C. Origin and Development of Northeastern University. Boston: Cuneo, 1961.

OREAD COLLEGIATE INSTITUTE

1136   Wright, Martha Burt, ed. History of the Oread Collegiate Institute, Worcester, Massachusetts. New Haven: Tuttle, Morehouse and Taylor, 1905.

RADCLIFFE COLLEGE

1137   Briggs, Le Baron. "An Experiment in Faith: Radcliffe College." Atlantic Monthly 143 (1929): 105-109.

1138   Baker, Christine. The Story of Fay House. Cambridge: Harvard University Press, 1929.

MASSACHUSETTS 121

1139 Maguire, Mary H. "The Curtain-raiser to the Founding of Radcliffe College." <u>Cambridge Historical Society Publications</u> 36 (1957): 23-39.

SAINT JOHN'S SEMINARY

1140 Sexton, John E., and Riley, Arthur J. <u>History of Saint John's Seminary, Brighton</u>. Boston: Roman Catholic Archbishop of Boston, 1945.

SALEM STATE COLLEGE

1141 Pitman, J.A. "The Salem Normal School." <u>Elementary School Journal</u> 30 (1930): 416-430.

SIMMONS COLLEGE

1142 Beasley, Gertrude. <u>My First Thirty Years</u>. Paris: Three Mountains Press, 1925.

1143 Keeton, Morris, and Hilberry, Conrad. <u>Struggle and Promise: A Future for Colleges</u>. New York: McGraw-Hill, 1969, pp. 113-148.

1144 Mark, Kenneth L. <u>Delayed by Fire, Being the Early History of Simmons College</u>. Concord, N.H.: Rumford Press, 1945.

SMITH COLLEGE

1145 Dunn, Esther Cloudman. <u>Pursuit of Understanding; Autobiography of an Education</u>. New York: Macmillan, 1945. [Dunn was Professor of English.]

1146 Greene, Louisa D. <u>Foreshadowings of Smith College</u>. Portland, Me.: Southworth Press, 1928.

1147 Hanscom, Elizabeth Deering, and Greene, H.F. <u>Sophia Smith and the Beginnings of Smith College</u>. Northampton: Smith College, 1925.

1148 Rhees, Harriet S. <u>Laurenus Clark Seelye</u>. New York: Houghton Mifflin, 1933. [Seelye was First President, 1873-1910.]

1149 Seelye, Laurenus C. <u>The Early History of Smith College</u>. Boston: Houghton Mifflin, 1923.

1150 Thorp, Margaret (Farrand). <u>Neilson of Smith</u>. New York: Oxford University Press, 1956. [W.A. Neilson was President, 1917-1939.]

SOUTHEASTERN MASSACHUSETTS UNIVERSITY

1151 Cass, Walter James. "A History of Southeastern Massachusetts Technological Institute in Cultural Perspective." Doctoral dissertation, Boston University, 1966.

SPRINGFIELD COLLEGE

1152 Doggett, Lawrence Locke. Man and a School; Pioneering in Higher Education at Springfield College. New York: Association Press, 1943.

1153 Runquist, Kenneth. "An Historical Study of the Development of Teacher Preparation in Physical Education at Springfield College with Special Reference to the Curriculum." Doctoral dissertation, Columbia Teachers College, 1953.

SUFFOLK UNIVERSITY

1154 Archer, Gleason. Building a School: A Fearless Portrayal of Men and Events in the Old Bay State, 1906-1919. Boston: Privately Printed, 1915. [Author was Founder and First President.]

1155 Archer, Gleason. The Impossible Task. Boston: Suffolk Law School Press, 1926.

TUFTS UNIVERSITY

1156 Miller, Russell E. Light on the Hill: A History of Tufts College, 1852-1952. Boston: Beacon Press, 1966.

1157 Carmichael, Leonard. Tufts College, Its Science and Technology, a Centennial View, 1852-1952. New York: Newcomen Society in North America, 1952.

1158 Finn, John Joseph. "History of Tufts College, Boston, Massachusetts." Phi Chi Quarterly 36 (1939): 365-376.

1159 Start, Alaric Bertrand, ed. History of Tufts College, Published by the Class of 1897. Boston: Tufts College, 1896.

WELLESLEY COLLEGE

1160 Converse, Florence. Wellesley College; A Chronicle of the Years, 1875-1938. Wellesley: Hathaway House Book-Shop, 1939.

1161 Burgess, Dorothy. Dream and Deed: The Story of Katherine Lee Bates. Norman, Okla.: University of Oklahoma Press, 1952. [Bates was Professor of English, 1881-1925.]

1162 Frederick, Peter J. "Vida Dutton Scudder: The Professor as Social Activist." New England Quarterly 43 (1970): 407-433. [Scudder was Professor of Literature, 1892-1927.]

1163 Gager, C. Stuart. "Wellesley College and the Development of Botanical Education in America." Science n.s. 67 (1928): 171-178.

1164 Hackett, Alice Payne. Wellesley, Part of the American Story. New York: E.P. Dutton, 1949.

1165 Hazard, Caroline, ed. An Academic Courtship. Cambridge: Harvard University Press, 1940. [Letters between Alice Freeman, President 1881-1888, and George Herbert Palmer.]

1166 Hazard, Caroline. From College Gates. Boston: Houghton Mifflin, 1925.

1167 Kingsley, Mrs. Florence (Morse). The Life of Henry Fowle Durant, Founder of Wellesley College. New York: Century, 1924.

1168 Palmer, George H. The Life of Alice Freeman Palmer. Boston and New York: Houghton Mifflin, 1924. [A.F. Palmer was President, 1881-1888.]

1169 Scudder, Vida D. One Journey. New York: E.P. Dutton, 1937.

WESTFIELD STATE COLLEGE

1170 Massachusetts W.P.A. The State Teachers College at Westfield. Boston: State Department of Education, 1941.

WHEATON COLLEGE

1171 Shepard, Grace. "Female Education at Wheaton College." New England Quarterly 6 (December 1933): 803-834.

WILLIAMS COLLEGE

1172 Rudolph, Frederick. *Mark Hopkins and the Log: Williams College 1836-1872*. New Haven: Yale University Press, 1956. [Hopkins was President, 1836-1872.]

1173 Bascom, John. *Things Learned by Living*. New York: Putnam, 1913. [Author was Professor of Philosophy, 1850-1872.]

1174 Botsford, E. Hubert. *Fifty Years at Williams*. 5 vols. Pittsfield: McClelland Press, 1928-1940.

1175 Denison, J.H. *Mark Hopkins: A Biography*. New York: Scribner's, 1935.

1176 Durfee, Calvin. *A History of Williams College*. Boston: A. Williams and Co., 1860.

1177 Jones, Robert A. "Consciousness and Sociology: The Intuitionism of John Bascom, 1827-1911." Doctoral dissertation, University of Pennsylvania, 1969.

1178 Perry, Carroll. *A Professor of Life: A Sketch of Arthur Latham Perry of Williams College, by His Son, Carroll Perry*. Boston: Houghton Mifflin, 1923. [Perry was Professor of History, 1853-1891.]

1179 Smallwood, William M. "The Williams Lyceum of Natural History, 1835-1888." *New England Quarterly* 10 (1937): 553-557.

WORCESTER COLLEGE FOR THE BLIND

1180 Bell, Donald. *An Experiment in Education: The History of Worcester College for the Blind, 1866-1966*. New York: Humanities Press, 1967.

WORCESTER POLYTECHNIC INSTITUTE

1181 Tymeson, Mildred McClay. *Two Towers: The Story of Worcester Tech, 1865-1965*. Worcester: Worcester Polytechnic Institute, 1964.

1182 Crew, Henry. "Thomas C. Mendenhall." *National Academy of Sciences Biographic Memoirs* 16 (1936): 239-251. [Mendenhall was President, 1894-1901.]

MASSACHUSETTS

1183 Johnson, Donald E., and Mooney, James E. *Pioneer Class*. Worcester: LaVigne Press, 1966.

1184 Taylor, Herbert F. *Seventy Years of the Worcester Polytechnic Institute*. Worcester: Davis Press, 1937.

Michigan

GENERAL REFERENCES

1185 Dunbar, Willis Frederick. *The Michigan Record in Higher Education.* Detroit: Wayne State University Press, 1963.

1186 Barnes, Richard Alan. "The Development of Teacher Education in Michigan." Doctoral dissertation, University of Chicago, 1940.

1187 Dunbar, Willis Frederick. "Early Denominational Academies and Colleges in Michigan." *Michigan History* 24 (1940): 451-466.

1188 Dunbar, Willis Frederick. "The Influence of the Protestant Denominations on Higher Education in Michigan 1817-1900." Doctoral dissertation, University of Michigan, 1939.

1189 Dunbar, Willis Frederick. "Public Versus Private Control of Higher Education in Michigan, 1817-1855." *Mississippi Valley Historical Review* 22 (1935): 385-406.

1190 Fallon, Jerome Anthony. "The Influence of the Summer School Movement on the State of Michigan, 1874-1931, With Special Reference to the University of Michigan." Doctoral dissertation, University of Michigan, 1960.

1191 Glazer, Stanford H. "Development of Michigan College Counselling Programs--1940-1950." Doctoral dissertation, Wayne State University, 1954.

1192 Green, Grace Helen. "Michigan Public Junior Colleges: A Decade of Development, 1914-1923." Doctoral dissertation, University of Michigan, 1968.

1193 Henning, Sister Gabrielle. "A History of Changing Patterns of Objectives in Catholic Higher Education for Women in Michigan." Doctoral dissertation, Michigan State University, 1969.

MICHIGAN

1194 Hoyt, Charles Oliver, and Ford, R.C. John D. Pierce, Founder of the Michigan School System; A Study of Education in the Northwest. Ypsilanti: Scharf Tag, Label & Box Co., 1905.

1195 McLaughlin, Andrew C. History of Higher Education in Michigan. Washington, D.C.: U.S. Bureau of Education, 1891.

1196 Magnuson, Roger Paul. "The Concern of Organized Business with Michigan Education, 1910-1940." Doctoral dissertation, University of Michigan, 1963.

1197 Ringenberg, William C. "Church Colleges vs. State University." Michigan History 55 (1971): 305-320.

1198 Ringenberg, William C. "College Life in Frontier Michigan." Michigan History 54 (1970): 91-107.

1199 Ringenberg, William C. "The Protestant College on the Michigan Frontier." Doctoral dissertation, Michigan State University, 1970.

1200 Rodehorst, Wayne Leroy. "An Analysis of the Introduction of Vocational-Technical Education Programs in Michigan Community Colleges Established Before 1930." Doctoral dissertation, Michigan State University, 1965.

1201 Ross, Margery Roberta. "Influences Affecting the Development of Undergraduate Social Work Education in Seven Michigan Colleges from 1920 to 1955." Doctoral dissertation, University of Michigan, 1958.

1202 Schlafmann, Norman J. "An Examination of the Influence of the State Legislature on the Educational Policies of the Constitutionally Incorporated Colleges and Universities of Michigan Through Enactment of Public Acts from 1851 Through 1970." Doctoral dissertation, Michigan State University, 1970.

1203 Sebaly, Avis L. "A Study of the Rise of the State Normal Schools in Michigan into Teachers Colleges." Doctoral dissertation, University of Michigan, 1950.

1204 Williams, Wolcott B. "Two Early Efforts to Found Colleges in Michigan, at Delta and at Marshall." Michigan Historical Society Collections 30 (1906): 525-549.

INSTITUTIONAL HISTORIES

ADRIAN COLLEGE

1205 Hay, Fanny, et al. The Story of a Noble Devotion: Adrian College, 1845-1945. Adrian: Adrian College Press, 1945.

1206 Kauffman, Albert W. "Early Years of Adrian College." Michigan History 13 (1929): 50-74.

ALBION COLLEGE

1207 Gildart, Robert. Albion College, 1835-1960: A History. Albion: Albion College, 1960.

1208 Brunger, Ronald A. "Albion College: The Founding of a Frontier School." Michigan History 61 (1967): 130-153.

1209 Reed, George R. "The Contributions of Thomas Milton Carter to Teacher Education, Albion College 1923-1962." Doctoral dissertation, Michigan State University, 1970.

ANDREWS UNIVERSITY

1210 Vande Vere, Emmett K. The Wisdom Seekers: The Intriguing Story of the Men and Women Who Made the First Institution for Higher Learning Among Seventh Day Adventists. Nashville, Tenn.: Southern Publishing, 1972.

1211 Cadwallader, Edward M. "Educational Principles in the Writings of Ellen G. White." Doctoral dissertation, University of Nebraska, 1949.

BENTON HARBOR COLLEGE

1212 Edgcumbe, Victoria C. "Benton Harbor College and Its President, Dr. George S. Edgcumbe." Michigan History 6 (1922): 375-385.

CALVIN COLLEGE

1213 Semi-Centennial Committee. Calvin College and Theological School. Grand Rapids: n.p., 1926.

1214 Rooks, Albert J. "Calvin College, Grand Rapids, 1894-1927." Michigan History 11 (1927): 532-553.

CENTRAL MICHIGAN UNIVERSITY

1215 Wesley, Charles H. Central State College: Its Birth and Growth. Ann Arbor: Edwards Brothers, 1953.

MICHIGAN

1216 Larzelene, Claude S. "The Central Michigan Normal School at Mt. Pleasant." Michigan History 3 (1919): 235-246.

DETROIT, UNIVERSITY OF

1217 Dionne, Narcisse Eutrope. Gabriel Richard, Sulpicien, Curé et Second Fondateur de la Ville de Detroit. Quebec: Typographie Laflamme and Proulx, 1911.

1218 Doran, William T. "Historical Sketch of the University of Detroit." Michigan History 2 (1918): 154-164.

DUNS SCOTUS COLLEGE

1219 Casey, Edgar. Saint Anthony Shrine Duns Scotus College: A Brief History and Guide. Cincinnati: n.p., 1930.

EASTERN MICHIGAN UNIVERSITY

1220 Isbell, Egbert R. A History of Eastern Michigan University 1849-1965. Ypsilanti: Eastern Michigan University, 1971.

1221 Eastern Michigan University. The First One Hundred Years, Michigan State Normal College, Ypsilanti, Michigan. Ypsilanti: Eastern Michigan University, 1949.

1222 Eastern Michigan University. Michigan State Normal College, Seventy-Fifth Anniversary, A Souvenir History. Ypsilanti: Eastern Michigan University, 1928.

1223 Putnam, Daniel. A History of the Michigan State Normal School (Now Normal College) at Ypsilanti, Michigan 1849-1899. Ypsilanti: Scharf Tag, Label & Box Co., 1899.

FERRIS STATE COLLEGE

1224 Byrnes, Lawrence W. "Ferris Institute as a Private School, 1884-1952." Doctoral dissertation, Michigan State University, 1970.

FLINT COMMUNITY COLLEGE

1225 Prahl, Marie. "Case Study of the Development of a Junior College into a Community College." Doctoral dissertation, University of Michigan, 1967.

GENERAL MOTORS INSTITUTE

1226 Young, Clarence H., and Tuttle, Robert. *The Years 1919-1969... A History of G.M.I.* Flint: General Motors Institute, 1969.

1227 Sobey, Albert. *Whither Destiny; Pioneering Education and Training in and for Industry Through General Motors Institute. An Autobiography Written for His Son.* Unpublished. 1953.

GRAND RAPIDS JUNIOR COLLEGE

1228 Baxter, E. Ray. *Grand Rapids Junior College: Fifty Years of Leadership, 1914-1964.* Grand Rapids: n.p., 1964.

1229 Davis, Jesse Buttrick. *The Saga of a Schoolmaster: An Autobiography.* Boston: Boston University Press, 1956. [Author was President, 1914-1920.]

GRAND VALLEY STATE COLLEGE

1230 Swets, Marinus Matthius. "A Study of the Establishment of Grand Valley State College." Doctoral dissertation, Michigan State University, 1962.

HILLSDALE COLLEGE

1231 Moore, Vivian Elsie (Lyon). *The First Hundred Years of Hillsdale College.* Ann Arbor: Ann Arbor Press, 1944.

HOPE COLLEGE

1232 Wichers, Wynand. *A Century of Hope, 1866-1966.* Grand Rapids: Eerdmans, 1968.

1233 Stegenga, Preston L. *Anchor of Hope: The History of an American Denominational Institution, Hope College.* Grand Rapids: Eerdmans, 1954.

1234 Vennema, Ame. "Rise and Progress of Hope College." *Michigan History* 4 (1920): 287-298.

MICHIGAN

KALAMAZOO COLLEGE

1235 Mulder, Arnold. The Kalamazoo College Story; The First Quarter of the Second Century of Progress 1933-1958. Kalamazoo: Kalamazoo College, 1958.

1236 Goodsell, Charles, and Dunbar, Willis Frederick. Centennial History of Kalamazoo College, 1833-1933. Kalamazoo: Kalamazoo College, 1933.

MICHIGAN STATE UNIVERSITY

1237 Kuhn, Madison. Michigan State: The First Hundred Years, 1855-1955. East Lansing: Michigan State University Press, 1955.

1238 Baker, Ray Stannard. Native American; The Book of My Youth. New York: Scribner's, 1941. [Author was Undergraduate.]

1239 Beal, W.J. History of Michigan Agriculture College. East Lansing: The Agriculture College, 1915.

1240 Blaisdell, Thomas C., ed. Semi-Centennial Celebration of Michigan State Agricultural College, May 26-31, 1907. Chicago: University of Chicago Press, 1908.

1241 Cullen, Maurice R. "The Presidency of Jonathan LeMoyne Snyder at Michigan Agricultural College, 1896-1915." Doctoral dissertation, University of Michigan, 1964.

1242 Haigh, Henry A. "Old Days and Early Authors of Michigan State College." Michigan History 13 (1929): 165-195.

1243 White, Katherine. "Student Activism at Michigan State University During the 1960's." Doctoral dissertation, Michigan State University, 1972.

1244 Yoder, Mabel Bristol. "Life at Michigan State University at the Turn of the Century." Michigan History 39 (1955): 327-332.

MICHIGAN, UNIVERSITY OF

1245 Peckham, Howard H. The Making of the University of Michigan, 1817-1967. Ann Arbor: University of Michigan Press, 1967.

1246 Adams, C.K. Historical Sketch of the University of Michigan. Ann Arbor: University of Michigan Press, 1876.

1247 Andrews, Charles M. "These Forty Years." American Historical Review 30 (1925): 225-250.

1248 Angell, James Burrill. "A Memorial Discourse on the Life and Services of Henry Simmons Frieze." In Selected Addresses, by James Burrill Angell. New York: Longmans, Green, 1912. [Frieze was Professor of Latin and twice Acting President, 1854-1889.]

1249 Angell, James Burrill. Reminiscences. New York: Longmans, Green, 1912. [Author was President, 1872-1909.]

1250 Bennet, Wells. "Alexander J. Davis, Architect; His Designs for the First Building of the University of Michigan." Michigan Alumnus (Quarterly Review) 43 (1937): 414-420.

1251 Bonesteel, Roscoe. John Montieth: A Man of Conscience. Detroit: Wayne State University Press, 1966.

1252 Bordin, Ruth. The University of Michigan: A Pictorial History. Ann Arbor: University of Michigan Press, 1967.

1253 Campbell, Edward D. History of the Chemical Laboratory of the University of Michigan, 1856-1916. Ann Arbor: University of Michigan, 1916.

1254 Cooley, Mortimer E. Scientific Blacksmith. Ann Arbor: University of Michigan Press, 1947. [Author was Professor of Engineering and Dean, 1881-1928.]

1255 Cross, Arthur L. "The University of Michigan and the Training of Her Students for the War." Michigan History 4 (1920): 112-140.

1256 Damm, Helmut H. "The University of Michigan from 1850 to 1917 as a Leading Center of German Influences During the Nation's Economic Take-Off." Doctoral dissertation, University of Michigan, 1970.

1257 Davis, C.O. "History, Organization, and Administration of the Teachers Appointment Office of the University of Michigan." School Review 20 (1912): 532-558.

1258 Drachler, Norman. "Religion and the University of Michigan." Doctoral dissertation, University of Michigan, 1948.

1259 Dunbar, Willis Frederick. "The University and Its Branches, Michigan's Second Experiment in Educational Centralization." Michigan Alumnus (Quarterly Review) 46 (1940): 303-315.

MICHIGAN

1260 Eggertsen, Claude, ed. Studies in the History of the School of Education, University of Michigan (1868-1954). Ann Arbor: University of Michigan Press, 1955.

1261 Farrand, Elizabeth M. History of the University of Michigan. Ann Arbor: Register Publishing House, 1885.

1262 Guthe, Carl E. "The Museums at Michigan." Michigan Alumnus (Quarterly Review) 43 (1937): 469-477.

1263 Hazzard, Florence W. "Life of Eliza Mosher." Unpublished manuscript, Michigan Historical Collections, University of Michigan. [Mosher was First Dean of Women, 1896-1902.]

1264 Hinsdale, Burke. History of the University of Michigan. Ann Arbor: University of Michigan, 1906.

1265 Holli, Melvin G., and Tompkins, C. David. "Mortimer E. Cooley: Technocrat as Politician." Michigan History 52 (1968): 133-146.

1266 Hornberger, Theodore. "The Gilded Years of Lecturing: The History of the Student Lecture Association from 1864 to 1884." Michigan Alumnus 42 (1936): 154-167.

1267 Hornberger, Theodore. "Lectures and Lecturers in the Early Days: The Background and First Ten Years of the Student Lecture Association." Michigan Alumnus 42 (1936): 80-92.

1268 Huber, John. The Admission of Women to the University of Michigan. Ann Arbor: Michigan Historical Collections #18, 1970.

1269 Isbell, Egbert R. "The Catholepistemiad, or University, of Michigania." In University of Michigan Historical Essays, edited by A. E. Boak, pp. 159-182. Ann Arbor: University of Michigan Press, 1937.

1270 Laird, David B. "The Regents of the University of Michigan and the Legislature of the State, 1920-1950." Doctoral dissertation, University of Michigan, 1972.

1271 Liu, Yung-szi. "The Academic Achievement of Chinese Graduate Students at the University of Michigan (1907-1950)." Doctoral dissertation, University of Michigan, 1955.

1272 McGuigan, Dorothy. A Dangerous Experiment: One Hundred Years of Women's Education at the University of Michigan. Ann Arbor: Center for the Continuing Education for Women, 1970.

1273 Maxwell, Howard B. "The Formative Years of the University Alumni Movement as Illustrated by Studies of the University of Michigan and Columbia, Princeton, and Yale Universities, 1854-1918." Doctoral dissertation, University of Michigan, 1964.

1274 Michigan University. Records of the University of Michigan, 1817-1837. Ann Arbor: University of Michigan, 1935.

1275 Nyikos, Michael. "A History of the Relationship between Athletic Administration and Faculty Governance at the University of Michigan, 1945-1968." Doctoral dissertation, University of Michigan, 1970.

1276 Perry, Charles M. Henry Philip Tappan--Philosopher and University President. Ann Arbor: University of Michigan Press, 1933. [Tappan was First President, 1852-1861.]

1277 Peterson, Reuben. "Landmarks in the Medical School; A Survey of the History of the University of Michigan Medical School and Its Hospital." Michigan Alumnus (Quarterly Review) 45 (1939): 196-202.

1278 Poret, George Cleveland. The Contributions of William Harold Payne to Public Education. Nashville, Tenn.: George Peabody University, 1930. [Payne was First Professor of Education, 1879-1888.]

1279 Price, Richard Rees. The Financial Support of the University of Michigan: Its Origin and Development. Cambridge: Cambridge University Press, 1924.

1280 Ringenbery, William. "Church College vs. State University." Michigan History 55 (1971): 305-320.

1281 Ruthven, Alexander G. A Naturalist in Two Worlds. Ann Arbor: University of Michigan Press, 1963. [Ruthven was President, 1929-1951.]

1282 Sagendorph, Kent. Michigan: The Story of the University. New York: E.P. Dutton, 1948.

1283 Schurtz, Shelby B. Beta Theta Pi at Michigan. Privately Printed, 1928.

1284 Schurtz, Shelby B. "Gabriel Richard and the University of Michigan." Michigan History 19 (1935): 5-18.

1285 Shaw, Wilfred B. "Early Days of the University of Michigan." Michigan History 16 (1932): 439-463.

1286 Shaw, Wilfred B., ed. From Vermont to Michigan: Correspondence of James Burrill Angell, 1869-1871. Ann Arbor: University of Michigan Press, 1936.

1287 Shaw, Wilfred B. "Ninety Years Ago." Michigan Alumnus (Quarterly Review) 44 (1938): 112-125, 230-246.

1288 Shaw, Wilfred B. Support of the University of Michigan from Sources Other Than Public Funds or Student Fees, 1817-1931. Ann Arbor: University of Michigan Press, 1934.

MICHIGAN

1289 Shaw, Wilfred B. The University of Michigan. New York: Harcourt, Brace and Howe, 1920.

1290 Shaw, Wilfred B., ed. The University of Michigan, An Encyclopedic Survey. 8 vols. Ann Arbor: University of Michigan Press, 1941-1958.

1291 Smith, Ira M. "University of Michigan: Trend of Admission Requirements in the College of Literature, Science, and the Arts." Michigan History 14 (1930): 207-220.

1292 Smith, S.W. Harry Burns Hutchins and the University of Michigan. Ann Arbor: University of Michigan Press, 1951. [Hutchins was President.]

1293 Smith, S.W. James Burrill Angell: An American Influence. Ann Arbor: University of Michigan Press, 1954.

1294 Snyder, Sam R. "Academic Freedom at the University of Michigan: The Nickerson Case." Doctoral dissertation, University of Michigan, 1970.

1295 Spill, William A. "University of Michigan: Beginnings--I, II, III." Michigan History 12 (1928): 635-661; 13 (1929): 41-54, 227-244.

1296 Stratton, Rev. C.C., ed. Autobiography of Bishop Erastus O. Haven. New York: Phillips and Hunt, 1883. [Haven was Professor of Latin, President 1862-1868.]

1297 vanDeWater, Peter E. "President Alexander Grant Ruthven of Michigan and His Relations to His Faculty, Students, and Regents." Doctoral dissertation, University of Michigan, 1970.

1298 Van Eyck, Daniel K. "President Clarence Cook Little and the University of Michigan." Doctoral dissertation, University of Michigan, 1964.

1299 Vaughan, Victor C. A Doctor's Memories. Indianapolis: Bobbs-Merrill, 1926. [Author was Dean of Medical School, 1891-1921.]

1300 Wenley, Robert M. The Life and Work of George Sylvester Morris. New York: Macmillan, 1917. [Morris was Professor of Philosophy.]

1301 Wenley, Robert M. "The University of Michigan in the War." Michigan History 2 (1918): 690-701.

1302 Whiteney, Allen S. Training Teachers at the University of Michigan, 1879-1921. Ann Arbor: University of Michigan Press, 1931.

1303 Wilbee, Victor Roy. "The Religious Dimensions of Three Presidencies in a State University: Presidents Tappan, Haven, and Angell at the University of Michigan." Doctoral dissertation, University of Michigan, 1967.

1304 Wilson, Lois Mayfield. "Henry P. Tappan's Conceptions of the Structuring of University Functions." Doctoral dissertation, Stanford University, 1954.

MONTEITH COLLEGE

1305 Keeton, Morris, and Hilberry, Conrad. Struggle and Promise: A Future for Colleges. New York: McGraw-Hill, 1969, pp. 183-218.

NORTHERN MICHIGAN UNIVERSITY

1306 Hilton, Miriam E. Northern Michigan University: The First Seventy-Five Years. Forthcoming.

OAKLAND UNIVERSITY

1307 Riesman, David, et al. Academic Values and Mass Education: The Early Years of Oakland and Monteith. New York: Doubleday, 1971.

1308 Stoutenburg, Herbert N., Jr. "Oakland University: Its First Four Years; An Historical Analysis of Its Development and Its Administrative Policies." Doctoral dissertation, Michigan State University, 1968.

SACRED HEART SEMINARY

1309 Sacred Heart Seminary. Fiftieth Anniversary Book. Detroit: Sacred Heart Seminary, 1969.

SPRING ARBOR COLLEGE

1310 Snyder, Howard A. One Hundred Years at Spring Arbor: A History of Spring Arbor College, 1873-1973. Winona Lake, Ind.: Light and Life Press, 1973.

WAYNE STATE UNIVERSITY

1311 Hanawalt, Leslie L. *A Place of Light: The History of Wayne State University. A Centennial Publication*. Detroit: Wayne State University Press, 1968.

1312 Halperin, Samuel. *A University in the Web of Politics*. New Brunswick, N.J.: Eaglewood Institute of Politics, 1960.

1313 Irwin, James R. "Wayne University--A History." Doctoral dissertation, Wayne State University, 1953.

1314 Rosenblum, Sanders F. "Wayne State University." *Michigan History* 42 (1958): 223-226.

WESTERN MICHIGAN UNIVERSITY

1315 Knauss, James O. *The First Fifty Years 1903-1953, A History of Western Michigan College of Education*. Kalamazoo: Western Michigan College of Education, 1953.

1316 Burnham, Ernest. "A Historical Sketch of Western State Normal School, Kalamazoo." *Michigan History* 9 (1925): 501-514.

1317 Dunham, E. Alden. *Colleges of the Forgotten Americans*. New York: McGraw-Hill, 1969.

1318 Knauss, James O. *History of Western State Teachers College 1904-1929*. Kalamazoo: Western Michigan Teachers College, 1929.

1319 Various Faculty Members. *Twenty Years 1904-1924*. Kalamazoo: Western State Normal School, 1924.

Minnesota

GENERAL REFERENCES

1320 Minnesota Commission on Higher Education. *Higher Education in Minnesota*. Minneapolis: University of Minnesota Press, 1950.

1321 Greer, John N. *History of Education in Minnesota*. Washington, D.C.: U.S. Government Printing Office, 1902.

1322 Jarchow, Merrill E. *Private Liberal Arts Colleges in Minnesota: Their History and Contributions*. St. Paul: Minnesota Historical Society, 1974.

1323 Meyer, Ray Francis. "A History of the Separate, Two Year Public and Private Junior Colleges of Minnesota, 1905-55." Doctoral dissertation, University of Minnesota, 1957.

1324 Prochnow, Larry A. "The Story of Science in Minnesota's Denominational Colleges, 1850-1910." Master's thesis, University of Minnesota, 1970.

1325 Williams, Ward R. "Post-High School Education in Minnesota 1952-53." Doctoral dissertation, University of Minnesota, 1955.

INSTITUTIONAL HISTORIES

AUGSBURG COLLEGE

1326 Chrislock, Carl Henry. *From Fjord to Freeway: One Hundred Years. Augsburg College*. Minneapolis: Augsburg College, 1969.

BEMIDJI STATE COLLEGE

1327 Lee, Arthur O. College in the Pines; A History of Bemidji State College. Minneapolis: Dillon Press, 1970.

1328 Lee, Arthur O. "Paternalistic President: Manfred W. Deputy of Bemidji State College." Minnesota History 42 (1971): 178-185. [Deputy was President, 1919-1947.]

BETHEL COLLEGE

1329 Olson, A., and Olson, V.A. Seventy-Five Years: A History of Bethel Theological Seminary, St. Paul, Minnesota, 1871-1946. Chicago: Conference Press, 1946.

CARLETON COLLEGE

1330 Headley, Leal A., and Jarcow, Merrill E. Carleton: The First Century. Northfield: Carleton College, 1966.

1331 Leonard, Delavan L. The History of Carleton College: Its Origin and Growth Environment and Builders. Chicago: Revell, 1904.

CONCORDIA COLLEGE (ST. PAUL)

1332 Overn, Oswald B. A History of Concordia College, St. Paul, Minnesota. St. Paul: Concordia College, 1967.

GUSTAVUS ADOLPHUS COLLEGE

1333 Lund, Doniver Adolph. Gustavus Adolphus College; A Centennial History, 1862-1952. St. Peter: Gustavus Adolphus College Press, 1963.

1334 Peterson, Conrad. Gustavus Adolphus College, A History of Eighty Years, 1862-1942. Rock Island, Ill.: Augustana Book Concern, 1942.

1335 Peterson, Conrad. Remember Thy Past; A History of Gustavus Adolphus College 1862-1952. St. Peter: Gustavus Adolphus College Press, 1953.

HAMLINE UNIVERSITY

1336 Pace, Charles N., ed. Hamline University. St. Paul: Hamline University Alumni Association, 1939.

1337 Asher, Hellen D. "A Frontier College of the Middle West: Hamline University, 1854-69." Minnesota History 9 (1928): 363-378.

MACALESTER COLLEGE

1338 Dupre, Huntley. Edward Duffield Neill. St. Paul: Macalester College Press, 1949. [Neill was President, 1874-1884.]

1339 Fund, Henry D. A History of Macalester College. St. Paul: Macalester College Board of Trustees, 1910.

1340 Kagin, Edwin. James Wallace (1849-1939) of Macalester. Garden City: Doubleday, 1957. [Wallace was Professor of Greek and President, 1887-1926.]

MINNESOTA, UNIVERSITY OF

1341 Gray, James. Open Wide the Door; The Story of the University of Minnesota. New York: Putnam, 1958.

1342 Buck, Solon J., ed. William Watts Folwell: The Autobiography and Letters of a Pioneer of Culture. Minneapolis: University of Minnesota Press, 1933. [Folwell was First President, 1869-1884, and Professor of Political Science, 1875-1907.]

1343 Coffman, Lotus Delta. University of Minnesota 1920-1930. A Decade in the History of the University of Minnesota. Minneapolis: University of Minnesota Press, 1930.

1344 Dawald, Victor F. "The Social Philosophy of Lotus Delta Coffman." Doctoral dissertation, University of Wisconsin, 1951. [Coffman was President, 1920-1938.]

1345 Firkins, Oscar W. Cyrus Northrop; A Memoir. Minneapolis: University of Minnesota Press, 1925. [Northrop was President, 1884-1909.]

1346 Ford, Guy S. The Making of the University: An Unorthodox Report. Minneapolis: University of Minnesota Press, 1940. [Author was Professor and Administrator, 1913-1941.]

1347 Ford, Guy S. On and Off the Campus. Minneapolis: University of Minnesota Press, 1938.

MINNESOTA 141

1348 Gibson, William C. "Frank Fairchild Wesbrook, 1868-1918: A Pioneer Medical Educator in Minnesota and British Columbia." Journal of the History of Medicine and Allied Sciences 22 (1967): 357-379. [Wesbrook was Professor of Medicine, 1895-1913.]

1349 Gilfillan, John B. "History of the University of Minnesota." Minnesota Historical Society Collections 12 (1908): 43-84.

1350 Gray, James. The University of Minnesota, 1851-1951. Minneapolis: University of Minnesota Press, 1951.

1351 Johnson, E. Bird, ed. Forty Years of the University of Minnesota. Minneapolis: University of Minnesota Press, 1910.

1352 Leonard, William E. "Early College Silhouettes." Minnesota History 16 (1935): 178-186.

1353 Randall, Eugene. Reminiscences and Reflections. St. Paul: n.p., 1935. [Author was Dean of the College of Agriculture.]

1354 Whitney, Helen. Maria Sanford, 1836-1920. Minneapolis: University of Minnesota, 1922. [Sanford was Professor of English, 1880-1909.]

1355 Wiberg, Charles E. "A History of the University of Minnesota Chapter of the American Association of University Professors." Doctoral dissertation, University of Minnesota, 1964.

1356 Youngquist, Bernard Edward. "A Critical Study and Analysis of the University of Minnesota Schools of Agriculture." Doctoral dissertation, University of Minnesota, 1959.

MINNESOTA, UNIVERSITY OF, AT MORRIS CAMPUS

1357 Munson, Corliss D. "A Description of the Changing Profile of the University of Minnesota Morris 1960-65." Master's thesis, University of Minnesota, 1966.

SAINT BENEDICT, COLLEGE OF THE

1358 McDonald, Grace. With Lamps Burning. St. Joseph: St. Benedict's Priory, 1957.

SAINT CLOUD STATE COLLEGE

1359 Cates, Edwin. A Centennial History of St. Cloud State College. Minneapolis: Dillan Press, 1968.

1360 Brainard, Dudley S. History of St. Cloud State Teachers College. St. Cloud: St. Cloud State Teachers College, 1954.

SAINT JOHN'S UNIVERSITY

1361 Barry, Colman James. Worship and Work; St. John's Abbey and University, 1856-1956. Collegeville: St. John's Abbey, 1956.

1362 Hoffmann, Alexius. St. John's University; A Sketch of Its History. Collegeville: Record Press, 1907.

SAINT OLAF COLLEGE

1363 Benson, William C. High on Manitou; A History of St. Olaf College, 1874-1949. Northfield: St. Olaf College Press, 1949.

1364 Gross, I.F. "The Beginnings of St. Olaf College." Norwegian-American Historical Association Studies 5 (1930): 110-121.

1365 Kelsey, Roger R. "Fram! Fram! Christmenn, Crossmenn: The St. Olaf Program, 1912-1952." Doctoral dissertation, George Peabody University, 1954.

SAINT THOMAS, COLLEGE OF

1366 College of St. Thomas. Tradition of Excellence; A Tribute and a Testimonial. St. Paul: The Mother's Club, College of St. Thomas, St. Thomas Military Academy, 1957.

1367 Keenan, Edward Patrick. The Story of St. Thomas College. St. Paul: College of St. Thomas, 1935.

1368 Keeton, Morris, and Hilberry, Conrad. Struggle and Promise: A Future for Colleges. New York: McGraw-Hill, 1969, pp. 307-348.

WINONA STATE COLLEGE

1369 Talbot, Jean. First State Normal School 1860, Winona State College, 1960. Winona: Winona State College, 1961.

MINNESOTA

1370 Ruggles, C.O. *Historical Sketch and Notes: Winona State Normal School, 1860-1910*. Winona: Jones & Kroeger, 1910.

1371 Selle, Erwin S., ed. *The Winona State Teachers College: Historical Notes, 1910-1935*. Winona: n.p., 1935.

Mississippi

GENERAL REFERENCES

1372 Lucas, Aubrey Keith. "The Mississippi Legislature and Mississippi Public Higher Education: 1890-1960." Doctoral dissertation, Florida State University, 1966.

1373 Mayes, Edward. History of Education in Mississippi. Washington, D.C.: U.S. Government Printing Office, 1899.

1374 Scott, Roy V. "Land Grants for Higher Education in Mississippi: A Survey." Agricultural History 43 (1969): 357-368.

1375 Stark, Grace W. "Beginnings of Teacher Training in Mississippi." Doctoral dissertation, George Peabody University, 1946.

INSTITUTIONAL HISTORIES

ALCORN A & M COLLEGE

1376 Sewell, George A. "A Hundred Years of History: Alcorn A & M College Observes Centennial (1871-1971)." Negro History Bulletin 34 (1971): 78-80.

BLUE MOUNTAIN COLLEGE

1377 Sumrall, Robbie Neal. A Light on a Hill, A History of Blue Mountain College. Nashville, Tenn.: Penson, 1947.

MISSISSIPPI

DELTA STATE COLLEGE

1378 Kethley, William Marion. "A Brief History of Delta State College." Journal of Mississippi History 19 (1957): 173-184.

JACKSON STATE COLLEGE

1379 Coombs, Orde. "Jackson State College." Change 5 (October 1973): 34-39.

JEFFERSON COLLEGE

1380 Hamilton, William B. "Jefferson College and Education in Mississippi." Journal of Mississippi History 3 (1941): 259-276.

MISSISSIPPI COLLEGE

1381 Weathersby, W.H. "A History of Mississippi College." Mississippi Historical Society Publication 5 (1925): 184-220.

MISSISSIPPI STATE UNIVERSITY

1382 Bettersworth, John K. People's College; A History of Mississippi State. University, Ala.: University of Alabama Press, 1953.

1383 Colvard, Dean W. The Land Grant Way in Mississippi; The Story of Mississippi State University. New York: Newcomen Society in North America, 1962.

1384 Lee, Stephen Dill. The Agricultural and Mechanical College of Mississippi. Its Origin, Object, Management and Results, Discussed in a Series of Papers. Jackson: Clarion-Ledger, 1889.

MISSISSIPPI, UNIVERSITY OF

1385 Cabaniss, James Allen. The University of Mississippi: Its First Hundred Years. Hattiesburg: University and College Press of Mississippi, 1971.

1386 Barrett, Russell H. Integration at Ole Miss. Chicago: Quadrangle, 1965.

1387 Cabaniss, James A. *A History of the University of Mississippi.* University: University of Mississippi, 1949.

1388 Gillespie, Neal C. "Ole Miss: A New Look at Her First President." *Journal of Mississippi History* 30 (1968): 275-280.

1389 Hooker, G.C. "The Origin and History of the University of Mississippi." Doctoral dissertation, Stanford University, 1931.

1390 Shackelford, Walter Malcolm. "A History of Teacher Education at the University of Mississippi." Doctoral dissertation, University of Mississippi, 1959.

1391 Waddel, John N. *Memorials of Academic Life: Being an Historical Sketch of the Waddel Family.* Richmond, Va.: Presbyterian Committee of Publication, 1891. [Author was President, 1865-1874.]

MISSISSIPPI VALLEY STATE COLLEGE

1392 Tinsley, Sammy. "A History of Mississippi Valley State College." Doctoral dissertation, University of Mississippi, 1972.

SOUTHERN MISSISSIPPI, UNIVERSITY OF

1393 Bacon, John P. "History of Intercollegiate Athletics at the University of Southern Mississippi, 1912-1942." Master's thesis, University of Southern Mississippi, 1967.

1394 Fagerberg, Siegfred W. "History of the Athletic Programs at the University of Southern Mississippi, 1949-1969." Doctoral dissertation, University of Southern Mississippi, 1970.

TOUGALOO COLLEGE

1395 Campbell, Clarice T. "History of Tougaloo College." Doctoral dissertation, University of Mississippi, 1970.

UTICA JUNIOR COLLEGE

1396 Washington, Walter. "Utica (Mississippi) Junior College, 1903-1957: A Half Century of Education for Negroes." Doctoral dissertation, University of Southern Mississippi, 1970.

Missouri

GENERAL REFERENCES

1397 Snow, Marshall S. *Higher Education in Missouri*. Washington, D.C.: U.S. Bureau of Education, 1898.

1398 DeWoody, George M. "Development of the Educational Provisions of the Missouri Constitution of 1945." Doctoral dissertation, University of Missouri, 1949.

1399 Eisenman, Harry J. "Origins of Engineering Education in Missouri." *Missouri History Review* 63 (1969): 451-460.

1400 Grimes, Lloyd E. "The Development of Constitutional and Statutory Provisions for Education in Missouri Since 1874." Doctoral dissertation, University of Missouri, 1944.

1401 Mileham, Hazel B. "The Junior College Movement in Missouri." Doctoral dissertation, Yale University, 1934.

1402 Shankland, Wilbur M. "Medical Education in Saint Louis, 1836 to 1861." Doctoral dissertation, Washington University, 1953.

1403 Stevens, Walter. *A Centennial History of Missouri, 1820-1920*. St. Louis: S.J. Clarke, 1921.

INSTITUTIONAL HISTORIES

CENTRAL MISSOURI STATE COLLEGE

1404 Jones, Robert C. *One Hundred Years; 1871 Central Missouri State College 1971*. Warrensburg: Central Missouri State College, 1970.

1405   Anders, Leslie. *Education for Service: Centennial History of Central Missouri State College*. Warrensburg: Central Missouri State College, 1971.

CONCORDIA COLLEGE

1406   Fuerbringer, Ludwig Ernest. *Eighty Eventful Years; Reminiscences*. St. Louis: Concordia Public House, 1944. [Author was President, 1931-1943.]

1407   Sommer, M.S. "Reminiscences of My Student Days at Concordia Seminary, St. Louis, Missouri, from 1889 to 1892." *Concordia Historical Institute Quarterly* 12 (1939): 14-21.

CULVER-STOCKTON COLLEGE

1408   Peters, George L. *Dreams Come True; A History of Culver-Stockton College (Founded Christian University 1853)*. Canton: Culver-Stockton College, 1941.

DRURY COLLEGE

1409   Pope, Richard M. "Drury College: An Interpretation." Doctoral dissertation, University of Chicago, 1955.

HARRIS TEACHERS COLLEGE

1410   Harris, Ruth M. *Stowe Teachers College and Her Predecessors*. Boston: Christopher Publishing House, 1967.

IBERIA JUNIOR COLLEGE

1411   *A Half Century of Progress, 1890-1940*. Iberia: Iberia Junior College, 1940.

IMMACULATE CONCEPTION SEMINARY

1412   Malone, Edward E. *Conception; Colony, Abbey and Schools*. Elkhorn, Neb.: Michaeleen Press, 1971.

MISSOURI

KANSAS CITY ART INSTITUTE

1413 Owens, Mazee Bush, ed. A History of Community Achievement, 1885-1964. Kansas City: Jaderslice Committee of the Art Institute, 1964.

KEMPER COLLEGE

1414 Richardson, Jack. "Kemper College in Missouri." Historical Magazine of the Protestant Episcopal Church 30 (June 1961): 111-126. [Existed 1837-1845.]

LINCOLN UNIVERSITY

1415 Savage, William Sherman. The History of Lincoln University. Jefferson City: Lincoln University, 1939.

1416 Peters, Dustin A. "Lincoln University in the Nineteenth Century: The Founding and Development of a Laboratory of Leadership and Race Relations." Negro History Bulletin 34 (1971): 80-83.

MARILLAC COLLEGE

1417 Monahan, Danno. "History of Marillac College, 1955-1969." Doctoral dissertation, St. Louis University, 1972.

MARION COLLEGE

1418 McKee, Howard. "The Marion College Episode in Northeast Missouri History." Missouri Historical Review 36 (April 1942): 299-319.

MARYVILLE COLLEGE OF THE SACRED HEART

1419 Holland, Dorothy G. "Maryville-The First Hundred Years." Missouri Historical Society Bulletin 29 (April 1973): 145-162.

MISSOURI, UNIVERSITY OF, AT COLUMBIA

1420 Stephens, Frank. History of the University of Missouri. Columbia: University of Missouri Press, 1962.

1421 Hogan, Percy Anderson. "History of the University of Missouri Law School." *Missouri Law Review* 5 (1940): 269-292.

1422 Sawyer, Robert McLaran. "The Gaines Case; Its Background and Influence on the University of Missouri and Lincoln University 1936-1950." Doctoral dissertation, University of Missouri Press, 1966.

1423 Severance, Henry O. *Richard Henry Jesse: President of the University of Missouri, 1891-1908.* Columbia: University of Missouri Press, 1937.

1424 Stephens, Frank F. *A History of the University of Missouri.* Columbia: University of Missouri Press, 1962.

1425 Viles, Jonas. *The University of Missouri, A Centennial History.* Columbia: University of Missouri Press, 1939.

1426 Weaver, John C. "Footsteps in the Corridors Behind Us." *Missouri Historical Review* 62 (1968): 213-234. [Author was President, 1966-1971.]

1427 Williams, Walter. "The Record of Walter Williams (1864-1935) as President of the University of Missouri." *School and Society* 42 (1935): 137-143.

MISSOURI, UNIVERSITY OF, AT KANSAS CITY

1428 Decker, Clarence Raymond, and Bell, Mary. *A Place of Light; The Story of a University Presidency.* New York: Hermitage House, 1954.

MISSOURI, UNIVERSITY OF, AT ROLLA

1429 Mann, Clair V., and Mann, Bonita H. *A Brief History of Missouri School of Mines and Metallurgy, A Division of the University of Missouri, Located at Rolla, Missouri.* Rolla: n.p., 1939.

1430 Eisenman, Harry. "Origins of Engineering Education in Missouri." *Missouri Historical Review* 63 (1969): 451-460.

MONTICELLO FEMALE SEMINARY

1431 Young, Homer F. "Origin and Early History of Monticello Female Seminary, 1834-1865." Doctoral dissertation, Washington University, 1951.

MISSOURI

NORTHEAST MISSOURI STATE COLLEGE

1432 Ryle, Walter H. *Centennial History of the Northeast Missouri State Teachers College.* St. Louis: Comfort, 1972.

1433 DelPizzo, Ferdinand. "The Contributions of John Kirk (1851-1937) to Teacher-Education." Doctoral dissertation, Washington University, 1955. [Kirk was President, 1899-1925.]

1434 Simmons, Lucy. *History of Northeast Missouri State Teachers College.* Kirksville: Auten, 1927.

NORTHWEST MISSOURI STATE COLLEGE

1435 Dykes, Mattie M. *Behind the Birches; A History of Northwest Missouri State College.* Maryville: Northwest Missouri State College, 1958.

PARK COLLEGE

1436 McAfee, Joseph E. *College Pioneering: Problems and Phases of the Life at Park College during its Early Years.* Kansas City: Alumni Parkana Committee, 1938.

1437 Hawley, Pauline A. "Park College and Its Illinois Founder." *Journal of the Illinois State Historical Society* 13 (1920): 224-228.

PRITCHETT COLLEGE

1438 Smith, T. Berry. "Pritchett College, Glascow, Missouri." *Missouri Historical Review* 26 (1932): 223-235.

SAINT LOUIS COLLEGE OF PHARMACY

1439 Winkelmann, John P. *History of the St. Louis College of Pharmacy.* St. Louis: Privately Printed, 1964.

SAINT LOUIS UNIVERSITY

1440 Adams, Rita Grace, et al. *Saint Louis University--One Hundred Fifty Years.* St. Louis: St. Louis University, 1968.

1441 Bowdern, Thomas Stephen. St. Louis University. St. Louis: St. Louis University, 1928.

1442 Faherty, William Barnaby. "Nativism and Midwestern Education: The Experience of Saint Louis University, 1832-1856." History of Education Quarterly 8 (1968): 447-458.

1443 Ganss, George E. The Jesuit Educational Tradition and Saint Louis University; Some Bearings for the University's Sesquicentennial, 1818-1968. St. Louis: Sesquicentennial Committee of St. Louis University, 1969.

1444 Heithaus, Claude H. The Truth About Saint Louis University. St. Louis: St. Louis University, 1940.

1445 Hill, Walter Henry. Historical Sketch of the Saint Louis University; The Celebration of Its Fiftieth Anniversary or Golden Jubilee on June 24, 1879. St. Louis: P. Fox, 1879.

1446 Kenny, Laurence J. "Pioneer Catholic Universities." U.S. Catholic History Society Record 31 (1940): 145-148.

1447 St. Louis University. Memorial Volume of the Diamond Jubilee of Saint Louis University, 1829-1904. St. Louis: Press of Little and Becker, 1904.

SAINT MARY'S SEMINARY

1448 Poole, Stafford. "The Founding of Missouri's First College, Saint Mary's of the Barrens, 1815-1818." Missouri Historical Review 65 (1970): 1-21.

SOUTHEAST MISSOURI STATE COLLEGE

1449 Mattingly, A.H. Centennial History of Southeast Missouri State University. Forthcoming.

SOUTHWEST MISSOURI STATE COLLEGE

1450 Ellis, Roy. Shrine of the Ozarks: A History of Southwest Missouri State College 1905-1965. Springfield: Southwest Missouri State College, 1968.

STEPHENS COLLEGE

1451 Crighton, John C. Stephens: A Story of Educational Innovation. Columbia: American Press, 1970.

MISSOURI

1452 Amkrum, Ward E. "The Implementation of Educational Philosophy and a Program of Educational Research in the Curricular Growth of Stephens College." Doctoral dissertation, University of Missouri, 1951.

WASHINGTON UNIVERSITY

1453 Bulger, Harold. "Early Years of the Missouri Medical College." Washington University Medical Alumni Quarterly 2 (1939): 193-204.

1454 Coates, Charles P. History of the Manual Training School of Washington University. Washington, D.C.: U.S. Government Printing Office, 1923.

1455 Compton, Arthur. Atomic Quest: A Personal Narrative. New York: Oxford University Press, 1956. [Author was President, 1945-1953.]

1456 Eliot, Charlotte C. William Greenleaf Eliot: Minister, Educator, Philanthropist. Boston: Houghton Mifflin, 1904.

1457 Hagedorn, Herman. Brookings: A Biography. New York: Macmillan, 1957. [Robert S. Brookings, Major Benefactor.]

1458 Hayes, Donn W. "A History of Smith Academy of Washington University." Doctoral dissertation, Washington University, 1950.

1459 Stevens, Walter B. St. Louis: The Fourth City. 1764-1911. St. Louis: S.J. Clarke, 1911.

WESTMINSTER COLLEGE

1460 Parrish, William E. Westminster College: An Informal History, 1851-1969. Fulton: Westminster College, 1971.

1461 Fisher, M.M., and Rice, John J. History of Westminster College, 1851-1903. Columbia: Press of E.W. Stephens, 1903.

1462 Lamkin, Charles Facklar. A Great Small College: A Narrative History of Westminster College, Fulton, Missouri, 1946. St. Louis: Horace Barks Press, 1946.

WILLIAM JEWELL COLLEGE

1463 Hester, Hubert. Jewell Is Her Name: A History of William Jewell College. Liberty: William Jewell College, 1967.

Montana

GENERAL REFERENCES

1464 Durham, George H. <u>The Administration of Higher Education in Montana</u>. Helena: Montana Legislative Council, 1958.

1465 Stout, Thomas, ed. <u>Montana: Its Story and Biography</u>. New York: American Historical Society, 1921. Vol. I, ch. 22, pp. 493-554.

INSTITUTIONAL HISTORIES

MONTANA, UNIVERSITY OF

1466 Merriam, Harold G. <u>The University of Montana; A History</u>. Missoula: University of Montana Press, 1970.

1467 American Federation of Teachers. <u>The Keeney Case: Big Business, Higher Education, and Organized Labor</u>. Chicago: American Federation of Teachers, 1939.

1468 Gutfeld, Arnon. "The Levine Affair (1919): A Case Study in Academic Freedom (State University of Montana)." <u>Pacific Historical Review</u> 39 (1970): 19-38.

WESTERN MONTANA COLLEGE

1469 Spiegle, Edward. "Historical Study of the Formation and Early Growth of Western Montana College of Education." Master's thesis, Western Montana College of Education, 1952.

Nebraska

GENERAL REFERENCES

1470 Caldwell, Howard Walter. <u>Education in Nebraska</u>. Washington, D.C.: U.S. Government Printing Office, 1902.

1471 Hickman, Glen E. "The History of Teacher Education in Nebraska." Doctoral dissertation, University of Oregon, 1948.

1472 Horton, Agnes. "Federal Land Grants Relating to Higher Education in Nebraska: Their Acquisition and Disposition." Doctoral dissertation, University of Denver, 1957.

1473 Sawyer, R. McLaran. "No Teacher for the School: The Nebraska Junior Normal School Movement." <u>Nebraska History</u> 52 (Summer 1971): 191-203.

1474 Weyer, Frank. <u>Presbyterian Colleges and Academies in Nebraska</u>. Hastings: Democrat Printing Co., 1940.

INSTITUTIONAL HISTORIES

CONCORDIA TEACHERS COLLEGE

1475 Brandhorst, Carl T. <u>A Short Story of Concordia Teachers College, Seward, Nebraska by One Who Has Known Her Since 1912</u>. Seward: n.p., 1969.

1476 Simon, Martin T. "A History of Concordia Teachers College, Seward, Nebraska." Doctoral dissertation, University of Oregon, 1953.

DANA COLLEGE

1477 Christensen, William E. *Saga of the Tower: A History of Dana College and Trinity Seminary.* Blair: Luthern Publishing House, 1959.

HASTINGS COLLEGE

1478 Weyer, Frank E. *Hastings College: Seventy-Five Years in Retrospect, 1882-1957.* Hastings: Tribune, 1957.

LUTHER ACADEMY

1479 Dowie, James I. "Luther Academy, 1883-1903; A Facet of Swedish Pioneer Life in Nebraska." Doctoral dissertation, University of Minnesota, 1957.

NEBRASKA COLLEGE

1480 Barnds, William J. "Nebraska College, the Episcopal School at Nebraska City, 1868-1885." *Nebraska History* 52 (Summer 1971): 169-190.

NEBRASKA, UNIVERSITY OF

1481 Manley, Robert N. *Centennial History of the University of Nebraska.* Lincoln: University of Nebraska Press, 1969.

1482 Biehn, Albert Lawrence. "The Development of the University of Nebraska, 1871-1900." Master's thesis, University of Nebraska, 1934.

1483 Crawford, Robert Platt. *These 50 Years: A History of the College of Agriculture of the University of Nebraska.* Lincoln: University of Nebraska, 1925.

1484 Hannah, James Joseph. "The Ideas and Plans in the Founding of the University of Nebraska 1869-1875." Master's thesis, University of Nebraska, 1951.

1485 Howard, George E. *Evolution of the University.* Lincoln: The Association, 1890.

1486 Murray, Floyd B. "A History of Summer Sessions at the University of Nebraska." Master's thesis, University of Nebraska, 1942.

1487 Parks, Walter Wayne. "A History of Teacher Placement at the University of Nebraska." Doctoral dissertation, University of Nebraska, 1963.

1488 Sawyer, R. McLaran. *History of the University of Nebraska.* Lincoln: University of Nebraska Press, 1960 (Vol. 1). Lincoln: Centennial Press, 1973 (Vol. 2).

1489 Swisher, Jacob A. "The Cradle of the University." *Palimpsest* 28 (1947): 129-143.

1490 Taylor, Wilson L. "At the University." *Palimpsest* 24 (1943): 285-292.

1491 Walsh, Thomas R. "Charles Bessey: Land-Grant College Professor." Doctoral dissertation, University of Nebraska, 1972. [Bessey was Professor of Botany, 1884-1899, and Dean, 1909-1915.]

1492 Walsh, Thomas R. "Charles E. Bessey and the Transformation of the Industrial College." *Nebraska History* 52 (Winter 1971): 383-409.

NEBRASKA WESLEYAN UNIVERSITY

1493 Winship, Frank Loren. "A History of Nebraska Wesleyan University." Master's thesis, University of Nebraska, 1930.

PERU STATE COLLEGE

1494 Longfellow, Ernest. *The Normal on the Hill.* Grand Island: Augustine Co., 1967.

1495 McCann, Lloyd E. "Henry H. Straight, Educator." *Nebraska History* 35 (March 1953): 59-71.

UNION COLLEGE

1496 Dick, Everett Newfon. *Union: College of the Golden Cords.* Lincoln: Union College Press, 1967.

1497 Rees, David D., and Dick, Everett. *Union College: Fifty Years of Service.* Lincoln: Union College Press, 1941.

WAYNE STATE COLLEGE

1498 Nebraska State Teachers College, Wayne. <u>Nebraska Normal College: A History of Nebraska Normal College, the Faculty, Students, the Progress and Development of the New School...</u> Lincoln: n.p., 1939.

YORK COLLEGE

1499 Larsen, Dale R. "A History of York College." Doctoral dissertation, University of Nebraska Teachers College, 1966.

Nevada

GENERAL REFERENCES

1500 Wren, Thomas, ed. <u>A History of Nevada</u>. New York: Lewis, 1904. [Chs. 22 and 23, pp. 206-224, about higher education.]

INSTITUTIONAL HISTORIES

NEVADA, UNIVERSITY OF

1501 Doten, Samuel B. <u>An Illustrated History of the University of Nevada</u>. Carson City: University of Nevada Press, 1924.

1502 Capen, Samuel P. <u>Survey of the University of Nevada</u>. U.S. Bureau of Education Bulletin 1917, #19. Washington, D.C.: U.S. Government Printing Office, 1917.

1503 Newman, Frank C. <u>The Legal Position of the University of Nevada as an Agency of the Government of the State of Nevada</u>. Reno: University of Nevada Press, 1953.

New Hampshire

GENERAL REFERENCES

1504 Bush, George. <u>History of Education in New Hampshire</u>. Washington, D.C.: U.S. Government Printing Office, 1898.

INSTITUTIONAL HISTORIES

COLBY JUNIOR COLLEGE

1505 Rowe, Henry K. <u>A Centennial History, 1837-1937</u>. New London: Colby Junior College, 1937.

DARTMOUTH COLLEGE

1506 Richardson, Leon B. <u>History of Dartmouth College</u>. 2 vols. Hanover: Dartmouth College, 1932.

1507 Chapman, Carleton B. <u>Dartmouth Medical School: The First 175 Years</u>. Hanover: University Press of New England, 1972.

1508 Chase, Frederick. <u>A History of Dartmouth College and the Town of Hanover, New Hampshire</u>. 2 vols. Cambridge: J. Wilson & Son, 1891 (Vol. 1). Concord: Rumford Press, 1913 (Vol. 2).

1509 Crehore, Albert Cushing. <u>Autobiography</u>. Gates Mills: William G. Berner, 1944. [Crehore was Professor of Physics, 1874-1878.]

1510 Dixon, Frank H. "Statistics of Vocations of Dartmouth College Graduates." <u>Yale Review</u> 10 (1901-1902): 84-88.

NEW HAMPSHIRE

1511 Flint, W.W. "Dartmouth College in the 1840s: Extracts from Lyman Flint's Expense Book." <u>Historical New Hampshire</u> 7 (November 1951): 1-24.

1512 Hardy, Arthur Sherburne. <u>Things Remembered</u>. Boston and New York: Houghton Mifflin, 1923. [Hardy was Professor of Mathematics, 1874-1893.]

1513 Lord, John K. <u>History of Dartmouth College, 1769-1909</u>. 2 vols. Concord: n.p., 1913.

1514 McCallum, James Dow. <u>Eleazar Wheelock, Founder of Dartmouth College</u>. Hanover: Dartmouth College, 1939.

1515 McClure, David, and Parish, Elijah. <u>Memoirs of The Reverend Eleazar Wheelock</u>. Newburyport: Edward Little and Co., 1811.

1516 Mecklin, John M. <u>My Quest for Freedom</u>. New York: Harcourt, Brace & Howe, 1945. [Mecklin was Professor of Sociology.]

1517 Newmyer, R. Kent. "Daniel Webster as Tocqueville's Lawyer: The Dartmouth College Case Again." <u>Journal of Legal History</u> 11 (1967): 127-147.

1518 Quint, Wilder D. <u>The Story of Dartmouth</u>. Boston: Little, Brown, 1914.

1519 Shirley, J.M. <u>The Dartmouth College Cases and the Supreme Court of the United States</u>. Chicago: Jones, 1895.

1520 Stites, Francis N. "The Dartmouth College Case, 1819." Doctoral dissertation, Indiana University, 1968.

1521 Tilton, Asa C. "The Dartmouth Literary or Debating Societies." <u>Granite Monthly</u> 52 (1920): 157-169, 202-213, 249-263.

1522 Tucker, William J. <u>My Generation: An Autobiographical Interpretation</u>. Boston: Houghton Mifflin, 1919. [Author was President, 1893-1909.]

FRANCONIA COLLEGE

1523 Ruopp, Richard, and Jerome, John. "Death in a Small College." In <u>Five Experimental Colleges</u>, edited by Gary MacDonald, pp. 114-157. New York: Harper and Row, 1973.

NEW HAMPSHIRE TECHNICAL COLLEGE

1524 Washburn, George. "New Hampshire College of Agriculture and Mechanic Arts." <u>New England Magazine</u> 33 (January 1906): 497-506.

NEW HAMPSHIRE, UNIVERSITY OF

1525   Marston, Philip M., ed. History of the University of New
       Hampshire 1866-1941. Durham: The Record Press, 1941.

PLYMOUTH STATE COLLEGE

1526   Bagley, Norton R. One Hundred Years of Service: A History of
       Plymouth State College, Plymouth, New Hampshire 1871-1971.
       Plymouth: Plymouth State College Alumni Association, 1971.

New Jersey

GENERAL REFERENCES

1527 Burr, Nelson R. <u>Education in New Jersey, 1630-1871</u>. Princeton: Princeton University Press, 1942.

1528 Chapman, Ira. "Education in New Jersey." In <u>The Story of New Jersey</u>, edited by William Myers, Vol. 1, ch. 23, pp. 424-523. New York: Lewis, 1945.

1529 Murray, David. <u>History of Education in New Jersey</u>. Washington, D.C.: U.S. Government Printing Office, 1899.

INSTITUTIONAL HISTORIES

ALMA WHITE COLLEGE

1530 Lawrence, Evan Jerry. "Alma White College: A History of Its Relationship to the Development of the PILLAR OF FIRE." Doctoral dissertation, Columbia University Teachers College, 1965.

BLOOMFIELD COLLEGE

1531 Taylor, Harry. <u>Bloomfield College: The First Century; 1868-1968</u>. Hibernia: Lars and Associates, 1970.

DOUGLASS COLLEGE

1532 Schmidt, George P. <u>Douglass College</u>. New Brunswick: Rutgers, 1968.

DREW UNIVERSITY

1533 Cunningham, John T. *University in the Forest: The Story of Drew University.* Madison: Public Affairs Office of Drew University, 1971.

1534 Sitterly, Charles F. *The Building of Drew University.* New York: Methodist Book Concern, 1938.

DREXEL INSTITUTE OF TECHNOLOGY

1535 McDonald, Edward D., and Hinton, Edward M. *Drexel Institute of Technology, 1891-1941.* Camden: Haddon Craftsmen, 1942.

EVELYN COLLEGE

1536 Healy, Frances. "A History of Evelyn College for Women, Princeton, New Jersey, 1887-1897." Doctoral dissertation, Ohio State University, 1967.

FAIRLEIGH DICKINSON UNIVERSITY

1537 Sammartino, Peter. *Of Castles and Colleges.* New York: A.S. Barnes, 1972.

MONTCLAIR STATE COLLEGE

1538 Davis, Earl C. "The Origin and Development of the New Jersey State Teachers College at Montclair 1908-1951." Doctoral dissertation, New York University, 1955.

NEWARK STATE COLLEGE

1539 Bennett, Hugh Francis. "A History of the University of Newark 1908-1946." Doctoral dissertation, New York University, 1956.

PATERSON STATE COLLEGE

1540 White, Kenneth B. *Paterson State College; A History 1855-1966.* Paterson: Student Cooperative Association of Paterson State College, 1967.

NEW JERSEY

PRINCETON UNIVERSITY

1541 Wertenbaker, Thomas J. *Princeton, 1746-1896*. Princeton: Princeton University Press, 1946.

1542 Alexander, S.D. *Princeton College During the Eighteenth Century*. Randolph: n.p., 1872.

1543 Baker, Ray S., ed. *Woodrow Wilson: Life and Letters, 1890-1910*. Garden City: Doubleday, 1927. [Wilson was President, 1902-1910.]

1544 Baldwin, James Mark. *Memories*. Boston: Stratford, 1926. [Author was Professor of Psychology, 1893-1903.]

1545 Beam, Jacob. *The American Whig Society of Princeton University*. Princeton: The Society, 1933.

1546 Bragdon, Henry W. *Woodrow Wilson: The Academic Years*. Cambridge: Belknap Press of Harvard University Press, 1967. [Wilson was Professor, 1890-1901, and President, 1902-1910.]

1547 Broderick, Francis L. "Pulpit, Physics, and Politics: The Curriculum of the College of New Jersey, 1746-1794." *William and Mary Quarterly*, 3d series, 6 (1949): 42-68.

1548 Collins, Varnum L. *President Witherspoon: A Biography*. 2 vols. Princeton: Princeton University Press, 1925. [Witherspoon was President, 1768-1794.]

1549 Collins, Varnum L. *Princeton*. New York: Oxford University Press, 1914.

1550 Come, Donald R. "The Influence of Princeton on Higher Education in the South Before 1825." *William and Mary Quarterly*, 3d series, 2 (1945): 359-396.

1551 Condit, Kenneth H. *A History of the College of Engineering of Princeton University*. Princeton: Princeton University Press, 1962.

1552 Greiff, Constance M. *Princeton Architecture*. Princeton: Princeton University Press, 1967.

1553 Haines, George Lemar. "The Princeton Theological Seminary 1925-1960." Doctoral dissertation, New York University, 1965.

1554 Jackson, Katherine Gauss, and Haydn, Hiram. *Christian Frederick Gauss (1878-1951)*. New York: Random House, 1957. [Gauss was Dean of the College, 1925-1945.]

1555 Lane, Wheaton J., ed. Pictorial History of Princeton. Princeton: Princeton University Press, 1923.

1556 MacLean, John. History of the College of New Jersey from Its Origin in 1746 to the Commencement of 1854. 2 vols. Philadelphia: J.B. Lippincott, 1877.

1557 McCosh, James. The Life of James McCosh. New York: Scribner's, 1896. [McCosh was President, 1868-1888.]

1558 McCosh, James. Twenty Years of Princeton College. Being Farewell Address, Delivered June 20, 1888. New York: Scribner's, 1888.

1559 Marsden, Donald. The Long Kickline: A History of the Princeton Triangle Club. Princeton: Princeton Triangle Club and Princeton University, 1968.

1560 Norris, Edwin M. The Story of Princeton. Boston: Little, Brown, 1917.

1561 Olson, Alison B. "The Founding of Princeton University: Religion and Politics in 18th Century New Jersey." New Jersey Historical Quarterly 87 (Autumn 1969): 133-150.

1562 Osborn, Henry F. Howard Crosby Butler, 1872-1922. Princeton: Princeton University Press, 1923. [Butler was Professor of Archeology, 1901-1922.]

1563 Paterson, William. Glimpses of Colonial Society and the Life at Princeton College, 1766-73. Philadelphia: J.B. Lippincott, 1903.

1564 Perry, Bliss. And Gladly Teach. Boston: Houghton Mifflin, 1935. [Author was Professor of English, 1893-1900.]

1565 Schmidt, George P. Princeton and Rutgers--The Two Colonial Colleges of New Jersey. Princeton: Van Nostrand, 1964.

1566 Scott, William B. Some Memories of a Paleontologist. Princeton: Princeton University Press, 1939. [Author was Professor of Geology, 1884-1930.]

1567 Scovel, Raleigh. "Orthodoxy at Princeton: A Social and Intellectual History of Princeton Theological Seminary, 1812-1860." Doctoral dissertation, University of California, 1970.

1568 Sigmund, Paul. "Princeton in Crisis and Change." Change 5 (1973): 34-42.

1569 Tarkington, Booth. "Young Literary Princeton Fifty Years Ago." Princeton University Library Chronicle 7 (November 1945): 1-6.

NEW JERSEY

1570 Veysey, Lawrence. "The Academic Mind of Woodrow Wilson." *Journal of American History* 49 (March 1963): 613-634.

1571 Wallace, George R. *Princeton Sketches: The History of Nassau Hall*. New York: G.P. Putnam's, 1893.

1572 Weiner, Charles. "Joseph Henry's Lectures in Natural Philosophy: Teaching and Research in Physics, 1832-1847." Doctoral dissertation, Case Western Reserve University, 1965.

1573 Williams, John R. *Academic Honors in Princeton University 1748-1902*. Princeton: Princeton University, 1902.

RIDER COLLEGE

1574 Brower, Walter A. "Rider College: The First One Hundred Years." Doctoral dissertation, Temple University, 1965.

RUTGERS, THE STATE UNIVERSITY

1575 McCormick, Richard P. *Rutgers: A Bicentennial History*. New Brunswick: Rutgers University Press, 1966.

1576 Bogart, John. *The John Bogart Letters: 42 Letters to John Bogart of Queens College and 5 From Him, 1776-1782*. New Brunswick: Rutgers College, 1914.

1577 Chute, William J. "The Educational Thought of Theodore Frelinghuysen." *Rutgers University Library Journal* 18 (December 1953): 20-27. [Frelinghuysen was President, 1850-1862.]

1578 Cowen, David. *Medical Edition: The Queens-Rutgers Experience, 1792-1830*. New Brunswick: Rutgers Medical School, 1966.

1579 Demarest, William H. *A History of Rutgers College, 1766-1924*. New Brunswick: Rutgers College, 1924. [Author was President, 1905-1924.]

1580 Lukac, George J., ed. *Aloud to Alma Mater*. New Brunswick: Rutgers University Press, 1966.

1581 McMahon, Ernest E., and Miers, Earl Schenck. *The Chronicles of Colonel Henry*. New Brunswick: Thatcher-Anderson Co., 1935. [Henry Rutgers.]

1582 Ravitch, Diane. "The Dreams of Livingston College." *Change* 1 (May-June 1969): 36-39.

1583 Schmidt, George P. *Princeton and Rutgers: The Two Colonial Colleges of New Jersey*. New Brunswick: Rutgers University Press, 1964.

1584 Vittum, Henry Earl. "The Development of the Curriculum of Rutgers College of Rutgers, the State University, 1862-1958." Doctoral dissertation, New York University, 1962.

1585 Woodward, Mildred R. "The Athenian Society of Queen's College." Rutgers University Library Journal 3 (1939): 13-19.

SAINT ELIZABETH, COLLEGE OF

1586 McEniry, Blanche Marie. Three Score and Ten, History of College of St. Elizabeth (1899-1969). Kearny: Jones Publishing, 1969.

SETON HALL UNIVERSITY

1587 Sullivan, Edwin V., Keller, William J., et al. The Summit of a Century, the Centennial Story of Seton Hall University, 1856-1956. South Orange: Seton Hall University, 1956.

1588 Kemmelly, Edward Francis. "A Historical Study of Seton Hall College." Doctoral dissertation, New York University, 1944.

STEVENS INSTITUTE OF TECHNOLOGY

1589 Furman, Franklin DeRonde. A History of Stevens Institute of Technology. Hoboken: Stevens Institute of Technology, 1905.

TRENTON STATE COLLEGE

1590 Franz, Evelyn B. "Trends in the Preparation of Teachers for the Elementary Schools at the New Jersey State Teachers College at Trenton, 1855-1956." Doctoral dissertation, Rutgers University, 1959.

1591 Fromm, Glenn E. "A History of the New Jersey State Teachers College at Trenton 1855-1950." Doctoral dissertation, New York University, 1951.

UPSALA COLLEGE

1592 Lawson, Evald Benjamin. Pages from Early History of Upsala College. East Orange: Upsala College, 1943.

VINELAND TRAINING SCHOOL

1593 McCaffrey, Katherine Regina. "Founders of the Training School at Vineland, New Jersey: S. Olin Garrison, Alexander Johnson, Edward R. Johnstone." Doctoral dissertation, Columbia University Teachers College, 1965.

New Mexico

GENERAL REFERENCES

1594 Coan, Charles F. *A History of New Mexico*. Chicago: American Historical Society, 1925. [Vol. I, ch. 27, pp. 484-495, and ch. 30, pp. 528-540, about higher education.]

1595 Haas, Frances. "Education in New Mexico: A Study of the Development of Education in a Changing Social Order." Doctoral dissertation, University of Chicago, 1955.

1596 Reed, Deward H. "The History of Teachers Colleges in New Mexico." Doctoral dissertation, George Peabody College for Teachers, 1948.

1597 Tipps, Garland Emory. "A Half-Century of Graduate Education in New Mexico." Doctoral dissertation, George Peabody College for Teachers, 1966.

INSTITUTIONAL HISTORIES

EASTERN NEW MEXICO UNIVERSITY

1598 Mann, A. Eugene. "The History and Development of Eastern New Mexico University." Doctoral dissertation, Colorado State College, 1959.

NEW MEXICO MILITARY INSTITUTE

1599 Jackman, Eugene T. "The New Mexico Military Institute, 1891-1966: A Critical History." Doctoral dissertation, University of Mississippi, 1967.

NEW MEXICO

NEW MEXICO STATE UNIVERSITY

1600 Kropp, Simon F. *That All May Learn: New Mexico State University, 1888-1964*. Las Cruces: New Mexico State University, 1972.

NEW MEXICO, UNIVERSITY OF

1601 Hughes, Dorothy. *Pueblo on the Mesa: The First Fifty Years at the University of New Mexico*. Albuquerque: University of New Mexico Press, 1939.

1602 Reeve, Frank D. "The Old University of New Mexico and Sante Fe." *New Mexico Historical Review* 8 (1933): 201-210.

New York

GENERAL REFERENCES

1603 Doran, Kenneth Thompson. "New York, New Yorkers, and the Two-Year College Movement: A History of the Debate Over Structure in Higher Education." Doctoral dissertation, Syracuse University, 1962.

1604 Finegan, Thomas E. "Colonial Schools and Colleges in New York." New York State Historical Society Proceedings 16 (1918): 165-182.

1605 French, William M. "How We Began to Train Teachers in New York." New York History 17 (1936): 180-191.

1606 French, William M. "Teacher Training in New York, 1834-1934." Doctoral dissertation, Yale University, 1934.

1607 Goodhartz, Abraham F. "The Control of Free Higher Education in New York City." Doctoral dissertation, New York University, 1951.

1608 Hartstein, Jacob Isaac. "State Regulatory and Supervisory Control of Higher Education in New York from Its Beginning Through the Civil War." Doctoral dissertation, New York University, 1945.

1609 Hobson, Elsie G. Educational Legislation and Administration in the State of New York, 1777-1850. Chicago: n.p., 1918.

1610 Kaufman, Martin. "Edward H. Dixon and Medical Education in New York." New York History 51 (1970): 395-410.

1611 Mallon, Arthur. "The Development of the Municipal Teacher Training Colleges in New York City." Doctoral dissertation, New York University, 1935.

NEW YORK

INSTITUTIONAL HISTORIES

ADELPHI UNIVERSITY

1612   Barrows, Chester L. *Fifty Years of Adelphi College*. Garden City: Adelphi College Press, 1946.

ALBANY, STATE UNIVERSITY OF NEW YORK AT

1613   French, William M. *College of the Empire State: A Centennial History of the New York College for Teachers at Albany*. Albany: n.p., 1944.

1614   New York, State University at Albany. *A Historical Sketch of the State Normal School at Albany, New York*. Albany: n.p., 1884.

1615   Phelps, W.F. *David Perkins Page: His Life and His Teachings*. New York: E.L. Kellogg, 1892. [Page was First President, 1844-1848.]

ALFRED UNIVERSITY

1616   Norwood, John Nelson. *Fiat Lux: The Story of Alfred University*. Alfred: Alfred University, 1957.

AUBURN COMMUNITY COLLEGE

1617   Skinner, Albert T. "A History of Auburn Community College During Its Founding Period, 1953-1959." Doctoral dissertation, Syracuse University, 1960.

BARD COLLEGE

1618   Hopson, George B. *Reminiscences of St. Stephen's College*. New York: Edwin S. Gorham, 1910.

1619   Magee, Christopher W. "The History of St. Stephen's College 1860-1933." Unpublished senior thesis, Bard College, 1935.

BARNARD COLLEGE

1620 Mintz, Eleanor Streichler. *A History of Barnard College*. New York: Barnard College, 1964.

1621 Brewster, William T. "Barnard College, 1889-1909." *Columbia University Quarterly* 12 (March 1910): 151-171.

1622 Gildersleeve, Virginia C. *Many a Good Crusade*. New York: Macmillan, 1954. [Author was Dean, 1911-1947.]

1623 Meyer, Annie Nathan. *Barnard Beginnings*. New York: Riverside Press, 1935.

1624 Meyer, Annie Nathan. "Beginnings of Barnard College, Reminiscences of Annie Nathan Meyer." *Columbia University Quarterly* 27 (1935): 296-320.

1625 Miller, Alice Duer, and Myers, Susan. *Barnard College: The First Fifty Years*. New York: Columbia University Press, 1939.

1626 White, Marian Churchill. *A History of Barnard College*. New York: Columbia University Press, 1954.

BROCKPORT, STATE UNIVERSITY COLLEGE AT

1627 Dedman, W. Wayne. *Cherishing This Heritage: The Centennial History of the State University College at Brockport, New York*. New York: Appleton-Century-Crofts, 1969.

1628 Dunham, E. Alden. *Colleges of the Forgotten Americans*. New York: McGraw-Hill, 1969.

BROOKLYN COLLEGE

1629 Coulton, Thomas Evans. *A City College in Action: Struggle and Achievement at Brooklyn College 1930-1955*. New York: Harper, 1955.

BUFFALO, STATE UNIVERSITY COLLEGE AT

1630 Messner, Charles A., Rockwell, Harry W., and Wofford, Kate Vixon. *New York State Teachers College at Buffalo; A History 1871-1946*. Buffalo: William J. Keller Co., 1946.

1631 Grant, Margaret A. "The Preparation of Homemaking Teachers: Ten Years Of Experience at the New York State College for Teachers, Buffalo, New York." Doctoral dissertation, University of Buffalo, 1953.

BUFFALO, STATE UNIVERSITY OF NEW YORK AT

1632 Park, Julian. The Evolution of the College: A Century of Higher Education in Buffalo. University of Buffalo Studies, Vol. 15, #3. Buffalo: n.p., 1938.

1633 Bennis, Warren. The Learning Ivory Tower. San Francisco: Jossey Bass, 1972.

1634 Collins, Charles R. "The Herbartian Teachers College, University Of Buffalo School Of Pedagogy 1895-1898." Doctoral dissertation, State University of New York at Buffalo, 1969.

1635 Crone, Douglas C. "An Historical Study of the Growth and the Development of the Educational and Administrative Ideas of Samuel Paul Capen, 1902-1950." Doctoral dissertation, State University of New York at Buffalo, 1968.

1636 Park, Julian D. Samuel Paul Capen. Buffalo: University of Buffalo, 1957. [Capen was President, 1922-1946.]

CANISIUS COLLEGE

1637 Brady, Charles A. The First Hundred Years: Canisius College, 1870-1970. Buffalo: Holling Press, 1969.

1638 Harney, Thomas A. Canisius College: The First Nine Years 1870-1879. New York: Vantage, 1971.

CITY COLLEGE OF NEW YORK

1639 Rudy, S. Willis. The College of the City of New York: A History, 1847-1947. New York: City College Press, 1949.

1640 Cosenza, Mario E. The Establishment of the College of the City of New York as the Free Academy in 1847. New York: College of the City of New York, 1925.

1641 Gettleman, Marvin E. "John H. Finley at CCNY--1903-1913." History of Education Quarterly 10 (1970): 423-439. [Finley was President.]

1642 Heller, Louis G. The Death of the American University, with Special Reference to the Collapse of the City College of New York. New Rochelle: Arlington House, 1973.

1643 Keenan, Hubert J. "A View from the Tower: An Investigation of the Writings of John Huston Finley on the School and Higher Education From 1921 to 1940." Doctoral dissertation, New York University, 1970.

1644 Kriegel, Leonard. "Surviving the Apocalypse." Change 4 (Summer 1972): 54-62.

1645 Mosenthal, Philip J., ed. The City College: Memoirs of 60 Years. New York: G.P. Putnam's Sons, 1907.

CLARKSON COLLEGE OF TECHNOLOGY

1646 Stillman, Donald Gale. Clarkson at 75: A Portrait of the College. Syracuse: Salina Press, 1972.

1647 Sawyer, William E. Clarkson College. Potsdam: Clarkson, 1946.

COLGATE UNIVERSITY

1648 Williams, Howard D. A History of Colgate University, 1819-1969. New York: Van Nostrand Reinhold Co., 1969.

1649 Crawshaw, William Henry. My Colgate Years. Hamilton: Privately Printed, 1937. [Author was Professor of Literature, 1887-1930.]

COLUMBIA UNIVERSITY

1650 Coon, Horace. Columbia, Colossus on the Hudson. New York: E. P. Dutton, 1947.

1651 Barnard, F.A.P. The Rise of a University. New York: Columbia University Press, 1937.

1652 Barzun, Jacques, ed. A History of the Faculty of Philosophy, Columbia University. New York: Columbia University Press, 1957.

1653 Burgess, John W. *Reminiscences of an American Scholar.* New York: Columbia University Press, 1934. [Author was Professor of Political Science and Dean, 1876-1912.]

1654 Burrell, John A. *A History of Adult Education at Columbia University: University Extension and the School of General Studies, 1904-1954.* New York: Columbia University Press, 1954.

1655 Butler, Nicholas Murray. *Across the Busy Years.* 2 vols. New York: Scribner's, 1934. [Author was President, 1898-1944.]

1656 Cardozo, Ernest A. "The Philolexian Society at Columbia: Its History from 1892-1902." *Columbia Quarterly* 5 (1902): 30-37.

1657 Chute, William J. "The Life of Frederick A.B. Barnard to His Election as President of Columbia College in 1864." Doctoral dissertation, Columbia University, 1952.

1658 Columbia University. *School of Library Economy of Columbia College, 1887-1889: Documents for a History.* New York: School of Library Service, Columbia University, 1937.

1659 Cremin, Lawrence A., Shannon, David A., and Townsend, Mary E. *A History of Teachers College, Columbia University.* New York: Columbia University Press, 1954.

1660 Duer, William Alexander. *Reminiscences of an Old Yorker. By the late William A. Duer, L.L.D., President of Columbia College.* New York: Printed for W.L. Andrews, 1867. [Author was President, 1829-1842.]

1661 Edman, Irwin. *A History of Columbia College on Morningside.* New York: Columbia University Press, 1954.

1662 Elliot, Edward C., ed. *The Rise of a University.* 2 vols. New York: Columbia University Press, 1937.

1663 Finch, James R. *A History of the School of Engineering, Columbia University.* New York: Columbia University Press, 1954.

1664 First, Wesley, ed. *Columbia Remembered.* New York: Columbia University Press, 1967.

1665 Fox, Dixon R. *Herbert Levi Osgood: An American Scholar.* New York: Columbia University Press, 1924. [Osgood was Professor of History, 1890-1918.]

1666 Fox, George Henry. *Reminiscences.* New York: Medical Life Press, 1926. [Author was Professor of Medicine, 1881-1907.]

1667 Freidel, Frank. *Francis Lieber, Nineteenth-Century Liberal.* Baton Rouge: Louisiana State University Press, 1937. [Lieber was Professor of Political Science, 1857-1872.]

1668 Fulton, John. *Memoirs of Frederick A. P. Barnard.* New York: Macmillan, 1896. [Barnard was President, 1864-1889.]

1669 Gay, Frederick P. "A Half Century of Bacteriology at Columbia." *Columbia University Quarterly* 31 (1939): 112-129.

1670 Grant, William Harold. "The Development of Student Government: A History of the Board of Student Representatives of Columbia University, 1892-1925." Doctoral dissertation, Columbia University, 1965.

1671 Hendricks, L.V. *James Harvey Robinson: Teacher of History.* New York: King's Crown Press, 1946.

1672 Higgins, Frances Caldwell. *The Life of Naomi Norsworthy.* Boston: Houghton Mifflin, 1918. [Norsworthy was Professor of Education.]

1673 Hollingworth, Harry L. *Leta Stetter Hollingworth.* Lincoln: University of Nebraska Press, 1943. [L.S. Hollingworth was Professor of Psychology, Teachers College, 1919-1939.]

1674 Hoth, William E. "The Development of a Communications Skill Course: A History of the Undergraduate Program at Teachers College, Columbia University." Doctoral dissertation, Columbia Teachers College, 1955.

1675 Hoxie, R. Gordon. *A History of the Faculty of Political Science, Columbia University.* New York: Columbia University Press, 1955.

1676 Hoxie, R. Gordon. "John W. Burgess, American Scholar." Doctoral dissertation, Columbia University, 1951.

1677 Humphrey, David C. "King's College in the City of New York, 1754-1776." Doctoral dissertation, Northwestern University, 1968.

1678 Humphrey, David C. "Urban Manners and Urban Morals: The Controversy Over the Location of King's College." *New York History* 54 (1973): 5-23.

1679 Johnson, Henry. *The Other Side of Main Street.* New York: Columbia University Press, 1943.

1680 Joncich, Geraldine. *The Sane Positivist: A Biography of Edward L. Thorndike.* Middletown: Wesleyan University Press, 1968. [Thorndike was Professor of Education and Psychology, 1901-1940.]

1681 Keating, James M. "Seth Low and the Development of Columbia University, 1889-1901." Doctoral dissertation, Columbia University, 1973. [Low was President, 1889-1901.]

1682 Keep, Austin B. "The Library of King's College." Columbia University Quarterly 13 (June 1911): 275-284.

1683 Keppel, Frederick P. Columbia. New York: Oxford University Press, 1914.

1684 Keppel, Frederick P., ed. History of Columbia University, 1734-1904. New York: Columbia University Press, 1904.

1685 Koch, Ruth Mae. "The Professional Education of Student Personnel Workers in Higher Education at Teachers College, Columbia University, 1913-1938." Doctoral dissertation, Columbia University (Teachers College), 1966.

1686 Kurland, Gerald. Seth Low: The Reformer in an Urban and Industrial Age. New York: Twayne, 1972.

1687 Langstaff, J.B. "Anglican Origins of Columbia University." History Magazine of the Protestant Episcopal Church 9 (1940): 257-260.

1688 Levermore, Charles H. Samuel Train Dutton: A Biography. New York: Macmillan, 1922. [Dutton was Professor of Educational Administration, Teachers College, 1900-1915.]

1689 Mampoteng, Charles. "Benjamin Moore, Bishop of New York and President of Columbia College." Columbia University Quarterly 27 (1936): 165-189. [Moore was President, 1801-1811.]

1690 Mampoteng, Charles. "The Lutheran Governors of King's College." Columbia University Quarterly 27 (1935): 436-453.

1691 Matthews, Brander. "College in the 70's" Columbia University Quarterly 19 (March 1917): 129-144.

1692 Matthews, Brander. A History of Columbia University, 1754-1904. New York: Columbia University Press, 1904.

1693 Matthews, Brander. These Many Years; Recollections of a New Yorker. New York: Scribner's, 1917. [Author was Professor of Literature, 1892-1924.]

1694 Miner, Dwight C., ed. A History of Columbia College on Morningside. New York: Columbia University Press, 1954.

1695 Mix, Mary Daugherty. "New College of Teachers College: A History, 1932-1939." Doctoral dissertation, Columbia University, 1969.

1696 Moore, Clement Clarke. The Early History of Columbia College; An Address Delivered Before the Alumni on May 4, 1825, By Clement Clarke Moore of the Class of 1798. [A facsimile edition with an introduction by Milton Halsey Thomas.] New York: Columbia University Press, 1940.

1697 Mudge, Isodore G. "Student Periodicals at Columbia, 1813-1911." Columbia University Quarterly 13 (September 1911): 430-436.

1698 Osborn, Henry Fairfield. Fifty-Two Years of Research. New York: Scribner's, 1930. [Author was Professor of Biology, 1881-1935.]

1699 Pupin, Michael Idvorsky. From Immigrant to Inventor. New York: Scribner's, 1923. [Pupin was Professor of Engineering, 1889-1931.]

1700 Roach, Helen P. History of Speech Education at Columbia College, 1754-1949. New York: Bureau of Publications, Teachers College, Columbia University, 1950.

1701 Rosenhaupt, Hans. Graduate Students at Columbia University, 1940-1956. New York: Columbia University Press, 1958.

1702 Russell, James E. Founding Teachers College. New York: Columbia University Press, 1937. [Author was first Dean, 1897-1915.]

1703 Russo, Joseph L. Lorenzo DaPonte, Poet and Adventurer. New York: Columbia University Press, 1922. [DaPonte was Professor of Italian Literature, 1825-1839.]

1704 Schneider, Herbert, and Schneider, Carol, eds. Samuel Johnson, President of King's College. 4 vols. New York: Columbia University Press, 1929.

1705 Shrady, John. The College of Physicians and Surgeons, New York, and Its Founders, Officers, Instructors, Benefactors and Alumni; A History. New York, Chicago: Lewis, 1920.

1706 Snedden, David Samuel. Recollections of Over Half a Century Spent in Educational Work. Palo Alto: n.p., 1949. [Author was Professor of Education, 1905-1935.]

1707 Tannebaum, Frank. A Community of Scholars: The University Seminars at Columbia. New York: Praeger, 1965.

1708 Thompson, Daniel G. Ruggles of New York. Columbia University Press, 1946. [Samuel Ruggles was Trustee, 1836-1881.]

1709 Toepfer, Kenneth H. "James Earl Russell and the Rise of Teachers College: 1897-1915." Doctoral dissertation, Columbia University, 1964.

1710 Turner, Samuel Hulbeart. Autobiography of the Reverend Samuel Hulbeart Turner, D. D. New York: A.D.F. Randolph, 1863. [Author was Professor of Hebrew, 1830-1861.]

1711 Weld, William E., and Sewny, Kathryn W. Herbert E. Hawkes: Dean of Columbia College, 1918-1943. New York: Columbia University Press, 1958.

NEW YORK 181

1712 Whistler, Harvey Samuel. "The Life and Work of Theodore Thomas." Doctoral dissertation, Ohio University, 1942. [Thomas was Professor of Medicine.]

1713 Whittemore, Richard. "Nicholas Murray Butler and the Teaching Profession." History of Education Quarterly 1 (September 1961): 22-37.

1714 Wimmer, Curt Paul. The College of Pharmacy of the City of New York, Included in Columbia University in 1904; A History. Baltimore: Read-Taylor, 1929.

1715 Wooster, James Willet, Jr. Edward Stephen Harkness, 1874-1940. New York: Harper & Bros., 1949. [Harkness was Benefactor.]

1716 Ziegenfuss, George. "Intercollegiate Athletics at Columbia University." Doctoral dissertation, Columbia University, 1951

COOPER UNION

1717 Spalding, Charles S. Peter Cooper, a Critical Bibliography of His Life and Works. New York: Cooper Union, 1941.

CORNELL UNIVERSITY

1718 Bishop, Morris. A History of Cornell. Ithaca: Cornell University Press, 1962.

1719 Austen, Jessica Tyler, ed. Moses Coit Tyler: Selections from His Letters and Diaries. Garden City: Doubleday, Page & Co., 1911. [Tyler was Professor of American History and Literature, 1881-1900.]

1720 Beach, Mark. "Andrew Dickson White as Ex-president: The Plight of a Retired Reformer." American Quarterly 17 (Summer 1965): 239-247.

1721 Becker, Carl L. Cornell University: Founders and the Founding. Ithaca: Cornell University Press, 1943.

1722 Carron, M.T. The Contract Colleges of Cornell University. Ithaca: Cornell University Press, 1958.

1723 Coats, A.W. "Henry Carter Adams: A Case Study in the Emergence of the Social Sciences in the United States 1850-1900." Journal of American Studies 2 (October 1968): 177-198.

1724 Colman, Gould P. Education and Agriculture; A History of the New York State College of Agriculture. Ithaca: Cornell University, 1963.

1725 Comstock, Anna B. *The Comstocks of Cornell*. Ithaca: Comstock Publishing Associates, 1953.

1726 Dorf, Philip. *The Builder: A Biography of Ezra Cornell*. Ithaca: Pine Grove Press, 1965.

1727 Durand, William F. *Robert H. Thurston*. New York: American Society of Mechanical Engineers, 1929. [Thurston was Professor of Engineering, 1885-1903.]

1728 Hewett, Waterman Thomas. *Cornell University: A History*. 5 vols. New York: University Publishing Co., 1905.

1729 Hotchkiss, Eugene. "Jacob Gould Shurman and the Cornell Tradition." Doctoral dissertation, Cornell University, 1960. [Shurman was President, 1895-1914.]

1730 Howes, Raymond F. *A Cornell Notebook*. Ithaca: Cornell Alumni Association, 1971.

1731 Jones, Howard M. *Moses Coit Tyler*. Ann Arbor: University of Michigan Press, 1933.

1732 Parsons, Kermit Carlyle. *The Cornell Campus: A History of Its Planning and Development*. Ithaca: Cornell University Press, 1968.

1733 Peterson, Karl G. "Andrew Dickson White's Educational Principles: Their Sources, Development, Consequence." Doctoral dissertation, Stanford University, 1950.

1734 Rogers, Walter P. *Andrew D. White and the Modern University*. Ithaca: Cornell University Press, 1942. [White was First President, 1868-1885.]

1735 Rose, Flora, and Stocks, Esther. *A Growing College: Home Economics at Cornell University*. Ithaca: Cornell University, 1969.

1736 Stambaugh, Ben Franklin, Jr., "The Development of Post-graduate Studies at Cornell: The First Forty Years, 1868-1908." Doctoral dissertation, Cornell University, 1964.

1737 White, Andrew D. *Autobiography*. 2 vols. New York: Century, 1905.

1738 Wilkins, Burleigh T. *Carl Becker: A Biographical Study in American Intellectual History*. Cambridge: Massachusetts Institute of Technology Press, 1961. [Becker was Professor of History, 1917-1942.]

1739 Young, Charles V. *Courtney and Cornell Rowing*. Ithaca: Cornell Publications Printing Co., 1923. [Charles Edward Courtney, Rowing Coach, 1883-1916.]

CORTLAND, STATE UNIVERSITY COLLEGE AT

1740   Park, Bessie Louise. Cortland Our Alma Mater; A History of Cortland Normal School and State University of New York Teachers College at Cortland, 1869-1959. Ithaca: Cayuga Press, 1960.

1741   Brush, Carrie W. "The Cortland Normal School Response to Changing Needs and Professional Standards, 1866-1942." Doctoral dissertation, Columbia University, 1961.

1742   Park, Bessie Louise. A Survey of the Health, Physical Education and Recreation Program at Cortland State Teachers College. Cortland: State University of New York College at Cortland, 1947.

1743   State University College, Cortland. State Normal School, Cortland, New York, in the Early Nineteen Hundreds. Reminiscences and Pictures Contributed by Members of the Faculty and Classes of 1900 Through 1905. Compiled by a Volunteer Group of Alumni. Cortland: State Teachers College, 1949.

DOWNSTATE MEDICAL CENTER

1744   Jablons, A., ed. History of State University of New York College of Medicine at New York City. Brooklyn: Alumni Association, 1960.

ELMIRA COLLEGE

1745   Barber, W. Charles. Elmira College: The First Hundred Years. New York: McGraw-Hill, 1955.

1746   French, Ernestine. "Elmira College." New York State Historical Association Journal 11 (January 1930): 63-66.

1747   McDowell, Boyd. Simeon Benjamin, Founder of Elmira College, 1792-1868. Elmira: Snyder Bros. Printing Co., 1930.

1748   Meltzer, Gilbert. The Beginnings of Elmira College, 1851-1868. Elmira: Commercial Press, 1941.

1749   Palmer, Mrs. Anna Campbell. Joel Dorman Steele: Teacher and Author. New York: A. S. Barnes and Co., 1900. [Steele was President, 1866-1872.]

FINCH COLLEGE

1750 Parthemore, Janet Rayle. "A History of Findlay College." Unpublished. 1957.

FORDHAM UNIVERSITY

1751 McGinley, Lawrence J. Fordham, Part of an Ancient Tradition. New York: Newcomen Society in North America, 1954.

1752 Hassard, John R. Life of the Most Reverend John Hughes. New York: D. Appleton & Co., 1866. [Hughes was Founder.]

1753 Jerome, Judson. "Portrait of Three Experiments." Change 2 (July-August 1970): 40-54.

1754 Taaffe, Thomas G. A History of St. John's College, Fordham, New York. New York: The Catholic Publication Society, 1891.

FREDONIA, STATE UNIVERSITY COLLEGE AT

1755 Alumni Association of the State University College at Fredonia. Threshold: Normal School to Arts and Science College, 1867-1967. Fredonia: n.p., 1967.

1756 Bancroft, B. "The Historical Development of the Music Department of the State University College, Fredonia, New York." Doctoral dissertation, New York University, 1972.

1757 Ohles, John Ford. "The Historical Development of State University of New York College at Fredonia as Representative of the Evolution of Teacher Education in the State University of New York." Doctoral dissertation, State University of New York at Buffalo, 1964.

GENERAL THEOLOGICAL SEMINARY

1758 Dawley, Powel Mill. The Story of the General Theological Seminary: A Sesquicentennial History, 1817-1967. New York: Oxford University Press, 1969.

NEW YORK

GENESEO, STATE UNIVERSITY COLLEGE AT

1759 Fisher, Rosalind R. The Stone Strength of the Past; Centennial History of the State University College of Arts and Sciences at Geneseo. Buffalo: Keller, 1971.

1760 Dewey, Gene L. "A Bibliography of the History of State University Teachers College, Geneseo, New York." Unpublished manuscript, 1958.

1761 Mau, Clayton C. "Brief History of the State University Teachers College, Geneseo, New York." Unpublished manuscript, 1956.

HAMILTON COLLEGE

1762 Pilkington, Walter. Hamilton College: 1812-1962. Clinton: Hamilton College, 1962.

1763 Hamilton College. A Documented History of Hamilton College. Clinton: The College, 1922.

1764 North, S.N.D. Old Greek: An Old-time Professor in an Old-Fashioned College. New York: McClure, Phillips, 1905. [Author was Professor of Greek, 1843-1902.]

HARTWICK COLLEGE

1765 Heins, Henry Hardy. Throughout All the Years; Hartwick 1746-1946. Oneonta: Board of Trustees, Hartwick College, 1946.

HOBART AND WILLIAM SMITH COLLEGES

1766 Smith, Warren Harding. Hobart and William Smith: The History of Two Colleges. Geneva: Hobart and William Smith Colleges, 1958.

1767 Brown, Alan Willard. Hobart College; Oldest Episcopal College in U.S.A. New York: Newcomen Society in North America, 1956.

1768 Durfee, Walter H., and Schoen-Rene, Otto. William Smith College, 1908-1958; A History. Geneva: Hobart and William Smith Colleges, 1959.

1769 Turk, Milton H. Hobart, 1822-1922. Geneva: Hobart College, 1921.

HOFSTRA UNIVERSITY

1770 Palais, Elliott Samuel. "A Study of the Founding and Development of Student Government at Hofstra College." Doctoral dissertation, New York University, 1964.

HOUGHTON COLLEGE

1771 Wilson, Kenneth Lee. Consider the Years: Houghton College, 1883-1958. Houghton: Houghton College, 1958.

1772 Shea, Whitney J. "Houghton College and the Community." Doctoral dissertation, Columbia Teachers College, 1953.

HUNTER COLLEGE

1773 Burns, Mae A. "A Historical Background and Philosophical Criticism of the Curriculum of Hunter College of the City of New York from 1870-1938." Doctoral dissertation, Fordham University, 1937.

1774 Hunter, Thomas. The Autobiography of Thomas Hunter. New York: Knickerbocker Press, 1931. [Author was Founder and First President, 1870-1906.]

1775 Shuster, George N. The Ground I Walked On: Reflections of a College President. New York: Farrar, Straus and Cudahy, 1961.

JEWISH THEOLOGICAL SEMINARY

1776 Adler, Cyrus. I Have Considered the Days. Philadelphia: Jewish Publication Society of America, 1941. [Author was President, 1916-1940.]

JUILLIARD SCHOOL

1777 Damrosch, Frank. Institute of Musical Art (1905-1926). New York: Juilliard School of Music, 1936.

1778 Erskine, John. The Memory of Certain Persons. Philadelphia: J.B. Lippincott, 1947. [Author was President, 1927-1938.]

1779 Erskine, John. My Life as a Teacher. Philadelphia: J.B. Lippincott, 1948.

KEUKA COLLEGE

1780   Africa, Philip. Keuka College: A History. Valley Forge: Judson Press, 1973.

1781   Griffin, Z.F. The Builders of Keuka College. Penn Yan: Penn Yan Print Co., 1937.

LE MOYNE COLLEGE

1782   Kenney, James E. A History of Le Moyne College; The First Twenty-Five Years. Syracuse: Le Moyne College, 1972.

LONG ISLAND UNIVERSITY

1783   Gatner, Elliott S. "Long Island: The History of a Responsive and Relevant University, 1926-1968." Doctoral dissertation, Columbia University Teachers College, 1973.

1784   Long Island University. Preface to the Future. Greendale: Long Island University Press, 1967.

MANHATTAN COLLEGE

1785   Costello, C. Gabriel. The Tree Bore Fruit. New York: Manhattan College, 1953.

NEW PALTZ, STATE UNIVERSITY COLLEGE AT

1786   Lang, Elizabeth, and Lang, Robert. In a Valley Fair; A History of the State University College at New Paltz, New York. New Paltz: State University College of Education, 1960.

1787   Campbell, Loren D. "The Development of a Major Department of Health and Physical Education for Men and Women at the State Teachers College, New Paltz, New York." Doctoral dissertation, New York University, 1952.

1788   Klotzberger, Edward Lewis. "The Growth and Development of State Teachers College, New Paltz, State University of New York With Implications of Education in the State of New York." Doctoral dissertation, University of Connecticut, 1958.

NEW SCHOOL FOR SOCIAL RESEARCH

1789 Johnson, Alvin S. *Pioneer's Progress*. New York: Viking Press, 1952.

1790 Sale, J. Kirk. "The New School at Middle Age." *Change* 1 (July-August 1969): 37-45.

NEW YORK UNIVERSITY

1791 Jones, Theodore F. *New York University, 1832-1932*. New York: New York University Press, 1933.

1792 Chamberlain, Joshua L. *New York University: Its History, Influence, Equipment and Characteristics, with Biographical Sketches and Portraits of Founders, Benefactors, Officers and Alumni*. 2 vols. Boston: R. Herndon Co., 1901-1902.

1793 Freidus, Anne. "A History of the Division of General Education, New York University, 1934-1959." Doctoral dissertation, New York University, 1962.

1794 Horton, Byrne J. "The Origin of the Graduate School and the Development of Its Administration." Doctoral dissertation, New York University, 1939.

1795 Kriegel, Leonard. "The Education of an Academic." *Change* 3 (November 1971): 27-32.

1796 Lebowitz, Carl F. "A Historical Study of the School of Retailing, New York University, 1919-1963." Doctoral dissertation, New York University, 1965.

1797 MacCracken, Henry Mitchell, et al. *New York University*. New York and London: G.P. Putnam's, 1901.

1798 Wilson, Louis R. *Harry Woodburn Chase*. Chapel Hill: University of North Carolina Press, 1960. [Chase was President, 1933-1951.]

NEW YORK, STATE UNIVERSITY OF

1799 Carmichael, Oliver C., Jr. *New York Establishes a State University*. Nashville, Tenn.: Vanderbilt University Press, 1955.

1800 Gilbert, Amy M. *ACUNY: The Associated Colleges of Upper New York*. Ithaca: Cornell University Press, 1950.

1801 Greene, Robert J. "The Growth of Radio in the State University of New York." Doctoral dissertation, Syracuse University, 1970.

1802 Williams, Samuel A. "The Growth of Physical Education in the State Teachers Colleges of New York in Relation to Certain Socio-Economic Factors." Doctoral dissertation, New York University, 1950.

NEW YORK, UNIVERSITY OF THE STATE OF

1803 Abbott, Frank C. Government Policy and Higher Education: A Study of the Regents of the University of the State of New York 1784-1949. Ithaca: Cornell University Press, 1958.

1804 Alexander, Charles B. "New York State's Historic University." State Service 5 (August 1921): 364-371.

1805 Canuteson, Richard L. "An Historical Study of Some Effects of Dual Control in the New York State Educational System." Doctoral dissertation, Michigan State University, 1951.

1806 Finegan, Thomas E. Life and Public Services of Andrew Sloan Draper. Albany: University of State of New York, 1914. [Draper was First Commissioner of Education, 1904-1913.]

1807 Holmes, Keith D. "Frank Pierrepont Graves--His Influence upon American Education." Doctoral dissertation, Cornell University, 1952.

1808 Hough, Franklin B. Historical and Statistical Record of the University of the State of New York During the Century from 1784 to 1884. Albany: Weed, Parsons, and Co., 1885.

1809 Pine, John B. "Origin of the University of the State of New York." Educational Review 37 (March 1909): 284-291.

1810 Sherwood, Sidney. The University of the State of New York: History of Higher Education in the State of New York. Washington, D.C.: U.S. Bureau of Education, 1902.

NIAGARA UNIVERSITY

1811 McKey, Joseph P. History of Niagara University, 1856-1931. Niagara: Niagara University, 1931.

1812 History of the Seminary of Our Lady of Angels, Niagara University, Niagara County, New York, 1856-1906. Buffalo: Matthews-Northrup Works, 1906.

1813   That All May Know Thee: One Hundred Years, 1856-1956. Niagara: The University, 1956.

OLD WESTBURY, STATE UNIVERSITY COLLEGE AT

1814   Jerome, Judson. "Portrait of Three Experiments." Change 2 (July-August 1970): 40-54.

1815   Keyes, Ralph, Wofford, Harris, Grennan, Jacqueline, et al. "The College That Students Helped Plan." Change 1 (March-April 1969): 12-23.

1816   Wofford, Harris. "How Big the Wave?" In Five Experimental Colleges, edited by Gary MacDonald, pp. 158-193. New York: Harper and Row, 1973.

ONEONTA, STATE UNIVERSITY COLLEGE AT

1817   Brush, Carey W. In Honor and Good Faith: A History of the State University College at Oneonta, New York. Geneva: W. F. Humphrey Press, 1965.

OSWEGO, STATE UNIVERSITY COLLEGE AT

1818   Rogers, Dorothy. Oswego: Fountainhead of Teacher Education. New York: Appleton, 1961.

1819   Hollis, Andrew P. The Contribution of the Oswego Normal School to Educational Progress in the United States. Boston: D. C. Heath, 1898.

1820   Sheldon, Edward A. Autobiography. New York: Ives-Butler, 1911. [Author was President, 1862-1897.]

PACKER COLLEGIATE INSTITUTE

1821   Cahalan, Thomas L. "Silas Sadler Packard, Pioneer in American Business Education." Doctoral dissertation, New York University, 1955.

1822   Nickerson, M.L. A Long Way Forward: The First Hundred Years of the Packer Collegiate Institute. Brooklyn: Packer Collegiate Institute, 1945.

NEW YORK

PARSONS SCHOOL OF DESIGN

1823 Jones, Marjorie. "A History of the Parsons School of Design, 1896-1966." Doctoral dissertation, New York University, 1968.

PLATTSBURGH, STATE UNIVERSITY COLLEGE AT

1824 Cooper, Frank A. The Plattsburgh Idea in Education. Plattsburgh: Plattsburgh College Association, 1968.

1825 Diebolt, Alfred L. "Economic and Social Practices in Clinton County as Related to the Problems of the State Normal School in Plattsburgh, New York." Doctoral dissertation, New York University, 1939.

POLYTECHNIC INSTITUTE OF BROOKLYN

1826 Kastendieck, Miles. The Story of Poly. Wilmington: H. Matthews and Co., 1940.

POTSDAM, STATE UNIVERSITY COLLEGE AT

1827 Lahey, William C. The Potsdam Tradition. New York: Appleton-Century-Crofts, 1966.

PRATT INSTITUTE

1828 Office of the President. Pratt Institute, Some Basic Information on Its History, Purposes, and Achievements. Brooklyn: Pratt Institute, 1964.

RENSSELAER POLYTECHNIC COLLEGE

1829 Reznek, Samuel. Education for a Technological Society; Rensselaer Polytechnic Institute. Troy: Rensselaer Polytechnic Institute, 1968.

1830 Baker, Raymond P. A Chapter in American Education. New York: Scribner's, 1925.

1831 McAllister, Ethel M. "Amos Eaton, Scientist and Educator." Doctoral dissertation, University of Pennsylvania, 1940. [Eaton was Professor, 1824-1842.]

1832 Ricketts, P.C. History of the Rensselaer Polytechnic Institute 1824-1934. 3d ed. New York: Wiley, 1934.

ROCHESTER INSTITUTE OF TECHNOLOGY

1833 Hoke, George R. Blazing New Trails: The Biography of a Pioneer in Education. Rochester: Rochester Athenaeum and Mechanics Institute, 1937.

ROCHESTER, UNIVERSITY OF

1834 May, Henry. The University of Rochester: A History. [Edition by L. Klein forthcoming.]

1835 Ackerman, Carl W. George Eastman. New York: Houghton Mifflin, 1930.

1836 Adams, John Quincy. An Old Boy Remembers. Boston: Ruth Hill, 1935.

1837 Corner, Betsey C. "Rochester's Early Medical School." Rochester Historical Society Publication 7 (1928): 141-152.

1838 Kendrick, Asahel. Martin Brewer Anderson: A Biography. Philadelphia: American Baptist Publication Society, 1895. [Anderson was First President, 1851-1888.]

1839 May, Arthur J. "A University Dream That Failed." New York History 68 (April 1967): 160-181.

1840 Parkman, Aubrey. "David Jayne Hill." Doctoral dissertation, University of Rochester, 1961. [Hill was President, 1892-1897.]

1841 Perkins, Dexter. Yield of the Years: An Autobiography. Boston: Little, Brown, 1969. [Perkins was Professor of History.]

1842 Rosenberger, Jesse L. Rochester and Colgate: Historical Backgrounds of the Two Universities. Chicago: Chicago Press, 1925.

1843 Rosenberger, Jesse L. Rochester: The Making of a University. Rochester: The University, 1927.

1844 Slater, John R. Rhees of Rochester. New York: Harper, 1946. [Rhees was President, 1900-1935.]

1845 Valentine, Alan. Trial Balance: The Education of an American. New York: Pantheon, 1956. [Author was President, 1935-1949.]

NEW YORK

ROCKEFELLER UNIVERSITY

1846 Corner, G.W. A History of the Rockefeller Institute, 1901-1953. New York: Rochester Institute Press, 1964.

ROSARY HILL COLLEGE

1847 Dunn, Georgia. Hillsides, a Memoir of Rosary Hill College, 1948-1971. Forthcoming.

RUSSELL SAGE COLLEGE

1848 Lutz, Alma. Emma Willard, Daughter of Democracy. Boston: Houghton Mifflin, 1929.

1849 Patton, Julia. Russell Sage College: The First 25 Years, 1916-1941. Troy: Press of W. Snyder, 1941.

1850 Spears, George J. Russell Sage College: The Second Quarter Century, 1941-1966. Troy: Birkmayer, 1966.

SAINT BONAVENTURE UNIVERSITY

1851 Herscher, Irenaeus. The History of St. Bonaventure University. St. Bonaventure: St. Bonaventure University, 1951.

1852 Angelo, Rev. Mark V. "The History of St. Bonaventure University." Doctoral dissertation, Fordham University, 1958.

1853 Hammon, Walter. The First Bonaventure Men: The Early History of St. Bonaventure University and the Allegany Franciscans. St. Bonaventure: St. Bonaventure University, 1958.

SAINT JOHN'S COLLEGE

1854 Damiano, Roland, and Scimecca, Joseph. Crisis at St. John's: Strike and Revolution on the Catholic Campus. New York: Random House, 1967. Pp. 9, 213.

SAINT LAWRENCE UNIVERSITY

1855 Pink, Louis H., and Delmage, R.E. Candle in the Wilderness. New York: Appleton-Century-Crofts, 1957.

1856 Black, Malcolm S. *Sixty Years of St. Lawrence*. Canton: St. Lawrence University, 1916.

SAINT ROSE, COLLEGE OF

1857 Soulier, Catherine Francis. "The College of Saint Rose, 1920-1950." Master's thesis, College of St. Rose, 1951.

SARAH LAWRENCE COLLEGE

1858 Warren, Constance. *A New Design for Women's Education*. New York: Stokes, 1940.

SIENA COLLEGE

1859 Mooney, Donald J. "A History of Siena College from the Beginning to July, 1943." Master's thesis, Siena College, 1945.

SKIDMORE COLLEGE

1860 Decker, Maud K. *Charles Henry Keyes: A Biography by His Daughter*. Minneapolis: University Printing Co., 1937. [Keyes was First President, 1912-1925.]

SYRACUSE UNIVERSITY

1861 Galpin, W. Freeman. *Syracuse University*. 2 vols. Syracuse: Syracuse University Press, 1952-1960.

1862 Armstrong, George R., and Kranz, Marvin W., eds. *Forestry College: Essays on the Growth and Development of New York State's College of Forestry, 1911-1961*. Syracuse: Alumni Association, State University College of Forestry at Syracuse University, 1961.

1863 Charters, Alexander N. *The Hill and the Valley: The Story of University College at Syracuse University Through 1964*. Syracuse: Syracuse University Press, 1972.

1864 Charvat, Arthur. "A History of the Syracuse University History Department 1871-1922." Doctoral dissertation, Syracuse University, 1957.

1865 Cole, Edgar B. "The College of Fine Arts of Syracuse University, 1894-1922." Doctoral dissertation, Syracuse University, 1957.

NEW YORK

1866 Craven, Clifford J. "Why We Withdrew: An Investigation into the Reasons Male Students Left Syracuse University During the Year 1948 and into Their Attitude Toward the Institution." Doctoral dissertation, Syracuse University, 1951.

1867 Field, Earle. "The New York State College of Forestry at Syracuse University, the History, Founding and Early Growth, 1911-1922." Doctoral dissertation, Syracuse University, 1954.

1868 Galpin, William Freeman. Syracuse and Teacher Education, the First Fifty Years. Syracuse: Syracuse University Press, 1956.

1869 Hoyle, Raymond J., and Cox, Laurie D. "The New York State College of Forestry at Syracuse University, a History of Its First Twenty-Five Years 1911-1936." Syracuse: The College, 1936.

1870 Seward, Doris M. "A Historical Study of the Women's Residence Program at Syracuse University." Doctoral dissertation, Syracuse University, 1953.

UNION COLLEGE

1871 Fox, Dixon Ryan. Union College: An Unfinished History. Schenectady: Graduate Council, Union College, 1945.

1872 Feigenbaum, Rita. "The Early Portrait Collection of Union College, 1800-1850." Master's thesis, Union College, 1967.

1873 Hislop, Codman. Eliphalet Nott. Middletown, Conn.: Wesleyan University Press, 1972. [Nott was President, 1801-1866.]

1874 Hough, Frederick B. Historical Sketch of Union College. Washington, D.C.: U.S. Bureau of Education, 1876.

1875 Raymond, Andrew V. Union University. 3 vols. New York: Lewis, 1907.

UNION THEOLOGICAL SEMINARY

1876 Brown, William Adams. Teacher and His Times. New York: Scribner's, 1940. [Author was Professor of Theology, 1898-1936.]

1877 Stoddard, Francis H. The Life and Letters of Charles Butler. New York: Scribner's, 1903. [Butler was Co-founder.]

UNITED STATES MILITARY ACADEMY

1878 Ambrose, Stephen E. Duty, Honor, Country: A History of West Point. Baltimore: Johns Hopkins University Press, 1966.

1879 Cohane, Tim. Gridiron Grenadiers: The Story of West Point Football. New York: Putnam, 1948.

1880 Denton, Edgar III. "The Formative Years of the United States Military Academy 1775-1833." Doctoral dissertation, Syracuse University, 1964.

1881 Dillard, Walter S. "The United States Military Academy, 1865-1900." Doctoral dissertation, University of Washington, 1972.

1882 Farley, Joseph Pearson. West Point in the Early Sixties. Troy: Pafraets, 1902.

1883 Flipper, Henry Ossian. The Colored Cadet at West Point. Autobiography of Lt. Henry Ossian Flipper, U.S.A.: First Graduate of Color from the U.S. Military Academy. New York: Homer Lee and Co., 1878.

1884 Forman, Sidney. "West Point: A History of the United States Military Academy." Doctoral dissertation, Columbia University, 1949.

1885 Galloway, K. Bruce, and Johnson, Robert. West Point. New York: Simon and Schuster, 1973.

1886 Godson, William F. "A History of West Point, 1852-1902." Doctoral dissertation, Temple University, 1934.

1887 Griess, Thomas E. "Dennis Hart Mahan: West Point Professor and Advocate of Military Professionalism, 1830-1871." Doctoral dissertation, Duke University, 1969.

1888 MacArthur, Douglas. Reminiscences. New York: McGraw-Hill, 1964. [Author was Superintendent, 1919-1922.]

1889 McIver, George W. "North Carolinians at West Point Before the Civil War." North Carolina History Review 7 (January 1930): 15-45.

1890 Marszalek, John F. Court-Martial: A Black Man in America. New York: Scribner's, 1972. [About Johnson Whittaker.]

1891 Morrison, James L. "The United States Military Academy, 1833-1866: Years of Progress and Turmoil." Doctoral dissertation, Columbia University, 1970.

1892 Nye, Roger H. "The United States Military Academy in an Era of Educational Reform, 1900-1925." Doctoral dissertation, Columbia, 1968.

1893 Richardson, Robert C. West Point: An Intimate Picture of the National Military Academy and the Life of a Cadet. New York: G.P. Putnam's, 1917.

VASSAR COLLEGE

1894 Plum, Dorothy A., and Dowell, George B. The Magnificent Enterprize: A Chronicle of Vassar. Poughkeepsie: Vassar College, 1961.

1895 Brown, Louise F. Apostle of Democracy: The Life of Lucy Maymard Salmon. New York: Harper & Bros., 1943. [Salmon was Professor of History, 1888-1927.]

1896 Haight, Elizabeth H. The Life and Letters of James M. Taylor, 1848-1916. New York: E.P. Dutton, 1919. [Taylor was President, 1885-1914.]

1897 Haight, Elizabeth H., ed. Autobiography and Letters of Matthew Vassar, 1792-1868. New York: n.p., 1916.

1898 Johnson, Burgess. As Much As I Dare; A Personal Recollection. New York: Ives Washburn, 1944. [Author was Professor of English.]

1899 Keller, Dorothy. "Maria Mitchell, Early Woman Academician." Doctoral dissertation, University of Rochester, 1974. [Mitchell was Professor of Astronomy, 1865-1888.]

1900 Lossing, B.J. Vassar College and Its Founder. Alvord: New York, 1867.

1901 Norris, Mary H. The Golden Age of Vassar. Poughkeepsie: Vassar College, 1915.

1902 Taylor, James Monroe. Before Vassar Opened; A Contribution to the History of Higher Education of Women in America. Boston and New York: Houghton Mifflin, 1924.

1903 Taylor, James Monroe, and Haight, Elizabeth Hazelton. Vassar. New York: Oxford University Press, American branch, 1915.

1904 Wright, H. Sweeper in the Sky: The Life of Maria Mitchell, First Woman Astronomer in America. New York: Macmillan, 1949.

WELLS COLLEGE

1905 McKean, John Rosseel Overton. "Wells College Student Life 1868-1936." Doctoral dissertation, Cornell University, 1960.

WYANDANCH COLLEGE

1906 Ziegler, Jerome M. "'You Mean the Wyandanch College?'" Change 4 (June 1972): 48-52.

YESHIVA UNIVERSITY

1907 Klaperman, Gilbert. The Story of Yeshiva University, the First Jewish University in America. New York: Macmillan, 1969.

North Carolina

GENERAL REFERENCES

1908 Connor, R.D.W. "The Genesis of Higher Education in North Carolina." North Carolina History Review 28 (January 1951): 1-14.

1909 Coon, Charles L. North Carolina Schools and Academies, 1790-1840. Raleigh: Broughton Printing Co., 1915. [Colleges, pp. 641-721.]

1910 Drake, William Earle. Higher Education in North Carolina Before 1860. New York: Carlton Press, 1967.

1911 Farmer, Fannie Memory. "Legal Education in North Carolina, 1820-1860." North Carolina History Review 28 (July 1951): 271-297.

1912 Gobbel, Luther L. Church-State Relationships in Education in North Carolina Since 1776. Durham: Duke University Press, 1938.

1913 Ingram, Margaret Helen. "Development of Higher Education for White Women in North Carolina Prior to 1875." Doctoral dissertation, University of North Carolina, 1961.

1914 Logan, Frenise A. "The Movement in North Carolina to Establish a State Supported College for Negroes." North Carolina History Review 35 (April 1958): 167-180.

1915 Raper, Charles L. The Church and Private Schools in North Carolina. Greensboro: n.p., 1898.

1916 Segner, Kenyon B. "A History of the Community College Movement in North Carolina, 1927-1963." Doctoral dissertation, University of North Carolina, 1966.

1917 Teele, Arthur E. "Education of the Negro in North Carolina, 1862-1872." Doctoral dissertation, Cornell University, 1954.

1918 Young, Wade P. "A History of Agricultural Education in North Carolina." Doctoral dissertation, University of North Carolina, 1934.

INSTITUTIONAL HISTORIES

BELMONT ABBEY COLLEGE

1919 Doris, Sebastian. "Belmont Abbey: Its History and Educational Influence." Master's thesis, Catholic University of America, 1933.

BLACK MOUNTAIN COLLEGE

1920 Duberman, Martin. *Black Mountain: An Exploration in Community*. New York: E.P. Dutton, 1972.

1921 Adamic, Louis. "Education on a Mountain." *Harpers* 172 (1936): 516-530.

1922 Rice, John A. *I Came Out of the 18th Century*. New York: Harper, 1942. [Author was President, 1933-1939.]

CATAWBA COLLEGE

1923 Keppel, Alvin Robert. *A College of Our Own; A Brief History of Catawba College 1851-1951*. Salisbury: Catawba College, 1951.

CHOWAN COLLEGE

1924 McKnight, Edgar. *A History of Chowan College*. Murfreesboro: Chowan College, 1964.

DAVIDSON COLLEGE

1925 Shaw, Cornelia Rebeckah. *Davidson College*. New York: F.H. Revell Press, 1923.

1926 Lingle, W.L. *Memoirs of Davidson College*. Richmond, Va.: John Knox Press, 1947.

NORTH CAROLINA

DUKE UNIVERSITY

1927 Porter, Earl W. Trinity and Duke 1892-1924: Foundations of Duke University. Durham: Duke University Press, 1964.

1928 Chaffin, N.C. Trinity College, 1839-1892: The Beginnings of Duke University. Durham: Duke University Press, 1950.

1929 Crowell, John Franklin. Personal Recollections of Trinity College, North Carolina, 1887-1894. Durham: Duke University Press, 1939. [Author was President, 1887-1894.]

1930 Dowd, Jerome. The Life of Braxton Craven (1822-1882): A Biographical Approach to Social Science. Durham: Duke University Press, 1939. [Craven was First President of Trinity, 1849-1882.]

1931 Garber, Paul N. John Carlisle Kilgo, President of Trinity College, 1894-1910. Durham: Duke University Press, 1937.

1932 Gifford, James F. The Evolution of a Medical Center: A History of Medicine at Duke University to 1941. Durham: Duke University Press, 1972.

1933 Gifford, James F. "A History of Medicine at Duke University: Origins and Growth, 1865-1941." Doctoral dissertation, Duke University, 1970.

1934 Jenkins, John W. James B. Duke, Master Builder. New York: George H. Doran Co., 1927.

1935 Tilley, Nannie M. The Trinity College Historical Society, 1892-1941. Durham: Duke University Press, 1941.

FAYETTEVILLE STATE UNIVERSITY

1936 Murphy, Ella L. "Origin and Development of Fayetteville State Teachers College, 1867-1959. --A Chapter in the History of the Education of Negroes in North Carolina." Doctoral dissertation, New York University, 1960.

GUILFORD COLLEGE

1937 Gilbert, Dorothy Lloyd. Guilford: A Quaker College. Guilford: Guilford College, 1937.

HIGH POINT COLLEGE

1938 Pritchard, J.E. *A Brief History of the First Twenty-Five Years of High Point College*. High Point: n.p., 1953.

JOHNSON C. SMITH UNIVERSITY

1939 George, Arthur A. *100 Years 1867-1967: Salient Factors in the Growth and Development of Johnson C. Smith University*. Charlotte: Dowd Press, Inc., 1968.

MARS HILL COLLEGE

1940 McLeod, John Angus. *From These Stones*. Mars Hill: Mars Hill College, 1968.

MEREDITH COLLEGE

1941 Johnson, Mary Lynch. *History of Meredith College*. Raleigh: Edward and Broughton, 1972.

NORTH CAROLINA AGRICULTURAL AND TECHNICAL STATE UNIVERSITY

1942 Gibbs, Warmoth T. *History of North Carolina Agricultural and Technical College*. Dubuque: William C. Brown, 1966.

NORTH CAROLINA, UNIVERSITY OF, AT CHAPEL HILL

1943 House, Robert B. *The Light That Shines*. Chapel Hill: University of North Carolina Press, 1964.

1944 Battle, Kemp Plummer. *History of the University of North Carolina*. Raleigh: Edward and Broughton, 1907-1912.

1945 Battle, Kemp Plummer. *Memories of an Old-time Tarheel*. Chapel Hill: University of North Carolina Press, 1945. [Author was President, 1876-1901.]

1946 Caldwell, Joseph. *Autobiography and Biography of Rev. Joseph Caldwell*. Chapel Hill: J.B. Neathery, 1860. [Author was Professor of Mathematics, 1796-1804, 1812-1817; President, 1804-1812, 1817-1835.]

1947 Chamberlain, Hope Summerell. *Old Days in Chapel Hill Being the Life and Letters of Cornelia Phillips Spencer*. Chapel Hill: University of North Carolina Press, 1926.

1948 Connor, Robert Diggs Wimberly, ed. *A Documentary History of the University of North Carolina 1776-1799*. 2 vols. Chapel Hill: University of North Carolina Press, 1953.

1949 Coyner, Ruth E. "The South's First University Summer Normal School." *Peabody Journal of Education* 18 (1940): 173-182.

1950 Henderson, Archibald. *The Campus of the First State University*. Chapel Hill: University of North Carolina Press, 1949.

1951 Love, J.L. *'Tis Sixty Years Since: A Story of the University of North Carolina in the 1880's*. Chapel Hill: University of North Carolina, General Alumni Association, 1945.

1952 MacMillan, Dougald. *English at Chapel Hill 1795-1969*. Chapel Hill: University of North Carolina at Chapel Hill, Department of English, 1970.

1953 Noble, Alice. *The School of Pharmacy of the University of North Carolina*. Chapel Hill: University of North Carolina Press, 1961.

1954 Powell, William Stevens. *The First State University, a Pictorial History of the University of North Carolina*. Chapel Hill: University of North Carolina Press, 1972.

1955 Robinson, Blackwell P. "William Richardson Davie." Doctoral dissertation, University of North Carolina, 1953. [Davie was a Founder.]

1956 Scott, Tom. "A History of Intercollegiate Athletics at the University of North Carolina." Doctoral dissertation, Columbia Teachers College, 1955.

1957 Wagstaff, H.M. *Impressions of Men and Movements at the University of North Carolina*. Chapel Hill: University of North Carolina Press, 1950.

1958 Wilson, Louis Round. *The University of North Carolina*. Chapel Hill: University of North Carolina Press, 1957.

1959 Wilson, Louis Round. *The University of North Carolina Under Consolidation, 1931-1963, History and Appraisal*. Chapel Hill: University of North Carolina Consolidated Office, 1964.

NORTH CAROLINA, UNIVERSITY OF, AT GREENSBORO

1960 Bowles, Elisabeth Ann. A Good Beginning: The First Four Decades of the University of North Carolina at Greensboro. Chapel Hill: University of North Carolina Press, 1967.

1961 Holder, Rose Howell. McIver of North Carolina. Chapel Hill: University of North Carolina Press, 1957. [Charles D. McIver, President, 1892-1906.]

1962 Lathrop, Virginia Terrell. Educate a Woman: Fifty Years of Life at the University of North Carolina. Chapel Hill: University of North Carolina Press, 1942.

NORTH CAROLINA, UNIVERSITY OF, AT RALEIGH

1963 Lockmiller, David A. History of the North Carolina State College of Agriculture and Engineering of the University of North Carolina, 1889-1939. Raleigh: n.p., 1939.

PEMBROKE STATE UNIVERSITY

1964 Oxendine, Clifton. "Pembroke State College for Indians: Historical Sketch." North Carolina History Review 22 (January 1945): 22-33.

PFEIFFER COLLEGE

1965 Bangle, F.W. Dowd. "Pfeiffer Junior College—A Study of Missionary Education." Master's thesis, University of North Carolina, 1941.

QUEENS COLLEGE

1966 Hoyle, Hughes Bayne, Jr. "The Early History of Queens College to 1872." Doctoral dissertation, University of North Carolina, 1963.

SAINT ANDREW'S COLLEGE

1967 Burger, Nash K. "Battle Hill and St. Andrew's College." Journal of Mississippi History 4 (April 1942): 84-89.

NORTH CAROLINA 205

SAINT AUGUSTINE'S COLLEGE

1968   Halliburton, Cecil D. A History of Saint Augustine's College, 1867-1937. Raleigh: St. Augustine's College, 1937.

1969   Chitty, Arthur Ben. "St. Augustine's College, Raleigh, North Carolina." Historical Magazine of the Protestant Episcopal Church 35 (September 1966): 207-220.

SALEM COLLEGE

1970   Hixson, Ivay May. "Academic Requirements of Salem College, 1854-1909." North Carolina History Review 27 (October 1950): 419-429.

1971   Rondthaler, Howard E. "New Plans Against an Old Background, Salem College, 1866-1884." North Carolina History Review 27 (October 1950): 430-436.

SHAW UNIVERSITY

1972   Carter, Wilmoth A. Shaw's Universe. Washington, D.C.: National Publishing, Inc., 1973.

1973   Jenkins, Clara B. "A Historical Study of Shaw University, 1865-1963." Doctoral dissertation, University of Pittsburgh, 1964.

WAKE FOREST UNIVERSITY

1974   Paschal, George Washington. History of Wake Forest College. Wake Forest: Wake Forest College, 1935.

1975   Carpenter, Coy C. The Story of Medicine at Wake Forest University. Chapel Hill: University of North Carolina Press, 1971.

1976   Sikes, E.W. "The Genesis of Wake Forest College." North Carolina History Commission Publications 1 (1907): 538-557.

WESTERN CAROLINA UNIVERSITY

1977 Bird, William Ernest. <u>The History of Western Carolina College</u>.
     Chapel Hill: University of North Carolina Press, 1963.

YADKIN COLLEGE

1978 Michael, Olin Bain. <u>Yadkin College, 1856-1924; A Historic
     Sketch</u>. Salisbury: n.p., 1939.

North Dakota

GENERAL REFERENCES

1979 Heine, Clarence J. "A Study of the Decisions Made by the North Dakota Board of Higher Education From 1939 to 1969." Doctoral dissertation, University of Michigan, 1970.

1980 Olson, Gordon B. "The Status of Four-Year State Institutions of Higher Learning in North Dakota." Doctoral dissertation, University of North Dakota, 1953.

1981 Robinson, Elwyn. History of North Dakota. Lincoln: University of Nebraska Press, 1966. [Pp. 306-316 and 492-501 about higher education.]

1982 U.S. Office of Education. Higher Education in North Dakota. 2 vols. Washington, D.C.: U.S. Office of Education, 1958.

INSTITUTIONAL HISTORIES

DICKINSON STATE COLLEGE

1983 Belsheim, Osbourne T. The Story of Dickinson State: A History of Dickinson State College 1918-1968. Dickinson: Dickinson State College, 1968.

MAYVILLE STATE COLLEGE

1984 McMullen, Harvey M. "A Study to Identify the Role of Mayville State College and How It Serves the State and People of North Dakota." Doctoral dissertation, University of North Dakota, 1964.

NORTH DAKOTA STATE UNIVERSITY OF AGRICULTURE AND APPLIED SCIENCE

1985 Hunter, William Columbus. Beacon Across the Prairie; North Dakota's Land-Grant College. Fargo: Institute for Regional Studies, 1961.

NORTH DAKOTA, UNIVERSITY OF

1986 Geiger, Louis G. University of the Northern Plains. Grand Forks: University of North Dakota, 1958.

1987 Cummins, Cedric. "The University of Dakota: Higher Learning on the High Plains." North Dakota History 34 (Summer 1967): 243-257.

1988 Gillette, John M. "Social and Economic Background of the University of North Dakota in the 80's of the Last Century." University of North Dakota Quarterly Journal 13 (July 1923): 339-358.

1989 Massie, Mattie G. "Student Life During the First Decade of the University of North Dakota." University of North Dakota Quarterly Journal 13 (July 1923): 367-380.

1990 Quirke, Terence T. "Arthur Gray Leonard." North Dakota University Quarterly Journal 23 (1933): 147-156. [Leonard was Professor of Geology, 1903-1932.]

1991 Sprague, Homer B. "President Sprague's Administration of the University of North Dakota." University of North Dakota Quarterly Journal 7 (October 1916): 3-28. [Sprague was President, 1887-1891.]

1992 Vold, Lauriz. "The First Twenty-Five Years of the Law School of the University of North Dakota." University of North Dakota Quarterly Journal 14 (April 1924): 255-278.

VALLEY CITY STATE COLLEGE

1993 Hanna, Glenn Alden. "History of the Valley City State Teachers College." Master's thesis, University of North Dakota, 1951.

Ohio

GENERAL REFERENCES

1994 Knight, George W., and Commons, John R. <u>The History of Higher Education in Ohio</u>. Washington, D.C.: U.S. Bureau of Education, 1891.

1995 Barnes, Sherman B. "Learning and Piety in Ohio Colleges, 1900-1930." <u>Ohio History</u> 70 (July 1961): 214-243.

1996 Bosse, Richard C. "Origins of Lutheran Higher Education in Ohio." Doctoral dissertation, Ohio State University, 1969.

1997 Briggs, Harry H. "History of Teacher Training in Ohio Colleges and Universities." Doctoral dissertation, Case Western Reserve University, 1955.

1998 Eckelberry, Roscoe H. "An Early Proposal for a State Polytechnic School." <u>Ohio History</u> 39 (1930): 400-410.

1999 Hoover, Thomas N. "The Beginnings of Higher Education in the Northwest Territories." <u>Ohio History</u> 50 (July 1941): 244-267.

2000 Juettner, Otto. "The Rise of Medical Colleges in the Ohio Valley." <u>Ohio History</u> 22 (October 1913): 481-491.

2001 Kinnison, William Andrew. "The Impact of the Morrill Act on Higher Education in Ohio." Doctoral dissertation, Ohio State University, 1968.

2002 Leahy, John F., Jr. "The Development of a State-Wide Plan for Establishing Community Colleges in Ohio." Doctoral dissertation, Ohio State University, 1953.

2003 Thompson, W.O. "Universities in Ohio." <u>Ohio History</u> 12 (1903): 426-489.

INSTITUTIONAL HISTORIES

AKRON, UNIVERSITY OF

2004   Knepper, George W. New Lamps for Old: One Hundred Years of
        Urban Higher Education at the University of Akron. Akron:
        n.p., 1970.

2005   Spanton, A.I., ed. Fifty Years of Buchtel, 1870-1920. Akron:
        Buchtel College Alumni Association, 1922.

ANTIOCH COLLEGE

2006   Henderson, A.D., and Hall, Dorothy. Antioch College: Its Design
        for Liberal Education. New York: Harper, 1946.

2007   Clark, Burton R. The Distinctive College: Antioch, Reed and
        Swarthmore. Chicago: Aldine Publishing Co., 1970.

2008   Grant, Gerald. "Let a Hundred Antiochs Bloom!" Change 4
        (September 1972): 47-58.

2009   Karlen, Arno. "The Hazards of Innovation." Change 1 (1969):
        46-53.

2010   Messerli, Jonathan. Horace Mann; A Biography. New York: Knopf,
        1972. [Mann was President, 1851-1858.]

2011   Vallance, Harvard F. "A History of Antioch College." Doctoral
        dissertation, Ohio State University, 1936.

ASHLAND COLLEGE

2012   Miller, Clara W., and Mason, E. Glenn. A Short History of
        Ashland College. Ashland: Brethren Publishing Co., 1953.

ATHENAEUM

2013   Miller, Francis J. "A History of the Athenaeum of Ohio (1829-
        1960)." Doctoral dissertation, University of Cincinnati, 1963.

BALDWIN-WALLACE COLLEGE

2014 Feuchter, Clyde E., et al. A History of Baldwin University and German Wallace College. Berea: Baldwin-Wallace College, 1945.

BLUFFTON COLLEGE

2015 Smith, C. Henry., and Hirschler, E.J., eds. The Story of Bluffton College. Bluffton: Bluffton College, 1925.

BOWLING GREEN STATE UNIVERSITY

2016 Overman, James Robert. The History of Bowling Green State University. Bowling Green: Bowling Green State University, 1967.

2017 McThal, Kenneth. "From Normal College to State University, the Development of Bowling Green State University." Doctoral dissertation, Case Western Reserve University, 1947.

CASE WESTERN RESERVE

2018 Beman, Alan. "Charles Francis Thwing." Doctoral dissertation, University of Wisconsin, 1965. [Thwing was President of Western Reserve, 1890-1921.]

2019 Bunge, Helen L. "Changing the Basic Curriculum at the Frances Payne Bolton School of Nursing of Western Reserve University." Doctoral dissertation, Columbia University, 1950.

2020 Campbell, Thomas F. SASS: Fifty Years of Social Work Education. A History of the School of Applied Social Sciences, Case Western Reserve University. Cleveland: Western Reserve University Press, 1967.

2021 Corlett, William Thomas. Early Reminiscences, 1860-1904. Cleveland: Lakeside Press, 1920. [Author was Professor of Dermatology, 1885-1924.]

2022 Thwing, Charles F. Notes on the History of the College for Women of Western Reserve University for Its First Twenty-Five Years, 1888-1913. Cleveland: Western Reserve University Press, 1913.

2023 Waite, Frederick C. History of the School of Dentistry of Western Reserve University. Cleveland: n.p., 1940.

2024 Waite, Frederick C. <u>Western Reserve University Centennial History of the School of Medicine</u>. Cleveland: Western Reserve University Press, 1946.

2025 Waite, Frederick C. <u>Western Reserve University: The Hudson Era, 1826-1882</u>. Cleveland: Western Reserve University Press, 1943.

2026 Western Reserve University. <u>The Fiftieth Anniversary, Flora Stone Mather College of Western Reserve University, 1888-1938</u>. Cleveland: Western Reserve University Press, 1938.

2027 Williams, Howard R. "Edward Williams Morley." Doctoral dissertation, Case Western Reserve University, 1942. [Morley was Professor of Chemistry, 1869-1906.]

CEDARVILLE COLLEGE

2028 McDonald, Cleveland. "The History of Cedarville College." Doctoral dissertation, Ohio State University, 1965.

CINCINNATI, UNIVERSITY OF

2029 McGrane, Reginald C. <u>The University of Cincinnati</u>. New York: Harper, 1963.

2030 Coleman, Paul E. "Important Educational Achievements of the Cooperative Curriculum at University of Cincinnati." Doctoral dissertation, New York University, 1933.

2031 Ewing, James R. <u>The Public Services of Jacob Dolson Cox</u>. Washington, D.C.: Neale Publishing, 1902. [Cox was Dean of Law School, 1881-1897.]

2032 Lewis, John, Jr. "An Historical Study of the Origin and Development of the Cincinnati Conservatory of Music." Doctoral dissertation, University of Cincinnati, 1943.

2033 Nestor, William R. "The Development of the Student Personnel Program at the University of Cincinnati." Doctoral dissertation, University of Cincinnati, 1965.

2034 Orlando, Vincent A. "An Historical Study of the Origins and Development of the College of Music of Cincinnati." Doctoral dissertation, University of Cincinnati, 1946.

2035 Schwarberg, W.D. "A History of Physical Education at the University of Cincinnati." Doctoral dissertation, Columbia Teachers College, 1957.

OHIO

CLEVELAND STATE UNIVERSITY

2036 Earnest, G. Brooks. History of Fenn College. Forthcoming.

DAYTON, UNIVERSITY OF

2037 Wehrle, William Otto. A History of the University of Dayton. Dayton: University of Dayton, 1937.

2038 Brueck, John. Chronicles of Nazareth. Dayton: University of Dayton, 1948.

2039 Knust, Edward H., comp. Hallowed Memories; A Chronological History of Dayton. 2d ed. Dayton: University of Dayton, 1953.

2040 Knust, Edward H., comp. Miscellanea; Some Interesting Facts in the History of the University of Dayton, 1850-1950. Dayton: University of Dayton, 1951.

2041 Whetro, R. Kathleen. Highlights of Twenty-Five Years of Co-education at the University of Dayton. Dayton: University of Dayton, 1959.

DENISON UNIVERSITY

2042 Chessman, C. Wallace. Denison: The Story of an Ohio College. Granville: Denison University, 1957.

FARMERS' COLLEGE

2043 Becker, Carl M. "Freeman Cary and Farmers' College: An Ohio Educator and an Experiment in Nineteenth Century Practical Education." Bulletin of the Historical and Philosophical Society of Ohio 21 (July 1963): 151-175.

2044 Becker, Carl M. "Patriarch of Farmers' College: Dr. Robert H. Bishop." Cincinnati Historical Society Bulletin 23 (April 1965): 104-118.

HEBREW UNION COLLEGE

2045 Cohon, Samuel Simha. "The History of the Hebrew Union College." In American Jewish Historical Publications, #40. New York: American Jewish Historical Society, 1951.

2046 Philipson, David. "History of the Hebrew Union College, 1875-1925." In Hebrew Union College Annual, Jubilee Volume. Cincinnati: Hebrew Union College, 1925.

HEIDELBERG COLLEGE

2047 Williams, E.I.F. Heidelberg: Democratic Christian College, 1850-1950. Menasha: Banta, 1952.

HIRAM COLLEGE

2048 Treudley, M.B. Prelude to the Future: The First Hundred Years of Hiram College. New York: Association Press, 1950.

KENT STATE UNIVERSITY

2049 Shriver, Phillip R. The Years of Youth; A History of Kent State University. Kent: Kent State University Press, 1960.

2050 Davies, Peter. The Truth About Kent State: A Challenge to the American Conscience. New York: Noonday Press, 1972. [Many photographs of the events of May 1970.]

KENYON COLLEGE

2051 Smythe, George F. Kenyon College: Its First Century. New Haven: Yale University Press, 1924.

2052 Piatt, John J. How the Bishop Built His College in the Woods. Cincinnati: Western Literary Press, 1906.

2053 Smith, Walter George, and Grace, Helen. Fidelis of the Cross: James Kent Stone. New York: G.P. Putnam's, 1926. [Stone was Professor of Latin.]

2054 Walker, Cornelius. The Life and Correspondence of Reverend William Sparrow. Philadelphia: J. Hammond, 1876. [Sparrow was President, 1828-1841.]

LANE SEMINARY

2055 Myers, John. "Anti-Slavery Activities of Five Lane Seminary Boys in 1835-1836." Historical and Philosophical Society of Ohio Bulletin 21 (April 1963): 95-111.

OHIO

McNEELY NORMAL SCHOOL

2056 Eckeberry, R.H. "The McNeely Normal School and Hopedale Normal College." Ohio History 40 (1931): 86-136.

MALONE COLLEGE

2057 Osborne, Byron Lindley. The Malone Story; The Dream of Two Quaker Young People. Newton: United Printing, 1970.

MARIETTA COLLEGE

2058 Beach, Arthur G. A Pioneer College; The Story of Marietta. Chicago: John F. Cuneo Co., 1935.

2059 Dawes, Rufus C. "Marietta College and Early Education in the West." American Scholar 4 (1935): 373-376.

2060 Phillips, Josephine E. "The Infant School That Grew Up." Ohio History 47 (1938): 59-68.

MIAMI UNIVERSITY

2061 Havighurst, Walter. The Miami Years: 1809-1959. New York: G.P. Putnam's, 1958.

2062 Bradford, John E., ed. The James McBride Manuscripts; Selections Relating to the Miami University. Cincinnati: Press of Jennings and Graham, 1909.

2063 Rodabaugh, James H. "A History of Miami University from its Origin to 1885." Doctoral dissertation, Ohio State University, 1936.

2064 Rodabaugh, James H. "Miami University, Calvinism, and the Anti-Slavery Movement." Ohio History 48 (1939): 66-73.

2065 Smith, Ophia D. Fair Oxford. Oxford: Oxford Historical Press, 1947.

2066 Upham, Alfred H. Old Miami. Hamilton: Republican Publishing Co., 1909.

MOUNT UNION COLLEGE

2067 Osborne, Yost. A Select School: The History of Mount Union College and an Account of a Unique Education Experiment, Scio College. Alliance: Mount Union College, 1967.

MUSKINGUM COLLEGE

2068 Bright, John H. "Historical Development of Present Day Problems of Muskingum College." Doctoral dissertation, University of Cincinnati, 1951.

2069 Hoglund, A. William. "Muskingum College Student Rebels in the 'Jazz Age'." Ohio History 76 (Summer 1967): 146-158.

2070 McCracken, Charles W. "Developments in the Coordination of the Muskingum College Personnel Services During the Period from 1939 to 1950." Doctoral dissertation, Ohio University, 1951.

OBERLIN COLLEGE

2071 Barnard, John. From Evangelism to Progressivism at Oberlin College, 1866-1917. Columbus: Ohio State University Press, 1969.

2072 Barrows, Mary E. John Henry Barrows, A Memoir. Chicago: F.H. Revell Co., 1904. [J. Barrows was President, 1898-1902.]

2073 Bigglestone, W.E. "Oberlin College and the Negro Student, 1865-1940." Journal of Negro History 56 (1971): 198-219.

2074 Burroughs, Wilbur. "Oberlin's Part in the Slavery Conflict." Ohio History 20 (1911): 269-334.

2075 Ellsworth, Clayton. "Oberlin and the Anti-Slavery Movement Up to the Civil War." Doctoral dissertation, Cornell University, 1930.

2076 Finney, Charles G. An Autobiography. London: n.p., 1903. [Author was President, 1851-1866.]

2077 Fletcher, Robert. "Bread and Doctrine at Oberlin." Ohio History 49 (1940): 58-67.

2078 Fletcher, Robert. "The First Coeds." American Scholar 7 (1938): 78-93.

2079 Hendrick, Travis. "Charles Grandison Finney: Revivalist and Radical." Doctoral dissertation, Brown University, 1968.

2080 Hogeland, Ronald. "Coeducation of the Sexes at Oberlin College: A Study of Social Ideas in Mid-nineteenth Century America." Journal of Social History 6 (Winter 1972): 160-177.

2081 Keefe, Robert. "Fiscal Education at Oberlin College." Doctoral dissertation, Columbia University Teachers College, 1953.

2082 Keeton, Morris, and Hilberry, Conrad. Struggle and Promise: A Future for Colleges. New York: McGraw-Hill, 1969, pp. 88-112.

2083 Love, Donald M. Henry Churchill King of Oberlin. New Haven: Yale University Press, 1956. [King was President, 1903-1927.]

2084 Mahan, Asa. Autobiography. London: T. Woolmer, 1882. [Author was President, 1835-1850.]

2085 Rosell, Garth. "Charles G. Finney and the Rise of the Benevolence Empire." Doctoral dissertation, University of Minnesota, 1971.

2086 Strong, Sidney. "The Exodus of Students from Lane Seminary to Oberlin in 1834." Papers of the Ohio Church History Society 4 (1891): 1-16.

OHIO MEDICAL COLLEGE

2087 Juettner, Otto. Daniel Drake and His Followers. Cincinnati: Harvey Publishing Co., 1909.

OHIO STATE UNIVERSITY

2088 Pollard, James. History of the Ohio State University. Columbus: Ohio State University Press, 1952.

2089 Block, Robert F. "The Life of Lynn W. St. John and His Contributions to the Ohio State University and the Intercollegiate Athletics." Doctoral dissertation, Ohio State University, 1969.

2090 Good, H.G. The Rise of the College of Education of the Ohio State University. Columbus: College of Education, Ohio State University, 1960.

2091 Hitchcock, Embury A. My Fifty Years in Engineering. Caldwell, Idaho: Caxton Printers, 1939. [Author was Dean of Engineering, 1920-1936.]

2092 Kinnison, William A. Building Sullivant's Pyramid: An Administrative History of the Ohio State University, 1870-1907. Columbus: Ohio State University Press, 1971.

2093 Kovacic, Charles R. "The History of Intercollegiate Athletics at the Ohio State University." Doctoral dissertation, Columbia University Teachers College, 1953.

2094 McPherson, William. "History of the Development of Chemistry at Ohio State University." Journal of Chemical Education 8 (1931): 640-651.

2095 Mendenhall, Thomas C. History of Ohio State University, 1870-1910. 5 vols. Columbus: Ohio State University Press, 1920-1945.

2096 Ohio State University. The First One Hundred Years: A Family Album of the Ohio State University, 1870-1970. Columbus: Ohio State University Press, 1970.

2097 Peattie, Roderick. The Incurable Romantic. New York: Macmillan, 1941. [Author was Professor of Geology, 1925-1955.]

2098 Solomon, Eric. "Free Speech at Ohio State." Atlantic Monthly 115 (November 1965): 119-125.

2099 Weisenberger, Francis. "William Oxley Thompson: Clergyman and Educator." Journal of Presbyterian History 49 (1971): 80-97. [Thompson was President, 1899-1925.]

OHIO UNIVERSITY

2100 Hoover, Thomas N. The History of Ohio University. Athens: Ohio University Press, 1954.

2101 Fontaine, Paul H. Ohio University, the Baker Years. Athens: Ohio University Press, 1961.

2102 Lovenstein, Meno. The Decade of the University: Ohio University and the Alden Years. Athens: Ohio University Press, 1971.

2103 Marzloff, Clement L. Ohio University, the Historic College of the Old Northwest. Athens: Ohio University Press, 1910.

2104 Peters, William E. The Legal History of Ohio University. Cincinnati: Press of the Western Methodist Book Concern, 1910.

2105 Super, Charles W. A Pioneer College and Its Background. Salem, Mass.: Newcomb and Gauss, 1924.

OHIO 219

OHIO WESLEYAN UNIVERSITY

2106 Hubbart, Henry C. Ohio Wesleyan's First Hundred Years. Delaware: Ohio Wesleyan University, 1943.

OTTERBEIN COLLEGE

2107 Hancock, Harold B. History of Otterbein College, 1930-1972. Westerville: Otterbein College, 1971.

2108 Bartlett, Willard W. Education for Humanity: The Story of Otterbein College. Westerville: Otterbein College, 1934.

2109 Garst, Henry. Otterbein University, 1847-1907. Dayton: United Brethren Publishing House, 1907.

TOLEDO, UNIVERSITY OF

2110 Hickerson, Frank R. The Tower Builders: The Centennial Story of the University of Toledo. Toledo: University of Toledo Press, 1972.

WESTERN COLLEGE

2111 Nelson, Narka. The Western College for Women, 1853-1953. Oxford: Western College, 1967.

WILBERFORCE UNIVERSITY

2112 Killiam, Charles. "Wilberforce University: The Reality of Bishop Payne's Dream." Negro History Bulletin 34 (April 1971): 83-86.

2113 McGinnis, Frederick. History and Interpretation of Wilberforce University. Blanchester: Brown Publishing Co., 1941.

2114 Payne, Daniel. Recollections of Seventy Years. Nashville, Tenn.: Tennessee Publishing House of the A.M.E. Sunday School Union, 1888.

2115 Smith, Charles S. The Life of Daniel Alexander Payne. Nashville, Tenn.: Tennessee Publishing House of the A.M.E. Sunday School Union, 1894. [Payne was President, 1863-1876.]

2116 Talbert, Horace. The Sons of Allen. Xenia: Aldine Press, 1906.

WITTENBERG UNIVERSITY

2117 Lentz, Harold H. *A History of Wittenberg College, 1845-1945*. Columbus: F.J. Heer Printing Co., 1947.

2118 Bell, P.G. *A Portraiture of the Life of Samuel Sprecher*. Philadelphia: Lutheran Publication Society, 1907. [Sprecher was President.]

WOOSTER, COLLEGE OF

2119 Notestein, Lucy L. *Wooster of the Middle West*. New Haven: Yale University Press, 1937.

XAVIER UNIVERSITY

2120 O'Conner, Paul L. *Xavier University: 125 Years of Unchanging Vision*. New York: Newcomen Society in North America, 1956.

2121 McNulty, Helen P. "One Hundred and Ten Years of Education at Xavier." Doctoral dissertation, Fordham University, 1958.

Oklahoma

GENERAL REFERENCES

2122　Davison, Oscar W. "The History of Education in Oklahoma, 1907-1947." Doctoral dissertation, University of Oklahoma, 1950.

2123　Garrett, Kathleen. "Dartmouth Alumni in the Indian Territory." Chronicles of Oklahoma 32 (Summer 1953): 123-141. [About Cherokee and Choctow who attended Dartmouth, 1838-1915.]

2124　Gilmor, Francis R. "A Historical Study of the Oklahoma Agricultural Experiment Station." Doctoral dissertation, Oklahoma State University, 1967.

2125　Jackson, Joe C. "Summer Normals in Indian Territory after 1898." Chronicles of Oklahoma 37 (1959): 307-329.

2126　Litton, Gaston. History of Oklahoma. 2 vols. New York: Lewis, 1957. [Vol. 2, ch. 35, pp. 296-338, deals with higher education.]

2127　Watts, Fred G. "A Brief History of Early Higher Education Among the Baptists of Oklahoma, 1800-1915." Chronicles of Oklahoma 17 (1939): 26-34.

INSTITUTIONAL HISTORIES

BETHANY NAZARENE COLLEGE

2128　McConnel, Leona B. A History of the Town and College of Bethany, Oklahoma. Norman: n.p., 1935.

OKLAHOMA BAPTIST UNIVERSITY

2129 Owens, J.N. <u>Annals of Oklahoma Baptist University</u>. Shawnee: Historical Commission of the Baptist General Convention of Oklahoma, 1956.

OKLAHOMA CHRISTIAN COLLEGE

2130 Beeman, W.O. <u>Oklahoma Christian College: Dream to Reality, 1950-1970</u>. Delight, Arkansas: Gospel Light Publishing Co., 1970.

OKLAHOMA CITY UNIVERSITY

2131 Brill, Henry Elmore. <u>The Story of Oklahoma City University and Its Predecessors</u>. Oklahoma City: University Press, 1938.

2132 Smith, Cluster Q. <u>Building for Tomorrow</u>. Nashville, Tenn.: Parthenon Press, 1961.

OKLAHOMA PRESBYTERIAN COLLEGE

2133 Semple, Anne R. "The Origin and Development of the Oklahoma Presbyterian College." Doctoral dissertation, Oklahoma A and M University, 1955.

OKLAHOMA STATE UNIVERSITY

2134 Rulon, Philip R. "The Founding of the Oklahoma Agricultural and Mechanical College, 1890-1908." Doctoral dissertation, Oklahoma State University, 1968.

OKLAHOMA, UNIVERSITY OF

2135 Gittenger, Roy. <u>The University of Oklahoma, 1892-1942</u>. Norman: University of Oklahoma Press, 1942.

2136 Dellasega, Charles J. "The Development and Present Status of Education for Business at the University of Oklahoma." Doctoral dissertation, University of Oklahoma, 1953.

2137 Hubbell, John T. "The Desegregation of the University of Oklahoma, 1946-1950." <u>Journal of Negro History</u> 57 (1972): 370-384.

OKLAHOMA

2138 Long, Charles F. *With Optimism for the Morrow: A History of the University of Oklahoma*. Whole issue of the *Sooner Magazine* 38 (1965). Norman: University of Oklahoma Association, 1965.

OLD HIGH GATE COLLEGE

2139 Kinchen, Oscar A. "Oklahoma's First College: Old High Gate at Norman." *Chronicles of Oklahoma* 14 (1936): 312-323.

PHILLIPS UNIVERSITY

2140 Barron, Jack. *The Early Years of Phillips University, 1906-1912*. Enid: n.p., 1943.

2141 Marshall, Frank H. *Phillips University's First Fifty Years, 1906-1956*. 3 vols. Enid: Phillips University, 1957.

SOUTHWESTERN STATE COLLEGE

2142 Fiegel, Melvin F. "A History of Southwestern State College, 1903-1953." Doctoral dissertation, Oklahoma State University, 1968.

TULSA, UNIVERSITY OF

2143 Pi Alpha Mu. *History of the University of Tulsa, 1935-1958*. Tulsa: University of Tulsa Press, 1958.

Oregon

GENERAL REFERENCES

2144 Bryne, Charles D. Coordinated Control of Higher Education in Oregon. Palo Alto, Calif.: Stanford University Press, 1940.

2145 Gaston, Joseph. The Centennial History of Oregon, 1811-1911. Chicago: Clarke, 1912. [Vol. 1, ch. 21, pp. 573-615, is about higher education.]

2146 Larsell, O. "The Development of Medical Education in the Pacific Northwest." Oregon Historical Quarterly 27 (March 1926): 65-112.

2147 Nickerson, Francis B. "A History of the High School-College Relations Committee in Oregon." Doctoral dissertation, University of Oregon, 1959.

2148 Pemberton, H. Earl. "Early Colleges in Oregon." Oregon Historical Quarterly 33 (1932): 230-242.

2149 Santee, Joseph F. "The History and Status of Public Elementary Teacher Training in Oregon." Doctoral dissertation, University of Washington, 1939.

INSTITUTIONAL HISTORIES

CHRISTIAN COLLEGE

2150 Santee, Joseph F. "Christian College, 1866-1882." Oregon Historical Quarterly 42 (December 1941): 303-310.

2151 Santee, Joseph F. "History of Christian College at Monmouth." Oregon Historical Quarterly 42 (June 1941): 133-150.

OREGON

DALLAS COLLEGE

2152   Coad, Nola E. "A History of Dallas College." Master's thesis, University of Oregon, 1939.

LEWIS AND CLARK COLLEGE

2153   Montague, M.F. Lewis and Clark College, 1867-1967. Portland: Binfords Publishers, 1968.

LINFIELD COLLEGE

2154   Holmes, Kenneth L. Linfield's Hundred Years: A Centennial History of Linfield College. Portland: Binfords Publishers, 1956.

2155   Junasson, Jonas A. Bricks Without Straw: The Story of Linfield College. Caldwell, Id.: Caxton Printers, 1938.

MOUNT ANGEL COLLEGE

2156   Hodes, Ursala. "Mount Angel, Oregon, 1848-1912." Master's thesis, University of Oregon, 1932.

NORTHWESTERN CHRISTIAN COLLEGE

2157   Griffeth, Ross J. Crusaders for Christ. Eugene: Northwestern Christian College, 1971. [Includes accounts of merged colleges: Spokane University, Eugene Divinity School, Eugene Bible University, and Eugene Bible College.]

OREGON COLLEGE OF EDUCATION

2158   Stebbins, Ellis A. The Oregon College of Education Story. Monmouth: Oregon College of Education, 1973.

OREGON STATE UNIVERSITY

2159   Groshong, James W. The Making of a University, 1868-1968. Corvallis: Oregon State University, 1968.

2160 Knox, Warren B. *Eye of the Hurricane*. Corvallis: Oregon State University Press, 1973. [Author was President.]

2161 Santee, Joseph F. "Thomas M. Gatch, 1833-1913." *Oregon Historical Quarterly* 32 (1931): 114-122. [Gatch was President, 1897-1907.]

2162 Smith, John E. *Corvallis College*. Corvallis: n.p., 1953.

2163 Van Loan, Lillian S. "Historical Perspective of Oregon State College." Doctoral dissertation, Oregon State University, 1959.

OREGON, UNIVERSITY OF

2164 Sheldon, Henry D. *History of the University of Oregon*. Portland: Binfords and Mort, 1940.

2165 Colvin, Lloyd W. "A History of the School of Education at the University of Oregon." Doctoral dissertation, University of Oregon, 1964.

2166 Cunliffe, William E. "A History of the Reserve Officers Training Corps at the University of Oregon, 1919-1969." Doctoral dissertation, University of Oregon, 1969.

2167 Metzler, Ken. *Confrontation: The Destruction of a College President*. Los Angeles: Nash, 1973. [About President Charles E. Johnson.]

2168 Santee, Joseph F. "University of Oregon Admissions, 1876-1927." *Oregon Historical Quarterly* 30 (1929): 129-146.

2169 Santee, Joseph F. "The University Preparatory School, 1876-1904." *Oregon Historical Quarterly* 31 (1930): 152-159.

2170 Schafer, Joseph. *Prince Lucien Campbell*. Eugene: The University Press, 1926. [Campbell was President, 1902-1925.]

PACIFIC UNIVERSITY

2171 Long, Watt A. "A History of Pacific University." Doctoral dissertation, University of Oregon, 1932.

PHILOMATH COLLEGE

2172 Springer, C.G. "A History of Philomath College." Doctoral dissertation, University of Oregon, 1929.

OREGON

REED COLLEGE

2173 Clark, Burton R. The Distinctive College: Antioch, Reed, and Swarthmore. Chicago: Aldine, 1970.

SOUTHERN OREGON COLLEGE

2174 McNeal, Roy W. Southern Oregon College Cavalcade. Ashland: Southern Oregon College Foundation, 1972.

2175 Taylor, Arthur S., and Simpson, Hugh G. A History of Southern Oregon College, 1872-1959. Eugene: Oregon State Board of Higher Education, 1959.

2176 Tucker, William P. "The Ashland Normal School, 1869-1930." Oregon Historical Quarterly 32 (1931): 46-60, 165-176.

WILLAMETTE UNIVERSITY

2177 Gatke, Robert M. Chronicles of Willamette, the Pioneer University of the West. 2 vols. Portland: Binfords and Mort, 1943.

2178 Doney, Carl G. Cheerful Yesterdays and Confident Tomorrows. Portland: Binfords and Mort, 1942. [Author was President, 1915-1934.]

Pennsylvania

GENERAL REFERENCES

2179 Sack, Saul. <u>History of Higher Education in Pennsylvania</u>. 2 vols. Harrisburg: Pennsylvania Historical and Museum Commission, 1963.

2180 Amdruss, Harvey A. "The Development of Pennsylvania State Teachers Colleges as Institutions of Higher Education, 1927-1948." Doctoral dissertation, Pennsylvania State University, 1949.

2181 Bonder, James B. "The Growth and Development of the State Teachers Colleges of Pennsylvania." Doctoral dissertation, Temple University, 1953.

2182 Broomall, Lawrence W. "Will Grant Chambers: His Contributions to Teacher Education in the Commonwealth of Pennsylvania, 1909-1937." Doctoral dissertation, Pennsylvania State University, 1966. [Chambers was Dean of the School of Education at Penn State and at the University of Pittsburgh.]

2183 Buell, Harold E. "The Development of Higher Education Under the Methodist Episcopal Church in the Pittsburgh Area." Doctoral dissertation, University of Pittsburgh, 1950.

2184 Cornell, William A. "The Historical Development of the Patterns of Appropriations for Institutions of Higher Education by the General Assembly of the Commonwealth of Pennsylvania to 1960." Doctoral dissertation, State University of New York at Buffalo, 1963.

2185 Fleisher, Robert D. "The Development of the Relationships of Legal Fiscal Control to the Extent of State Aid for Higher Education as Applied to Pennsylvania, 1921-1953." Doctoral dissertation, University of Pittsburgh, 1954.

2186 Fruechtel, Warren B. "Relation of the State to Higher Education in Pennsylvania, 1776-1874." Doctoral dissertation, University of Pittsburgh, 1965.

2187 Graver, Lee A. "A History of the First Pennsylvania State Normal School." Doctoral dissertation, Rutgers University, 1954.

2188 Haskins, Charles H., and Hull, William I. A History of Higher Education in Pennsylvania. Washington, D.C.: U.S. Bureau of Education, 1902.

2189 Irby, Jon E. "Branch Campuses of Pennsylvania's State Colleges and Universities: Past, Present, and Future." Doctoral dissertation, Pennsylvania State University, 1973.

2190 Martin, Asa. "Pennsylvania's Land Grant Under the Morrill Act of 1862." Pennsylvania History 9 (April 1942): 85-117.

2191 Taylor, William S. The Development of the Professional Education of Teachers in Pennsylvania. Philadelphia: J.B. Lippincott, 1924.

2192 Tiger, Dennis D. "Business Degree Programs in Pennsylvania Colleges and Universities." Doctoral dissertation, University of Pittsburgh, 1966.

2193 Walkinshaw, Lewis G. "Higher Education in Mount Pleasant." Western Pennsylvania History Magazine 20 (1937): 275-286.

INSTITUTIONAL HISTORIES

ALBRIGHT COLLEGE

2194 Gingrich, F.W., and Barth, E.H. A History of Albright College, 1856-1956. Reading: F.A. Woerner Co., 1955.

2195 Barth, Eugene. "Schuylkill College: The Early Years." Historical Review of Berks County 35 (1969/70): 9-11, 24-31. [Schuylkill merged with Albright in 1929.]

ALLEGHENY COLLEGE

2196 Smith, Ernest A. Allegheny, A Century of Education, 1815-1916. Meadville: Allegheny College History Co., 1916.

BEAVER COLLEGE

2197 Higgins, Ruth L., and Sturgeon, Mary S. Beaver College, the First Hundred Years, 1853-1953. Jenkintown: n.p., 1954.

BRYN MAWR COLLEGE

2198 Meigs, Cornelia. What Makes a College? A History of Bryn Mawr. New York: Macmillan, 1956.

2199 Bailey, Margaret E. Good Bye, Proud World. New York: Scribner's, 1945.

2200 Finch, Edith. Carey Thomas of Bryn Mawr. New York: Harper, 1947. [Thomas was President, 1884-1922.]

2201 MacIntosh, Margaret T. Joseph Wright Taylor, Founder of Bryn Mawr College. Haverford: C.S. Taylor, 1936.

2202 Stimpson, Catherine R. "Women at Bryn Mawr." Change 6 (April 1974): 24-33.

BUCKNELL UNIVERSITY

2203 Oliphant, J. Orie. The Rise of Bucknell University. New York: Appleton-Century-Crofts, 1965.

2204 Harris, John H. Thirty Years as President of Bucknell. Washington, D.C.: W.F. Roberts Co., 1926. [Author was President, 1899-1919.]

2205 Theiss, Lewis E. Centennial History of Bucknell University, 1846-1946. Lewisburg: Bucknell University, 1946.

CARLISLE INDIAN SCHOOL

2206 Brunhouse, Robert L. "The Founding of the Carlisle Indian School." Pennsylvania History 6 (1939): 72-85.

CARNEGIE MELLON UNIVERSITY

2207 Cleeton, Glen U. The Story of Carnegie Tech. Pittsburgh: Carnegie Press, 1965.

2208 Tarbell, Arthur W. The Story of Carnegie Tech: Being a History of Carnegie Institute of Technology from 1900 to 1935. Pittsburgh: Carnegie Institute of Technology, 1937.

2209 Wall, Joseph F. Andrew Carnegie. New York: Oxford University Press, 1971.

CEDAR CREST COLLEGE

2210 Klein, Harry M. Cedar Crest College, 1867-1947. Allentown: Trustees of Cedar Crest College, 1948.

CHATHAM COLLEGE

2211 Dysart, Laberta. Chatham College: The First Ninety Years. Pittsburgh: Chatham College, 1960.

2212 McBane, Edith L. Pennsylvania College for Women: Historical Sketch, 1869-1944. Pittsburgh: Alumnae Association, 1944.

CLARION STATE COLLEGE

2213 Farmerie, Samuel A. Clarion State College: A Centennial History. Clarion: Alumni Association, 1968.

2214 Farmerie, Samuel A. "A Tom Thumb History of Clarion State College." Western Pennsylvania Historical Magazine 54 (1971): 349-358.

DELAWARE VALLEY COLLEGE OF SCIENCE AND AGRICULTURE

2215 Allman, Herbert D. A Unique Institution: The Story of the National Farm School. Philadelphia: Jewish Publication Society of America, 1935.

DICKINSON COLLEGE

2216 Sellers, Charles. Dickinson College: A History. Middletown, Conn.: Wesleyan University Press, 1973.

2217 Bonar, James A. "Benjamin Rush and the Theory and Practice of Republican Education in Pennsylvania." Doctoral dissertation, Johns Hopkins University, 1965.

2218   Bulwark of Liberty: Early Years at Dickinson. New York: F.H. Revell Co., 1950.

2219   Morgan, James H. Dickinson College, 1783-1933. Carlisle: Dickinson College, 1933.

2220   Neill, William. Autobiography. Philadelphia: Presbyterian Board of Publication, 1861. [Author was President, 1824-1829.]

DREXEL UNIVERSITY

2221   McDonald, Edward D., and Hinton, Edward M. Drexel Institute of Technology, 1891-1941: A Memorial History. Philadelphia: Drexel Institute, 1942.

DUQUESNE UNIVERSITY

2222   Clees, William J. "Duquesne University: Its Years of Struggle, Sacrifice, and Service." Doctoral dissertation, University of Pittsburgh, 1970.

EASTERN BAPTIST COLLEGE

2223   Baird, John A., Jr. The First Twenty Years of Eastern College. St. Davids: Eastern College, 1972.

EDINBORO STATE COLLEGE

2224   Neel, George W. "A History of the State Teachers College at Edinboro." Doctoral dissertation, Rutgers University, 1951.

ELIZABETHTOWN COLLEGE

2225   Schlosser, Ralph W. History of Elizabethtown College, 1899-1970. Elizabethtown: Elizabethtown College, 1971.

FRANKLIN AND MARSHALL COLLEGE

2226   Klein, Frederick S. Since 1787: The Franklin and Marshall College Story. Lancaster: Franklin and Marshall College, 1968.

PENNSYLVANIA

FRANKLIN INSTITUTE

2227 Sinclair, Bruce. "Science with Practice: Practice with Science. A History of the Franklin Institute, 1824-1837." Doctoral dissertation, Case Western Reserve University, 1966.

GETTYSBURG COLLEGE

2228 Hefelbower, Samuel G. The History of Gettysburg College, 1832-1932. Gettysburg: Gettyburg College, 1932.

2229 Breidenbaugh, E.S., ed. The Pennsylvania College Book, 1832-1882. Philadelphia: Lutheran Publication Society, 1882.

HARRISBURG AREA COMMUNITY COLLEGE

2230 Klotz, Richard R. The Rise and Demise of the Hersey Junior College. Manheim: Stiegel Printing Co., 1974. [Hersey founded 1938, merged with HACC 1965.]

HAVERFORD COLLEGE

2231 Jones, Rufus M. Haverford College: A History and an Interpretation. New York: Macmillan, 1933.

2232 Garrett, Philip C. A History of Haverford College for the First Sixty Years of Its Existence, 1830-1890. Porter: n.p., 1892.

2233 Jones, Rufus M. The Trail of Life in College. New York: Macmillan, 1929.

2234 Sharpless, Issac. The Story of a Small College, 1887-1917. Philadelphia: John C. Winston Co., 1918.

INDIANA UNIVERSITY OF PENNSYLVANIA

2235 Merryman, John. "Indiana University of Pennsylvania: From Private Normal School to Public University, 1871-1968." Doctoral dissertation, University of Pittsburgh, 1972.

JEFFERSON MEDICAL COLLEGE

2236 Gould, G.M. The Jefferson Medical College of Philadelphia. New York: Lewis, 1904.

2237 Gross, Samuel D. *Autobiography*. Philadelphia: George Barrie Co., 1887. [Author was Professor of Surgery, 1856-1879.]

2238 Quynn, Dorothy M. "Letters of a Maryland Medical Student in Philadelphia." *Maryland History Magazine* 31 (1936): 181-215.

JOHN AND MARY'S COLLEGE

2239 Edel, William W. *John and Mary's College Over Susquehanna*. New York: Newcomen Society in North America, 1956.

JUNIATA COLLEGE

2240 Ellis, Charles C. *Juniata College: The History of Seventy Years, 1876-1946*. Elgin, Ill.: Brethren Publishing House, 1947.

2241 Emmert, David. *Reminiscences of Juniata College: A Quarter Century, 1876-1901*. Huntington: Privately Printed, 1901.

KING'S COLLEGE

2242 Pi Delta Epsilon. *The Joyous Struggle*. Wilkes-Barre: King's College Press, 1973.

KUTZTOWN STATE COLLEGE

2243 Graver, Lee. "Kutztown State College-1864-1964." *Historical Review of Berks County* 29 (Fall 1964): 105-116.

LAFAYETTE COLLEGE

2244 Skillman, David B. *History of the First Century of Lafayette College*. 2 vols. Easton: Lafayette College, 1932.

2245 Clyde, John C. *Life of James H. Coffin*. Easton: n.p., 1881. [Coffin was Professor of Mathematics, 1846-1873.]

2246 Gendebien, Albert W. "Science the Handmaiden of Religion: The Origins of the Pardee Scientific Course at Lafayette College." *Pennsylvania History* 33 (April 1966): 127-152.

2247 Welch, Richard E. "What's the Image?" In *The New Professors*, edited by Robert O. Bowen, pp. 17-37. New York: Holt, Rinehart, and Winston, 1960.

PENNSYLVANIA

LA SALLE COLLEGE

2248 Donaghy, Thomas J. *Conceived in Crisis: A History of La Salle College, 1863-1965*. Philadelphia: Walther Press, 1966.

LEBANON VALLEY COLLEGE

2249 Wallace, Paul A. *Lebanon Valley College: A Centennial History*. Annville: Lebanon Valley College, 1966.

LEHIGH UNIVERSITY

2250 Bowen, Catherine D. *A History of Lehigh University*. South Bethlehem: Lehigh Alumni Bulletin, 1924.

2251 Billinger, R.D. "Thomas M. Brown, 1842-1904." *Journal of Chemical Education* 7 (December 1930): 2875-2886. [Brown was President, 1895-1904.]

LINCOLN UNIVERSITY

2252 Carr, George B. *John Miller Dickey: His Life and Times*. Philadelphia: Westminster Press, 1929. [Dickey was Founder.]

2253 Carter, James. *A Century of Service: In Memoriam to President Isaac Norton Rendall, D.D., and President John Ballard Rendall, D.D., Ll.D.* Philadelphia: Allen, Lane, and Scott, 1924.

2254 Paynter, John H. *Fifty Years After*. New York: Magent, 1940.

LOCK HAVEN STATE COLLEGE

2255 Wisor, Harold C. "A History of Teacher Education at Lock Haven State College, Lock Haven, Pennsylvania, 1870-1960." Doctoral dissertation, Lock Haven State College, 1966.

LOG COLLEGE

2256 Alexander, A. *Biographical Sketches of the Founder and Principal Alumni of the Log College*. Philadelphia: Printed by J.T. Robinson, 1851.

2257 Ingram, George H. "The Story of the Log College." *Presbyterian Historical Society Journal* 12 (1926): 487-511.

LYCOMING COLLEGE

2258 Williams, Charles S. <u>History of Lycoming College and its Predecessor Institutions: Williamsport Academy, Dickinson Seminary, and Williamsport Dickinson Junior College</u>. Baltimore: King Brothers, 1959.

MILLERSVILLE STATE COLLEGE

2259 Graver, Lee A. <u>A History of the First Pennsylvania State Normal School, Now the State Teachers College at Millersville</u>. Millersville: State Teachers College, 1955.

2260 Bair, Lawrence. "The Life and Educational Labors of James Pyle Wickersham, 1825-1891." Doctoral dissertation, University of Pittsburgh, 1939. [Wickersham was Principal, 1856-1866.]

MORAVIAN COLLEGE

2261 Reichel, William C. <u>A History of the Rise and Progress of the Moravian Seminary for Young Ladies at Bethlehem, Pennsylvania</u>. Philadelphia: J.B. Lippincott, 1881.

2262 Schwarze, William N. <u>History of the Moravian College and Theological Seminary</u>. Bethlehem: Moravian Historical Society, 1910.

MUHLENBURG COLLEGE

2263 Ochsenford, S.E. <u>Muhlenburg College: A History of the College and a Record of Its Men</u>. Allentown: n.p., 1892.

PENNSYLVANIA MILITARY COLLEGE

2264 Moll, Clarence R. "A History of the Pennsylvania Military College, 1821-1954." Doctoral dissertation, New York University, 1955.

PENNSYLVANIA STATE UNIVERSITY

2265 Dunaway, Wayland F. <u>History of the Pennsylvania State University</u>. State College: Pennsylvania State College, 1946.

PENNSYLVANIA 237

2266 Davidson, Edgar O. "The Development of Graduate Professional Education at the Pennsylvania State College with Reference to Other Collegiate Programs." Doctoral dissertation, Pennsylvania State University, 1953.

2267 Venuto, Louis J. The Creation of a College: The College of Mineral Industries at Pennsylvania State University. State College: n.p., 1966.

2268 Venuto, Louis J. "Dean Edward Steidle's Contributions to the Growth of the College of Mineral Industries at the Pennsylvania State University." Doctoral dissertation, Pennsylvania State University, 1965.

PENNSYLVANIA, UNIVERSITY OF

2269 Cheyney, Edward P. History of the University of Pennsylvania, 1740-1940. Philadelphia: University of Pennsylvania Press, 1940.

2270 Bell, Whitfield J. "Science and Humanity in Philadelphia, 1775-1790." Doctoral dissertation, University of Pennsylvania, 1947.

2271 Birch, Thomas R. The First One Hundred Years of the Zelosophic Society. Philadelphia: n.p., 1929.

2272 Bossard, James H. "A History of Sociology at the University of Pennsylvania." General Magazine of History and Chronology 33 (1931): 505-516.

2273 Buxbaum, Melvin. "Benjamin Franklin and William Smith, Their School and Their Dispute." History Magazine of the Protestant Episcopal Church 39 (December 1970): 361-382.

2274 Byrnes, Don R. "The Pre-Revolutionary Career of Provost William Smith." Doctoral dissertation, Tulane University, 1969.

2275 Corner, Betsy C. William Shippen, Jr.: Pioneer in American Medical Education. Philadelphia: American Philosophical Society, 1951.

2276 Corner, George W., ed. The Autobiography of Benjamin Rush. Philadelphia: American Philosophical Society, 1948.

2277 Darnell, Regnar. "The Emergence of Academic Anthropology at the University of Pennsylvania." Journal of the History of Behavioral Sciences 6 (January 1970): 80-92.

2278 Dickson, Samuel. "George Sharswood." American Law Register 15 (October 1907): 401-429. [Sharswood was Dean, 1852-1868, and Trustee, 1872-1883.]

2279 Fox, Bertha S. "Provost Smith and the Quest for Funds." *Pennsylvania History* 2 (1935): 225-238.

2280 Harshberger, John W. *The Life and Work of John Harshberger, Ph.D.: An Autobiography*. Lancaster: Lancaster Press, Inc., 1928. [Author was Professor of Botany, 1893-1929.]

2281 Hindle, Brook. *David Rittenhouse*. Princeton: Princeton University Press, 1964. [Rittenhouse was Professor of Astronomy.]

2282 Johnson, Emory R. *The Life of a University Professor: An Autobiography*. Philadelphia: n.p., 1943. [Author was Dean of the Wharton School of Business.]

2283 Johnson, Emory R. *The Wharton School, 1881-1931*. Philadelphia: University of Pennsylvania, 1931.

2284 Lewis, O.G. "The Life and Work of Edwin T. Darby." *General Magazine and Historical Chronicle* 40 (1938): 27-43. [Darby was Professor of Dentistry, 1878-1919.]

2285 Lippincott, Horace M. "Early Football." *General Magazine and Historical Chronicle* 38 (1935): 17-38.

2286 Lippincott, Horace M. "Early Undergraduate Life." *General Magazine and Historical Chronicle* 43 (1940): 38-52.

2287 Lively, Bruce R. "William Smith, the College and Academy of Philadelphia, and Pennsylvania Politics." *History Magazine of the Protestant Episcopal Church* 38 (1969): 237-258.

2288 Miller, Karl G. "Daughters of Pennsylvania." *General Magazine and Historical Chronicle* 39 (1937): 405-420.

2289 Mumford, Edward W. "A Brief History of the Howard Houston Hall." *General Magazine and Historical Chronicle* 41 (1939): 140-144.

2290 Nearing, Scott. *Education Frontiers: A Book About Simon Nelson and Other Teachers*. New York: T. Seltzer, Inc., 1925.

2291 Nichols, Roy F. *An Historian's Progress*. New York: Knopf, 1968. [Author was Professor of History, 1925-1966.]

2292 Nordell, Philip G. "The Academy Lotteries: A Chapter in the Early History of the University of Pennsylvania." *University of Pennsylvania Library Chronicle* 19 (1963): 51-76.

2293 Pennsylvania, University of. *School of Veterinary Medicine of the University of Pennsylvania, 1884-1934*. Philadelphia: Veterinary Alumni Association, 1935.

2294 Peters, William R. "The Contributions of William Smith, 1727-1803, to the Development of Higher Education in the United States." Doctoral dissertation, University of Michigan, 1968.

2295 Repplier, Agnes. *James William White, M.D.* Boston: Houghton Mifflin, 1919. [White was Professor of Surgery, 1889-1916.]

2296 Smith, Edgar Fahs. *The Life of Robert Hare, An American Chemist, 1781-1858.* Philadelphia: J.B. Lippincott, 1917. [Hare was Professor of Chemistry, 1818-1847.]

2297 Smith, Edgar Fahs. *James Woodhouse, A Pioneer in Chemistry.* Philadelphia: John C. Winston Co., 1918.

2298 Smith, Horace W. *The Life and Correspondence of the Reverend William Smith, D.D., First Provost of the College and Academy of Philadelphia. First President of Washington College, Maryland.* 2 vols. Philadelphia: Ferguson Bros. & Co., 1880.

2299 Stephenson, Mary V. *The First Fifty Years of the Training School for Nurses of the University of Pennsylvania.* Philadelphia: J.B. Lippincott, 1940.

2300 Stille, Charles J. "Reminiscences of a Provost, 1866-1880." *General Magazine and Historical Chronicle* 33 (1931): 311-348.

2301 Thorpe, Frances N. *Benjamin Franklin and the University of Pennsylvania.* Washington, D.C.: U.S. Bureau of Education, 1893.

2302 Thorpe, Francis N. *William Pepper: Provost of the University of Pennsylvania.* Philadelphia and London: J.B. Lippincott, 1904.

2303 Turner, William L. "The College, Academy, and Charitable School of Philadelphia: The Development of a Colonial Institution of Learning." Doctoral dissertation, University of Pennsylvania, 1952.

PHILADELPHIA COLLEGE OF PHARMACY AND SCIENCE

2304 England, Joseph W., ed. *The First Century of the Philadelphia College of Pharmacy, 1821-1921.* Philadelphia: n.p., 1922.

2305 Osol, Arthur, ed. *A Sesquicentennial of Service: A Narrative Overview of the Principal Happenings in the 150 Year History of the Philadelphia College of Pharmacy and Science, 1821-1971.* Philadelphia: Philadelphia College of Pharmacy and Science, 1971.

PHILADELPHIA COLLEGE OF TEXTILES AND SCIENCE

2306 Ward, Arthur. "The Philadelphia College of Textiles and Science." Master's thesis, University of Pennsylvania, 1963.

PHILADELPHIA NORMAL SCHOOL FOR GIRLS

2307   U.S. Commissioner of Education. Sketch of the Philadelphia Normal School for Girls. Washington, D.C.: U.S. Bureau of Education, 1888.

PITTSBURGH, UNIVERSITY OF

2308   Starrett, Agnes L. Through One Hundred and Fifty Years: The University of Pittsburgh. Pittsburgh: University of Pittsburgh Press, 1937.

2309   Greenberg, Daniel S. "Pittsburgh: The Rocky Road to Academic Excellence." Science 159 (February 4, 11, 18, 1966): 549-552, 658-662, 799-801.

2310   Ketchum, Carlton G. "Pitt: The Adolescent Years, 1908-1938." Western Pennsylvania Historical Magazine 54 (April 1971): 181-197.

2311   Schotter, Howard W. The Growth and Development of the Pennsylvania Railroad Company. Philadelphia: Press of Allen, Lane, and Scott, 1927. [Information on William Thaw, University Benefactor.]

SAINT JOSEPH'S COLLEGE

2312   Talbot, Francis X. Jesuit Education in Philadelphia: St. Joseph's College, 1851-1926. Philadelphia: St. Joseph's College, 1927.

SHIPPENSBURG STATE COLLEGE

2313   Hubley, John E. Hilltop Heritage: Shippensburg State's First Hundred Years. Shippensburg: Privately Printed, 1971.

2314   Hubley, John E. "A History of the Cumberland Valley State Normal School and the State Teachers College, Shippensburg, Pennsylvania." Doctoral dissertation, Pennsylvania State University, 1962.

SUSQUEHANNA UNIVERSITY

2315   Clark, William S., and Wilson, Arthur H. The Story of Susquehanna University. Selinsgrove: Susquehanna University Press, 1958.

PENNSYLVANIA

SWARTHMORE COLLEGE

2316 Babbidge, Homer D. "Swarthmore College in the Nineteenth Century: A Quaker Experience in Education." Doctoral dissertation, Yale University, 1953.

2317 Blanshard, Francis. *Frank Aydelotte of Swarthmore.* Middletown, Conn.: Wesleyan University Press, 1970. [Aydelotte was President, 1921-1940.]

2318 Brooks, Robert C. *Reading for Honors at Swarthmore: A Record of the First Five Years, 1922-1927.* New York: Oxford University Press, 1927.

2319 Johnson, Emily C. *Dean Bond of Swarthmore, A Quaker Humanist.* Philadelphia: J.B. Lippincott, 1927. [Elizabeth Bond was Dean, 1890-1906.]

2320 Magill, Edward H. *Sixty-Five Years in the Life of a Teacher, 1841-1906.* Boston: Houghton Mifflin, 1907. [Author was President, 1871-1889.]

2321 Swarthmore College Faculty. *An Adventure in Education: Swarthmore Under Frank Aydelotte.* New York: Macmillan, 1941.

TEMPLE UNIVERSITY

2322 Johnson, Robert L. *The Case for Temple University, One of America's Most Unique Institutions!* New York: Newcomen Society in North America, 1954.

VILLANOVA UNIVERSITY

2323 Breslin, Richard D. *Villanova: Yesterday and Today.* Villanova: Villanova University Press, 1972.

2324 Middleton, Thomas C. *Historical Sketch of the Augustinian Monastery, College, and Mission of the St. Thomas of Villanova, Delaware County, Pa., During the First Half Century of Their Existence, 1842-1892.* Villanova: Villanova College, 1893.

WAGNER FREE INSTITUTE OF SCIENCE

2325 Garmon, Emma E. "History of the Wagner Free Institute of Science and Its Contributions to Education." Doctoral dissertation, Temple University, 1942.

WASHINGTON AND JEFFERSON COLLEGE

2326 Coleman, Hellen T. *Banners in the Wilderness: The Early Years of Washington and Jefferson College*. Pittsburgh: University of Pittsburgh Press, 1956.

2327 Mosely, Edwin M. "Washington and Jefferson Colleges: A Microcosm of the Civil War." *Western Pennsylvania Historical Magazine* 45 (June 1962): 107-113.

WEST CHESTER STATE COLLEGE

2328 Sullivan, Mark. *The Education of an American*. New York: Doubleday, Doran and Co., 1938. [Author was Student at the Normal School, 1888-1892.]

WESTMINSTER COLLEGE

2329 Gamble, Paul. *Westminster's First Century*. New Willmington: Westminster College, 1952.

Puerto Rico

GENERAL REFERENCES

2330 Mendoza, Antonio C. <u>Historia de la Educacion en Puerto Rico, 1512-1826</u>. Washington, D.C.: Catholic University of America Press, 1937.

INSTITUTIONAL HISTORIES

PUERTO RICO, UNIVERSITY OF

2331 Aponte-Hernandez, Rafael. "The University of Puerto Rico: Foundations of the 1942 Reform." Doctoral dissertation, University of Texas, 1965.

2332 Parker, Paul. "Change and Challenge in Caribbean Higher Education: The Development of the University of the West Indies and the University of Puerto Rico." Doctoral dissertation, Florida State University, 1971.

Rhode Island

GENERAL REFERENCES

2333 Tolman, William H. *History of Higher Education in Rhode Island*. Washington, D.C.: U.S. Bureau of Education, 1898.

2334 Conlon, Noel P. "The College Scene in Providence, 1786-1787." *Rhode Island History* 27 (June 1968): 65-70.

INSTITUTIONAL HISTORIES

BROWN UNIVERSITY

2335 Bronson, Walter C. *History of Brown University, 1764-1914*. Providence: n.p., 1914.

2336 Brown, Robert P., Palmer, Henry R., et al., eds. *Memories of Brown*. Providence: Brown Alumni Magazine Co., 1909.

2337 Cape, Emily P. *Lester Frank Ward, A Personal Sketch*. New York: G.P. Putnam's, 1922. [Ward was Professor of Sociology.]

2338 Crane, Theodore R. *Francis Wayland: Political Economist as Educator*. Providence: Brown University Press, 1962. [Wayland was President, 1827-1855.]

2339 Fleming, Donald. *Science and Technology in Providence, 1860-1914*. Providence: Brown University Press, 1952.

2340 Freiberg, Malcolm. "Brown University's First 'College Edifice'." *Old Time New England* 50 (April 1960): 85-93.

2341 Guild, R.A. *Early History of Brown University, Including the Life, Times, and Correspondence of President Manning, 1756-1791*. Providence: Printed by Snow and Farnham, 1897.

2342 Hansen, James E. "Elisha Benjamin Andrews: An Educator's Odyssey." Doctoral dissertation, University of Denver, 1969. [Andrews was Professor of History and President, 1883-1898.]

2343 Hansen, James E. "Students and the Andrews Legend at Brown." Rhode Island History 30 (1970): 75-86.

2344 Hastings, William T. "The War of the Greeks at Brown." New England Quarterly 5 (1932): 533-554.

2345 Hawk, Grace E. Pembroke College in Brown University. Providence: Brown University Press, 1967.

2346 Hazard, Caroline. Memoir of the Rev. J. Lewis Diman. New York: Houghton Mifflin, 1887. [Diman was Professor of History and Political Economy, 1864-1881.]

2347 Mead, A.D. "Episodes and Personalities in the Development of Biology at Brown." Science 91 (1940): 301-305.

2348 Pomfret, Edwin B. "Student Interests at Brown, 1789-1790." New England Quarterly 5 (1932): 135-147.

2349 Randal, Otis E. The Dean's Window: A Portrayal of College Life and Activity as Seen from the Dean's Office. Boston: n.p., 1934.

2350 Robinson, Ezekiel G. Ezekiel Gilman Robinson: An Autobiography. Boston: Silver, Burdett & Co., 1896. [Author was President, 1872-1889.]

2351 Stern, Bernard J., ed. Diary of Lester Frank Ward. New York: G. P. Putnam's, 1935.

2352 van Horn, Harold E. "The Humanist as Educator: The Public Life of Henry Merritt Wriston." Doctoral dissertation, University of Denver, 1968. [Wriston was President, 1937-1955.]

2353 West, Earle Huddleston. "Life and Educational Contributions of Barnas Sears." Doctoral dissertation, George Peabody College for Teachers, 1961. [Sears was President, 1855-1867.]

2354 Wriston, Henry M. Academic Procession: Reflections of a College President. New York: Columbia University Press, 1959.

NAVAL WAR COLLEGE

2355 Gleaves, Albert. Life and Letters of Rear Admiral Stephen B. Luce. New York: G. P. Putnam's, 1925. [Luce was First President.]

2356 Taylor, Charles C. The Life of Admiral Mahan. New York: George H. Doran Co., 1920. [Mahan was President, 1886-1896.]

PROVIDENCE COLLEGE

2357 O'Neill, Daniel J. *Providence College, Early History*. Providence: n.p., 1929.

RHODE ISLAND COLLEGE

2358 Bicknell, Thomas W. *A History of the Rhode Island Normal School*. Providence: n.p., 1911.

2359 Carbone, Hector R. "The History of the Rhode Island Institute of Instruction and the Rhode Island Normal School as Agencies and Institutions of Teacher Education, 1845-1920." Doctoral dissertation, University of Connecticut, 1971.

RHODE ISLAND, UNIVERSITY OF

2360 Eschenbacher, Herman F. *The University of Rhode Island: A History of Land Grant Education in Rhode Island*. New York: Appleton-Century-Crofts, 1967.

South Carolina

GENERAL REFERENCES

2361 Colyer, Merriwether. *History of Higher Education in South Carolina.* Washington, D.C.: U.S. Bureau of Education, 1889.

2362 Elder, Fred. K. "Freedom in South Carolina as Shown by Church-State Relationships in Higher Education." Doctoral dissertation, University of North Carolina, 1940.

2363 Jackson, Luther P. "Educational Effects of the Freedman's Bureau in South Carolina, 1862-1872." *Journal of Negro History* 8 (January 1923): 1-40.

2364 Sanford, Paul L. "The Origins and Development of Higher Education for Negroes in South Carolina to 1920." Doctoral dissertation, University of New Mexico, 1964.

INSTITUTIONAL HISTORIES

CHARLESTON, COLLEGE OF

2365 Easterby, J.H. *A History of the College of Charleston, Founded 1770.* Charleston: Trustees of the College of Charleston, 1935.

2366 Chitty, Arthur B. "College of Charleston: Episcopal Claims Questioned." *Historical Magazine of the Protestant Episcopal Church* 37 (1968): 413-417.

CITADEL, THE

2367 Bond, Oliver J. The Story of the Citadel. Richmond, Va.: Garrett and Massie, 1936.

2368 Thomas, John P. The History of the South Carolina Military Academy. Charleston: Walker, Evans & Cogswell, 1893.

CLAFLIN COLLEGE

2369 Fitchett, E.H. "The Role of Claflin College in Negro Life in South Carolina." Journal of Negro Education 12 (1943): 42-68.

CLEMSON UNIVERSITY

2370 Barton, Don. The Carolina-Clemson Game, 1896-1966. Columbia: State Co., 1967.

COLUMBIA COLLEGE

2371 Ariail, James M. Columbia College, 1912-1968. Columbia: n.p., 1969.

2372 Durnin, Richard G. "William Harris: Schoolmaster, Churchman, and Columbia College President." Historical Magazine of the Protestant Episcopal Church 35 (December 1966): 287-295. [Harris was President, 1811-1829.]

2373 Griffin, Anne F. Columbia College Centennial Celebration, 1854-1954. Columbia: Farrell Press, 1956.

COLUMBIA SEMINARY

2374 Blackburn, George A. The Life and Work of John L. Girardeau. Columbia: State Co., 1916. [Girardeau was Professor of Theology, 1875-1895.]

2375 Eaton, Clement. "Professor James Woodrow and the Freedom of Teaching in the South." Journal of Southern History 28 (February 1962): 3-17. [Woodrow was Professor, 1861-1886.]

CONVERSE COLLEGE

2376 Gee, Mary W. Yes Ma'm Miss Gee. Charlotte, N.C.: Heritage House, 1957.

SOUTH CAROLINA

FURMAN UNIVERSITY

2377 Daniel, R.N. Furman University: A History. Greenville: The University, 1951.

2378 Cook, Harvey T. Life and Work of James C. Furman. Greenville: The University, 1926. [Furman was President, 1852-1879.]

2379 Kinlaw, Howard M. "Richard Furman as a Leader in Baptist Higher Education." Doctoral dissertation, George Peabody University, 1960.

2380 McGlothlin, William J. Baptist Beginnings in Education: A History of Furman University. Nashville, Tenn.: Sunday School Board of the Southern Baptist Convention, 1926.

LIMESTONE COLLEGE

2381 McMillan, Montague. Limestone College: A History, 1845-1970. Gaffney: Limestone College, 1970.

2382 Taylor, Walter C. History of Limestone College, Gaffney, S.C. Gaffney: Limestone College, 1937.

PRESBYTERIAN COLLEGE

2383 Jacobs, Thornwell. The Life of William Plumer Jacobs. Chicago: F.H. Revell Co., 1918. [Jacobs was Founder.]

SOUTH CAROLINA, UNIVERSITY OF

2384 Hollis, Daniel W. The University of South Carolina. 2 vols. Columbia: University of South Carolina Press, 1951 & 1956.

2385 Green, Edwin L. A History of the University of South Carolina. Columbia: State Co., 1916.

2386 Hungerpiller, J.G. The Life of Jonathon Maxcy, 1768-1820. Columbia: n.p., 1919. [Maxcy was President, 1804-1820.]

2387 LaBord, M. History of the South Carolina College. Charleston: n.p., 1874.

2388 Malone, Dumas. The Public Life of Thomas Cooper, 1783-1839. New Haven: Yale University Press, 1926. [Cooper was President, 1820-1834.]

2389 Palmer, Benjamin M. The Life and Letters of James Henly Thornwell. Richmond, Va.: Whittet and Shepperson, 1875. [Thornwell was President, 1837-1855.]

WOFFORD COLLEGE

2390 Wallace, David D. History of Wofford College, 1854-1949. Nashville, Tenn.: Vanderbilt University Press, 1951.

2391 Battle, Kemp Plummer. "Albert Micajah Shipp." In History of the University of North Carolina. 2 vols. Raleigh: Edwards & Broughton Printing Co., 1907 and 1912. [Shipp was President, 1859-1875.]

2392 Shyder, Henry N. An Educational Odyssey. New York: n.p., 1947. [Author was President, 1902-1942.]

South Dakota

GENERAL REFERENCES

2393 Martorana, S.V. *Higher Education in South Dakota*. 2 vols. Washington, D.C.: U.S. Office of Education, 1960.

2394 Kingsbury, George W. *History of South Dakota*. Chicago: S.J. Clarke, 1915. [Vol. 3, chs. 21 & 22, pp. 797-921, about higher education.]

INSTITUTIONAL HISTORIES

AUGUSTANA COLLEGE

2395 Erpestad, Emil. *A History of Augustana College*. Sioux Falls: Augustana Press, 1971.

DAKOTA STATE COLLEGE

2396 Lowry, V.A. *Forty Years at General Beadle*. Forthcoming.

DAKOTA WESLEYAN UNIVERSITY

2397 Coursey, Oscar W. *A History of Dakota Wesleyan University for Fifty Years, 1885-1935*. Mitchell: Dakota Wesleyan University, 1935.

SIOUX FALLS COLLEGE

2398 Jeschke, Reuben P. Dream of the Pioneers: A Brief and Informal History of Sioux Falls College. Sioux Falls: Sioux Falls College, 1968.

2399 Jeschke, Reuben P. A Decade of Growth. Sioux Falls: Sioux Falls College, 1968.

SOUTH DAKOTA SCHOOL OF MINES AND TECHNOLOGY

2400 O'Harra, C.C. "A Brief History of the South Dakota State School of Mines." The Black Hills Engineer 11 (January 1923): 13-71.

2401 Simmons, A.J. "Origin and Some Early History of the School of Mines." Pahasapa Quarterly 3 (December 1913): 5-12.

SOUTH DAKOTA STATE UNIVERSITY

2402 Seurey, Charles L. A History of South Dakota State College, 1884-1959. Brookings: South Dakota State College, 1959.

2403 Beadle, William H. Autobiography. Pierre: State Historical Society of South Dakota, 1938. [Author was President, 1889-1905.]

2404 Powers, William H. A History of South Dakota State College. Brookings: South Dakota State College, 1931.

SOUTH DAKOTA, UNIVERSITY OF

2405 Akeley, Lewis E. This Is What We Had in Mind: Early Memories of the University of South Dakota. Vermillion: University of South Dakota, 1959.

2406 Christol, Carl. The Early History of the University of South Dakota. Vermillion: n.p., 1964.

2407 Churchill, Edward P. Building Biology and the University of South Dakota. Vermillion: University of South Dakota, 1959.

2408 Cook, William A. "Early History of the University of South Dakota: The First Quarter Century, 1862-1887." South Dakota Historical Collections 13 (1926): 181-249.

SOUTH DAKOTA

2409 Cummins, Cedrick C. *As It Was in the Beginning: The University of South Dakota*. Vermillion: University of South Dakota, College of Arts and Sciences, 1966.

2410 Dow, John G. *Early History of the University, 1862-1889*. Vermillion: South Dakota Alumni Association, 1907.

2411 Haase, Richard T. *The History of Intercollegiate Football, Basketball, Track, and Baseball at the State University of South Dakota*. Vermillion: University of South Dakota, 1965.

2412 Hoy, Carl B. *According to Hoy: Memoirs of an Athletic Director*. Vermillion: University of South Dakota, 1960.

2413 Stockton, Frank T. *This Is What We Tried To Do In Cayote Land, 1917-1924*. Vermillion: University of South Dakota, 1960.

YANKTON COLLEGE

2414 Durand, George H. *Joseph Ward of Dakota*. Boston: Pilgrim Press, 1913. [Ward was Founder.]

2415 McMurtry, William J. *Yankton College: An Historical Sketch*. Yankton: n.p., 1907.

2416 Stewart, Edgar I. *Yankton College: The Second Twenty-Five Years*. Yankton: n.p., 1932.

Tennessee

GENERAL REFERENCES

2417 Merriam, Lucious S. *Higher Education in Tennessee*. Washington, D.C.: U.S. Bureau of Education, 1893.

2418 Clough, Richard B. "Teacher Institutes in Tennessee, 1870-1900." *Tennessee Historical Quarterly* 31 (1972): 61-73.

2419 Horton, Allison N. "Origin and Development of the State College Movement in Tennessee." Doctoral dissertation, George Peabody College for Teachers, 1954.

2420 Humphreys, Cecil C. "State Financial Support to Higher Education in Tennessee from 1930 to 1952." Doctoral dissertation, New York University, 1958.

2421 Ward, Richard H. "The Development of Baptist Higher Education in Tennessee." Doctoral dissertation, George Peabody College for Teachers, 1954.

2422 Witherington, Henry C. "History of State Higher Education in Tennessee." Doctoral dissertation, University of Chicago, 1931.

INSTITUTIONAL HISTORIES

CARSON-NEWMAN COLLEGE

2423 Carr, Isaac N. *History of Carson-Newman College, 1851-1959*. Jefferson City: n.p., 1959.

TENNESSEE

CUMBERLAND FEMALE COLLEGE

2424 Nunley, Joe E. "A History of Cumberland Female College, McMinnville, Tennessee." Doctoral dissertation, University of Tennessee, 1966.

CUMBERLAND UNIVERSITY

2425 Bone, Winstead P. A History of Cumberland University, 1842-1935. Lebanon: Privately Printed, 1935.

2426 Stephens, John V. The Cumberland University Theological School-Lebanon Theological Seminary. Cincinnati: n.p., 1939.

DAVID LIPSCOMB COLLEGE

2427 Neil, Robert G. "The History of David Lipscomb College." Master's thesis, George Peabody College for Teachers, 1938.

2428 Pittman, Samuel P. David Lipscomb College As I Have Known It. Nashville: McQuiddy, 1941.

2429 Young, Matt N. A History of Colleges Established and Controlled by Members of the Churches of Christ. Kansas City, Mo.: Old Paths Book Club, 1949.

FISK UNIVERSITY

2430 Jones, Thomas E. Progress at Fisk University: A Summary of Recent Years. Nashville: Fisk University, 1930.

2431 Richardson, Joe M. "Fisk University, the First Critical Years." Tennessee Historical Quarterly 29 (1970): 24-41.

GEORGE PEABODY COLLEGE FOR TEACHERS

2432 Beasley, Wallis. The Life and Educational Contributions of James Davis Porter. Nashville: Bureau of Publications, George Peabody College for Teachers, 1950. [Porter was President, 1902-1909.]

2433 Crabb, Alfred L. The Genealogy of George Peabody College for Teachers Covering a Period of One Hundred and Fifty Years. Nashville: n.p., 1935.

2434 Cullum, Edward N. "George Peabody College for Teachers, 1914-1937." Doctoral dissertation, George Peabody College for Teachers, 1963.

2435 Dillingham, George A. "Peabody Normal College in Southern Education, 1875-1909." Doctoral dissertation, George Peabody College for Teachers, 1970.

2436 Garrett, W.R. "The Genesis of Peabody College for Teachers." American History Magazine 8 (January 1903): 14-25.

2437 Hedges, William D. "Doctoral Candidates at George Peabody College for Teachers from 1919 to 1950." Doctoral dissertation, George Peabody College for Teachers, 1958.

2438 Kegley, Tracy M. "The Peabody Scholarship, 1877-1899." Doctoral dissertation, George Peabody College for Teachers, 1949.

LAMBUTH COLLEGE

2439 Clement, Sarah V. A College Grows: Lambuth. Jackson: McCowat-Mercer Press, 1972.

LANE COLLEGE

2440 Perry, Essie M. "Lane College Through Seventy-Five Years of Service." Jackson: Unpublished Manuscript, 1957.

LEE COLLEGE

2441 McBrayer, Richard T. Lee College, Pioneer of Pentecostal Education, 1918-1968. Cleveland: Pathway Press, 1968.

2442 Ray, Mauldon A. "A Study of the History of Lee College, Cleveland, Tennessee." Doctoral dissertation, University of Houston, 1963.

MARTHA WASHINGTON COLLEGE

2443 Curtis, Claude D. Three Quarters of a Century at Martha Washington College. Bristol: King Printing Co., 1928.

MEHARRY MEDICAL SCHOOL

2444 Mullowney, John J. America Gives a Chance. Tampa, Fla.: Tribune Press, 1940.

TENNESSEE 257

MIDDLE TENNESSEE STATE UNIVERSITY

2445 Pittard, Homer. *First Fifty Years: Middle Tennessee State College, 1911-1961*. Murfreesboro: Courier Printing Co., 1961.

NASHVILLE, UNIVERSITY OF

2446 Alstetter, Mabel, and Watson, Gladys. "The Western Military Institute, 1847-1861." *Filson Club Historical Quarterly* 10 (1936): 100-115.

2447 Haunton, Richard H. "Education and Democracy: The Views of Philip Lindsay." *Tennessee Historical Quarterly* 21 (June 1962): 131-139. [Lindsay was President, 1824-1850.]

2448 Howell, Isabel. "Montgomery Bell Academy: A Chapter in the History of the University of Nashville." Master's thesis, George Peabody College for Teachers, 1940.

2449 Kelton, Allen. "The University of Nashville, 1850-1875." Doctoral dissertation, George Peabody College for Teachers, 1969.

2450 Morgan, Kenimer H. "The University of Nashville, 1825-1850." Doctoral dissertation, George Peabody College for Teachers, 1960.

2451 Woolverton, John F. "Philip Lindsay and the Cause of Education in the Old Southwest." *Tennessee Historical Quarterly* 19 (March 1960): 3-22.

SOUTH, UNIVERSITY OF THE

2452 Baker, Lily G., ed. *Sewanee*. Sewanee: The University Press, 1932.

2453 Chitty, Arthur B. *Reconstruction at Sewanee: The Founding of the University of the South and Its First Administration, 1857-1872*. Sewanee: The University Press, 1954.

2454 DuBose, William. *Turning Points in My Life*. New York: Longmans, Green & Co., 1912. [Author was Professor and Chaplain, 1871-1918.]

2455 Dudney, R.G., ed. *Centennial Report of the Registrar of the University of the South*. Sewanee: The University Press, 1959.

2456 Fairbanks, George R. History of the University of the South at Sewanee, Tennessee, from Its Founding by the Southern Bishops, Clergy and Laity of the Episcopal Church in 1857 to the Year 1905. Jacksonville: H. and W.B. Drew Co., 1905.

2457 Gailor, Thomas F. Some Memories. Kingsport: Southern Publishers, 1937. [Author was President, 1908-1935.]

2458 Guerry, M. "Makers of Sewanee." Sewanee Review 41 (1933): 80-90, 237-243, 365-373, 483-494.

SOUTHWESTERN AT MEMPHIS

2459 Cooper, Waller R. Southwestern at Memphis, 1848-1948. Richmond, Va.: John Knox Press, 1949.

TENNESSEE TECHNOLOGICAL UNIVERSITY

2460 Smith, Austin W. The Story of Tennessee Tech. Nashville: McQuiddy Printing Co., 1957.

TENNESSEE, UNIVERSITY OF

2461 Montgomery, James R. The Volunteer State Forges Its University: The University of Tennessee, 1887-1919. Knoxville: University of Tennessee Press, 1966.

2462 Montgomery, James R. Threshold of a New Day: The University of Tennessee, 1919-1946. Knoxville: University of Tennessee Press, 1971.

2463 Folmsbee, Stanley J. Blount College and East Tennessee College, 1794-1840: The First Predecessors of the University of Tennessee. Knoxville: University of Tennessee Press, 1946.

2464 Folmsbee, Stanley J. East Tennessee University, 1840-1879: Predecessor of the University of Tennessee. Knoxville: University of Tennessee Press, 1959.

2465 Folmsbee, Stanley J. Tennessee Establishes a State University: First Years of the University of Tennessee, 1879-1887. Knoxville: University of Tennessee Press, 1961.

2466 Inman, Elmer B. "A History of the Development of the University of Tennessee, Martin Branch." Doctoral dissertation, University of Tennessee, 1960.

TENNESSEE

2467 O'Steen, Margaret, and O'Steen, Neal. Scholars and Scamps: The University of Tennessee in Pictures, 1794-1970. Knoxville: University of Tennessee Press, 1971.

TENNESSEE WESLEYAN COLLEGE

2468 Martin, LeRoy A. A History of Tennessee Wesleyan College, 1857-1957. Privately Printed, 1957.

TUSCULUM COLLEGE

2469 Ragan, Allen E. A History of Tusculum College, 1794-1944. Greenville: The Tusculum Sesquicentennial Committee, 1945.

VANDERBILT UNIVERSITY

2470 McGaw, Robert A. A Brief History of Vanderbilt University, 1873-1973. Nashville: Vanderbilt University Press, 1973.

2471 Croffut, William A. The Vanderbilts and the Story of Their Fortunes. Chicago: Clarke, 1886.

2472 Gross, John O. "The Bishops Versus Vanderbilt University." Tennessee Historical Quarterly 22 (March 1963): 53-65.

2473 Mims, Edwin. Chancellor Kirkland of Vanderbilt. Nashville: Vanderbilt University Press, 1940. [Kirkland was President, 1893-1937.]

2474 Mims, Edwin. A History of Vanderbilt University. Nashville: Vanderbilt University Press, 1946.

2475 Wadsworth, John. "A Biography of Cornelius Vanderbilt." Doctoral dissertation, Brown University, 1967.

WASHINGTON COLLEGE

2476 Carr, Howard E. Washington College: A Study of an Attempt to Provide Higher Education in Eastern Tennessee. Knoxville: S.B. Newman and Co., 1935.

2477 Foster, Isabelle. "Washington College and the Washington College Academy." Tennessee Historical Quarterly 30 (1971): 241-258.

Texas

GENERAL REFERENCES

2478 Lane, John J. *History of Education in Texas*. Washington, D.C.: U.S. Government Printing Office, 1903.

2479 Moseley, Carolyn. "Higher Education in Texas." Master's thesis, University of Texas, 1967.

2480 Parker, Edith H. "History of Land Grants for Education in Texas." Doctoral dissertation, University of Texas, 1952.

2481 Phelps, Ralph A., Jr. "The Struggle for Public Higher Education for Negroes in Texas." Doctoral dissertation, Southwestern Baptist University, 1949.

2482 Waddell, Fred. "An Historical Review of the Coordination of Higher Education in Texas." Doctoral dissertation, North Texas State University, 1972.

2483 Younker, Donna L. "Teacher Education in Texas, 1879-1919." Doctoral dissertation, University of Texas, 1963.

INSTITUTIONAL HISTORIES

ABILENE CHRISTIAN COLLEGE

2484 Morris, Don H., and Leach, Max. *Like Stars Shining Brightly: The Story of Abilene Christian College*. Abilene: Abilene Christian College Press, 1953.

ANGELO STATE UNIVERSITY

2485   Rawls, Ruth E. "Angelo State College, 1926-1965." Master's thesis, Southwest Texas State College, 1969.

AUSTIN COLLEGE

2486   Landolt, George L. Search for the Summit: Austin College Through Twelve Decades, 1849-1970. Sherman: Austin College Alumni Association, 1970.

2487   Ferguson, Dan. "The Antecedents of Austin College." Southwestern History Quarterly 53 (1950): 239-254.

BAYLOR UNIVERSITY

2488   Bragg, Jefferson D. "Baylor University, 1851-1861." Southwestern History Quarterly 49 (1945): 51-65.

2489   Bragg, Jefferson D. "Waco University." Southwestern History Quarterly 51 (1948): 213-224.

2490   Burleson, Georgia, and Haynes, Harry. The Life and Writings of Rufus C. Burleson. Waco: n.p., 1901. [Burleson was President, 1851-1861, 1886-1897.]

BETHANY NAZARENE COLLEGE

2491   Cantrell, Roy H. The History of Bethany Nazarene College. Fort Worth: Southwestern Baptist Theological Seminary, 1955.

BLINN MEMORIAL COLLEGE

2492   Schmidt, Charles F. History of Blinn Memorial College, 1883-1934. San Antonio: Lodovic Printing Co., 1935.

CARLTON COLLEGE

2493   Hay, Kenneth M. "The Life and Influence of Charles Carlton, 1821-1902." Bachelor of Divinity dissertation, Texas Christian University, 1939.

EAST TEXAS STATE UNIVERSITY

2494   Bledsoe, James M. A History of Mayo and His College. Commerce: n.p., 1946.

2495 Grinnan, James T. The History of East Texas State Teachers College During World War Two. Commerce: n.p., 1947.

2496 Hawkins, Matha L. "History of East Texas State Teachers College." Doctoral dissertation, University of Texas, 1936.

2497 McDowell, Henderson. "A Study of the Development of East Texas State Teachers College as Reflected by the Reports of the College Registrar and the State Auditor for the Years 1935-1941." Master's thesis, East Texas State Teachers College, 1942.

HARDIN-SIMMONS UNIVERSITY

2498 Richardson, Rupert N. Famous Are Thy Halls: Hardin-Simmons University As I Have Known It. Abilene: Abilene Printing Co., 1964.

2499 Crane, Royston C. "The Beginnings of Hardin-Simmons University." West Texas Historical Association Yearbook 16 (1940): 61-74.

HOWARD PAYNE COLLEGE

2500 Hinton, William H. "A History of Howard Payne College with Emphasis on the Life and Administration of Thomas H. Taylor." Doctoral dissertation, University of Texas, 1957.

HUSTON-TILLOTSON COLLEGE

2501 Shackles, Chrystine I. Reminiscences: The Story of Tillotson College and Samuel Huston College, 1928-1968. Austin: Best Publishing Co., 1973.

2502 Jones, William H. Tillotson College from 1930 to 1940, a Decade of Progress. Austin: n.p., 1940.

INCARNATE WORD COLLEGE

2503 Eagan, M. Clement. "A History of Incarnate Word College." Unpublished Manuscript. 1944.

KIDD-KEY COLLEGE

2504 Domatte, Rutho. "A History of Kidd-Key College." Southwestern History Quarterly 58 (1959): 263-278.

TEXAS

LAMAR UNIVERSITY

2505 Asbury, Ray. The South Park Story, 1891-1971, and the Founding of Lamar University, 1923-1941. Beaumont: South Park Historical Committee, 1972.

2506 Hutchison, Earl E. "The History of Lamar Junior College." Master's thesis, Texas Arts and Industries University, 1938.

2507 McLaughlin, Marvin L. "Reflections on the Philosophy and Practices of Lamar State College of Technology as Shown Through Its History." Doctoral dissertation, University of Houston, 1955.

LON MORRIS COLLEGE

2508 Jones, Glendell A. "History of Lon Morris College." Doctoral dissertation, North Texas State University, 1973.

MARY HARDIN-BAYLOR COLLEGE

2509 Walker, Thomas T. "Mary Hardin-Baylor College, 1845-1937." Doctoral dissertation, George Peabody College for Teachers, 1963.

MCKENZIE COLLEGE

2510 Osburn, John D. "McKenzie College." Southwestern History Quarterly 63 (1960): 533-553.

NORTH TEXAS STATE UNIVERSITY

2511 Rogers, James L. The Story of North Texas, from Texas Normal College, 1890, to North Texas State University, 1965. Denton: North Texas State University, 1965.

2512 Hall, Morris E. "The Development of North Texas State College, 1890-1949." Doctoral dissertation, New York University, 1954.

RICE UNIVERSITY

2513 Lovett, Edgar O. "The Meaning of the New Institution." Rice Institute Pamphlets 1 (1915): 45-132.

SOUTHERN METHODIST UNIVERSITY

2514 Thomas, Mary M. *Southern Methodist University: The First Twenty-Five Years, 1915-1940*. Dallas: Southern Methodist University Press, 1973.

SOUTHWEST TEXAS STATE UNIVERSITY

2515 Nichols, Tom W. *Rugged Summit*. San Marcos: Southwest Texas State University Press, 1970.

2516 Ball, Tommy R. "The Administration of John Garland Flowers, Third President of Southwest Texas State College." Doctoral dissertation, Southwest Texas State University, 1967. [Flowers was President, 1942-1964.]

2517 Henderson, Ruby. *Southwest Texas State Teachers College: A Documentary History*. Austin: Privately Printed, 1939.

2518 Smith, John Marvin. "The History and Growth of the Southwest Texas State Teachers College." Doctoral dissertation, University of Texas, 1930.

SOUTHWESTERN JUNIOR COLLEGE OF THE ASSEMBLIES OF GOD

2519 Farmer, Blake L. "Southwestern Assemblies of God College's Founding, Growth, and Development, 1927-1965." Doctoral dissertation, Baylor University, 1965.

SOUTHWESTERN UNIVERSITY

2520 Cody, Claude C. *The Life and Labors of Francis Asbury Mood, Founder of Southwestern University*. Chicago: F.H. Revell Co., 1886.

2521 Jones, Ralph W. "A History of Southwestern University, 1873-1949." Doctoral dissertation, University of Texas, 1960.

TARLETON STATE COLLEGE

2522 Davis, J. Thomas. *John Tarleton, Founder of Tarleton College*. Stephenville: Tarleton College, 1933.

TEMPLE JUNIOR COLLEGE

2523 Farrell, Harry C., Jr. "Temple Junior College: Its Founding, Growth, and Development, 1926-1964." Doctoral dissertation, Colorado State University, 1964.

TEXAS AGRICULTURAL AND MECHANICAL UNIVERSITY

2524 Perry, George S. *The Story of Texas A & M*. New York: McGraw-Hill, 1951.

2525 Cofer, David B. *Early History of Texas A & M College Through Letters and Papers*. College Station: Association of Former Students, 1952.

2526 Cofer, David B. *The First Five Administrators of Texas A & M College, 1876-1890*. College Station: Association of Former Students, 1952.

2527 Cofer, David B. *The Second Five Administrators of Texas A & M College, 1890-1905*. College Station: Association of Former Students, 1954.

2528 Ousley, Clarence. *The History of the Agricultural and Mechanical College of Texas*. College Station: A & M College of Texas, 1935.

2529 Payne, John. "David F. Houston's Presidency of Texas A & M." *Southwestern History Quarterly* 58 (1954): 22-35. [Houston was President, 1902-1905.]

TEXAS CHRISTIAN UNIVERSITY

2530 Hall, Colby D. *History of Texas Christian University, A College of the Cattle Frontier*. Fort Worth: Texas Christian University Press, 1947.

TEXAS TECHNOLOGICAL UNIVERSITY

2531 Andrews, Ruth H. *The First Thirty Years: A History of Texas Technological College, 1925-1955*. Lubbock: Texas Tech Press, 1956.

2532 Rutland, Robert. "The Beginnings of Texas Technological College." *Southwestern History Quarterly* 55 (1951): 231-239.

2533 Wade, Homer D. *The Establishment of Texas Technological College, 1916-1923*. Lubbock: Texas Technological College, 1956.

TEXAS, UNIVERSITY OF

2534 Long, Walter E. *For All Time to Come*. Austin: n.p., 1964.

2535 Battle, W.J. "A Concise History of the University of Texas, 1883-1950." *Southwestern History Quarterly* 54 (1951): 391-411.

2536 Benedict, Harry Y. *A Source Book Relating to the History of the University of Texas*. Austin: University of Texas Press, 1917.

2537 Berry, Margaret C. "Student Life and Customs, 1883-1938, at the University of Texas." Doctoral dissertation, Columbia University, 1965.

2538 Brewer, Thomas B. "The Old Department of History at the University of Texas, 1910-1951." *Southwestern History Quarterly* 70 (1966): 229-246.

2539 Cox, Alice C. "The Rainey Affair: A History of the Academic Freedom Controversy at the University of Texas, 1938-1946." Doctoral dissertation, University of Denver, 1970.

2540 Dugger, Ronnie. "The University of Texas: The Politics of Knowledge." *Change* 6 (February 1974): 30-39.

2541 Faculty and Staff. *The University of Texas Medical Branch at Galveston: A Seventy-Five Year History*. Austin: University of Texas Press, 1967.

2542 Garrison, George Pierce. "The First Twenty-Five Years of the University of Texas." *Southwestern History Quarterly* 60 (1956): 106-117.

2543 Hayes, Arthur R. "The Influence and Impact of Edwin Dubois Shurter on Teacher Education in Texas." Doctoral dissertation, University of Texas, 1952. [Shurter was Professor of Speech, 1899-1923.]

2544 Henderson, Joseph L. *Educational Memoirs*. Austin: Press of Von Boeckmann-Jones Co., 1940. [Author was Professor of Education, 1906-1940.]

2545 Hill, George A., Jr. "The Spirit of Santa Rica." *Southwestern History Quarterly* 48 (1944): 78-84. [About oil properties.]

2546 Jones, Ralph W. "The First Roots of the University of Texas Medical Branch at Galveston." *Southwestern History Quarterly* 65 (1962): 465-474.

TEXAS

2547 Lane, John J. A History of the University of Texas. Austin: n.p., 1891.

2548 Rainey, Homer P. The Tower and the Dome: A Free University Versus Political Control. Boulder, Colo.: Pruett, 1971. [Author was President, 1939-1944.]

2549 Roberts, O.M. "A History of the Establishment of the University of Texas." Southwestern History Quarterly 1 (1898): 233-265.

TEXAS WESLEYAN COLLEGE

2550 Corely, Carol W. A Brief Survey of the Development of Texas Wesleyan College and Judge George W. Armstrong. Denton: Texas Woman's University Library, 1970.

2551 Cox, John E. A Brief History of Texas Wesleyan College. Greeley, Colo.: Colorado State College Press, 1953.

TEXAS WOMAN'S UNIVERSITY

2552 Sone, Law. The History of Texas Woman's College, Fort Worth, Texas. Austin: Texas Woman's College, 1937.

2553 Texas Woman's University. A Summary History of the University, 1901-1961. Denton: Texas Woman's University, 1961.

TRINITY UNIVERSITY

2554 Everett, Donald E. Trinity University: A Record of One Hundred Years. San Antonio: Trinity University Press, 1963.

2555 Hornbeak, Samuel L. Trinity University, Project of Pioneers. San Antonio: Trinity University Development Council, 1951. [Author was President, 1908-1920.]

Utah

GENERAL REFERENCES

2556 Barker, Lincoln. "History of the State Junior Colleges of Utah." Doctoral dissertation, New York University, 1945.

2557 Benton, John E. "The Educational Program and Educational Policies Under Governor Simon Bamberger." Doctoral dissertation, University of Utah, 1962.

2558 Divett, Robert T. "Utah's First Medical College." Utah Historical Quarterly 31 (Winter 1963): 51-59.

2559 Sutton, Warren, ed. Utah: A Centennial History. New York: Lewis, 1949. [Vol. 3, ch. 24, pp. 1021-1056, about higher education.]

2560 Warrum, Noble, ed. Utah Since Statehood. Chicago: S.J. Clarke, 1919. [Ch. 27 & 28, pp. 359-410, about higher education.]

INSTITUTIONAL HISTORIES

BRIGHAM YOUNG UNIVERSITY

2561 Jensen, J. Marinus, ed. History of Brigham Young University. Unpublished. 1942.

2562 Smith, Keith. "Brigham Young University: The Early Years, 1875-1921." Doctoral dissertation, Brigham Young University, 1972.

UTAH STATE UNIVERSITY

2563 Ricks, Joel Edward. The Utah State Agricultural College: A History of Fifty Years, 1888-1938. Salt Lake City: Deseret News Press, 1938.

UTAH, UNIVERSITY OF

2564 Chamberlin, Ralph V. *The University of Utah: A History of Its First One Hundred Years, 1850-1950.* Salt Lake City: University of Utah Press, 1960.

2565 Culmsee, Carlton F. "Democracy Enrolls in College." *Utah Historical Quarterly* 30 (Summer 1962): 199-213.

2566 Willey, Darrell S. "A History of Teacher Training at the University of Utah." Doctoral dissertation, University of Utah, 1953.

WESTMINSTER COLLEGE

2567 Buzza, David E. "Contributions to a History of Utah's Westminster College." Master's thesis, University of Chicago, 1939.

Vermont

GENERAL REFERENCES

2568 Bush, George. *History of Education in Vermont*. Washington, D.C.: U.S. Government Printing Office, 1900.

2569 Norman, Albert. "Vermont State Colleges: Historical Approach to Contemporary Problems." *Vermont History* 32 (1964): 121-153 and 184-212.

2570 Waite, F.C. *The Story of a Country Medical College: A History of the Clinical School of Medicine and the Vermont Medical College, Woodstock, Vermont, 1827-1856*. Montpelier: Vermont Historical Society, 1945.

INSTITUTIONAL HISTORIES

BENNINGTON COLLEGE

2571 Jones, Barbara. *Bennington College: The Development of an Educational Idea*. New York: Harper and Bros., 1946.

2572 Newcomb, Theodore M. *Persistence and Change: Bennington College and Its Students After Twenty-Five Years*. New York: Wiley, 1967.

GODDARD COLLEGE

2573 Coyne, John, and Hebert, Thomas. "Goddard College: A Fresh Look at an Old Innovator." *Change* 3 (1971): 46-51.

2574 Keeton, Morris, and Hilberry, Conrad. *Struggle and Promise: A Future for Colleges*. New York: McGraw-Hill, 1969, pp. 221-242.

MIDDLEBURY COLLEGE

2575 Hamlin, Cyrus. *My Life and Times*. Boston: Congregational Sunday School and Publishing Society, 1893. [Author was President, 1880-1885.]

2576 Lee, William Storrs. *Father Went To College: The Story of Middlebury*. New York: Wilson-Erickson, Inc., 1936.

NORWICH UNIVERSITY

2577 Ellis, William A. *Norwich University, 1819-1911*. Montpelier: n.p., 1911.

VERMONT, UNIVERSITY OF

2578 Lindsay, Julian I. *Tradition Looks Forward: The University of Vermont, a History, 1791-1909*. Burlington: University of Vermont and State Agricultural College, 1954.

2579 Chapin, William A. *History of the University of Vermont College of Medicine*. Springfield, Mass.: Privately Printed, 1951.

2580 Feuer, Lewis. "James Marsh and the Conservative Transcendentalist Psychology." *New England Quarterly* 31 (March 1958): 3-31. [Marsh was President, 1826-1833.]

2581 Hentington, C.A. *The University of Vermont Fifty Years Ago*. Burlington: Whitney, 1892.

2582 Rozwenc, Edwin C. "Agricultural Education in Vermont." *Vermont History* 26 (April 1958): 68-111.

Virginia

GENERAL REFERENCES

2583 Bell, Sadie. *The Church, the State, and Education in Virginia*. Philadelphia: Science Press Printing Co., 1930.

2584 Blume, Clarence J. "The Growth and Development of Sixteen Colleges in the State of Virginia from 1910 to 1928." Master's thesis, University of Virginia, 1929.

2585 Bridges, Herbert L. "Admission Policies of Virginia Colleges." Doctoral dissertation, University of Virginia, 1929.

2586 Brown, Ralph M. "Agricultural Science and Education in Virginia Before 1860." *William and Mary Quarterly* 2d series 19 (1939): 197-213.

2587 Bruce, Alexander P. *Institutional History of Virginia in the 17th Century*. New York: Putnam, 1910.

2588 Capps, Marian P. "The Virginia Out-of-State Graduate Aid Program, 1936-1950." Doctoral dissertation, Columbia University Teachers College, 1954.

2589 Cato, William H. "The Development of Higher Education for Women in Virginia." Doctoral dissertation, University of Virginia, 1941.

2590 Hutcheson, James M. "Virginia's 'Darmouth College Case'." *Virginia Magazine of History and Biography* 51 (1943): 134-140.

2591 Maiden, Marvin G. "History of the Professional Training of Teachers in Virginia." Doctoral dissertation, University of Virginia, 1927.

VIRGINIA

INSTITUTIONAL HISTORIES

AVERETT COLLEGE

2592 Gray, David W. "A History of Averett College." Master's thesis, University of Richmond, 1961.

BRIDGEWATER COLLEGE

2593 Wayland, John W., ed. Fifty Years of Education Endeavor: Bridgewater College, 1880-1930, and Daleville College, 1890-1930. Staunton: McClure Co., 1930.

CLINCH VALLEY COLLEGE

2594 Zehmer, George B. The Story of the Founding of Clinch Valley College. Charlottesville: University Press of Virginia, 1958.

EASTERN MENNONITE COLLEGE

2595 Pellman, Hubert R. Eastern Mennonite College, 1917-1967: A History. Harrisonburg: Eastern Mennonite College, 1967.

ELIZABETH COLLEGE

2596 Robinson, Paul M. "A History of Elizabeth College, Salem, Virginia." Master's thesis, University of Virginia, 1948.

EMORY AND HENRY COLLEGE

2597 Stevenson, George J. Increase in Excellence: A History of Emory and Henry College. New York: Appleton-Century-Crofts, 1963.

HAMPDEN-SYDNEY COLLEGE

2598 Carlson, Alden L. "The Life and Educational Contributions of John Holt Rice." Doctoral dissertation, University of Virginia, 1954. [Rice was Professor of Theology, 1824-1831.]

2599 Grigsby, Hugh B. The Lives and Characters of the Early Presidents of Hampden-Sydney College. Richmond: Hermitage Press, 1913.

2600 Halsey, LeRoy J. *Memoir of the Life of Reverend Lewis Warner Green, D.D.* New York: Scribner's, 1871. [Green was President, 1848-1856.]

2601 McIlwaine, Richard. *Memories of Three Score Years and Ten.* New York: Neale, 1908. [Author was President, 1883-1904.]

2602 Swift, David. "Yankee in Virginia: James Marsh at Hampden-Sydney." *Virginia Magazine of History and Biography* 80 (1972): 312-332.

2603 Topping, Leonard W. "A History of Hampden-Sydney College in Virginia, 1771-1883." Master's thesis, Union Theological Seminary of Richmond, 1950.

HAMPTON INSTITUTE

2604 Carson, Suzanne C. "Samuel Chapman Armstrong, Missionary to the South." Doctoral dissertation, Johns Hopkins University, 1952. [Armstrong was First President, 1868-1893.]

2605 Graham, Edward K. "The Hampton Institute Strike of 1927: A Case Study in Student Protest." *American Scholar* 38 (1969): 668-681.

2606 Jackson, L.P. "The Origin of Hampton Institute." *Journal of Negro History* 10 (1925): 131-149.

2607 Robinson, William H. "The History of Hampton Institute, 1868-1949." Doctoral dissertation, New York University, 1955.

2608 Smith, S.L. "The Passing of the Hampton Library School." *Journal of Negro Education* 9 (1940): 51-58.

2609 Wright, Stephen J. "The Development of the Hampton-Tuskegee Pattern of Higher Education, 1865-1949." *Phylon* 10 (1949): 334-342.

HENRICO COLLEGE

2610 Land, Robert H. "Henrico and Its College." *William and Mary Quarterly* 2d series 18 (1938): 453-498.

2611 McCabe, W. Gordon. "The First University in America, 1619-1622." *Virginia History Magazine* 30 (1922): 133-156.

2612 Walne, Peter. "The Collections of Henrico College, 1616-1618." *Virginia Magazine of History and Biography* 80 (1972): 259-266.

VIRGINIA

HOLLINS COLLEGE

2613 Niederer, Frances. Hollins College: An Illustrated History. Charlottesville: University Press of Virginia, 1973.

2614 Logan, John A. Hollins, An Act of Faith for 125 Years. New York: Newcomen Society in North America, 1968.

2615 Smith, William R. Charles Lewis Cocke, Founder of Hollins College. Boston: R.G. Badger, 1921.

2616 Vickery, Dorothy S. Hollins College, 1842-1942: An Historical Sketch. Hollins College: Hollins College, 1942.

MADISON COLLEGE

2617 Dingeldine, Raymond C., Jr. Madison College: The First Fifty Years, 1908-1958. Harrisonburg: Madison College, 1959.

2618 Sandborn, William C. "The History of Madison College." Doctoral dissertation, George Peabody College for Teachers, 1954.

MARY BALDWIN COLLEGE

2619 Walters, Mary. A History of Mary Baldwin College. Staunton: Mary Baldwin College, 1942.

2620 Waddell, Joseph A. History of Mary Baldwin Seminary. Staunton: Augusta Press Co., 1905.

MARY WASHINGTON COLLEGE

2621 Carlson, Alden L. "A History of Mary Washington College." Master's thesis, University of Virginia, 1948.

MARYMOUNT COLLEGE

2622 Walsh, Walter. "The Growth and Development of Marymount College, Arlington, Virginia, 1948-1965." Master's thesis, Catholic University of America, 1966.

NEEDHAM LAW SCHOOL

2623 Brock, Robert K. <u>Needham Law School, 1821-1842, Cumberland County, Virginia, Founded and Conducted by Chancellor Creed Taylor</u>. Farmville: The Farmville Herald, 1935.

POTOMAC, COLLEGE OF THE

2624 Jerome, Judson. "Portrait of Three Experiments." <u>Change</u> 2 (1970): 40-54.

RADFORD COLLEGE

2625 Smith, Lewis, and Geissler, Lanora. <u>Radford College, A Sentimental Chronicle Through the First Half Century</u>. Radford: Radford College Alumnae Association, 1972.

2626 Moffett, McLedge. <u>A History of the State Teachers College at Radford, Virginia, 1910-1930</u>. Radford: Kingsport Press, 1933.

RANDOLPH-MACON WOMAN'S COLLEGE

2627 Cornelius, R.D. <u>The History of Randolph-Macon Woman's College</u>. Chapel Hill: University of North Carolina Press, 1951.

2628 Fitzgerald, Virginia. "A Southern College Boy Eighty Years Ago." <u>South Atlantic Quarterly</u> 20 (1920): 236-246.

RICHMOND, UNIVERSITY OF

2629 Gaines, R.E., and Taylor, George. <u>The First Hundred Years: Brief Sketches of the History of the University of Richmond</u>. Richmond: Whittet and Shepperson, 1932.

ROANOKE COLLEGE

2630 Eisenberg, William E. <u>The First Hundred Years of Roanoke College, 1842-1942</u>. Salem: Trustees of Roanoke College, 1942.

SAINT PAUL'S COLLEGE

2631 Woolverton, John F. "William Augustus Muhlenberg and the Founding of St. Paul's College." <u>History Magazine of the Protestant Episcopal Church</u> 29 (September 1960): 192-218.

VIRGINIA

STONEWALL JACKSON COLLEGE

2632 Britt, Samuel S. "A History of Stonewall Jackson College, 1868-1930." Master's thesis, University of Virginia, 1949.

SWEET BRIAR COLLEGE

2633 von Briesen, Martha, and Vickery, Dorothy. Sweet Briar College Through Seven Decades, 1901-1971. Richmond: Whittet and Shepperson, 1972.

2634 Stohlman, Martha L. The Story of Sweet Briar College. Princeton: Princeton University Press, 1956.

UNION SEMINARY

2635 Overy, David H. "Robert Lewis Dabney, Apostle of the Old South." Doctoral dissertation, University of Wisconsin, 1967. [Dabney was Professor of Theology.]

VIRGINIA COMMONWEALTH UNIVERSITY

2636 Sanger, William T. The Medical College of Virginia Before 1925 and University College of Medicine 1893-1913. Richmond: Medical College of Virginia Foundation, 1972.

VIRGINIA MILITARY INSTITUTE

2637 Couper, William. One Hundred Years at V.M.I. 4 vols. Richmond: Garrett and Massie, 1939.

2638 Smith, Francis H. The Virginia Military Institute, Its Building and Rebuilding. Lynchburg: J.P. Bell Co., 1912.

VIRGINIA POLYTECHNIC INSTITUTE AND STATE UNIVERSITY

2639 Kinnear, Duncan L. The First One Hundred Years: A History of Virginia Polytechnic Institute and State University. Blacksburg: Virginia Polytechnic Institute Education Foundation, 1972.

2640 Cochran, John P. "The Virginia Agricultural and Mechanical College: The Formative Half Century, 1872-1919, of Virginia Polytechnic Institute." Doctoral dissertation, University of Alabama, 1960.

VIRGINIA, UNIVERSITY OF

2641 O'Neal, William B. Pictorial History of the University of
Virginia. Charlottesville: University Press of Virginia,
1968.

2642 Abernethy, Thomas P. Historical Sketch of the University of
Virginia. Richmond: Dietz Press, 1948.

2643 Adams, Herbert B. Thomas Jefferson and the University of
Virginia. Washington, D.C.: U.S. Bureau of Education, 1888.

2644 Allen, Milton R. "A History of the Young Men's Christian
Association at the University of Virginia." Doctoral
dissertation, University of Virginia, 1947.

2645 Baker, G.E. "Thomas Jefferson on Academic Freedom." Bulletin
of the American Association of University Professors 39 (1953):
377-387.

2646 Barringer, Paul B. The University of Virginia: Its History,
Influence, Equipment and Characteristics with Biographical
Sketches and Portraits of Founders, Benefactors, Officers,
and Alumni. New York: Lewis, 1904.

2647 Bruce, Philip A. History of the University of Virginia 1819-
1919; The Lengthened Shadow of One Man. 5 vols. New York:
Macmillan, 1920.

2648 Cabell, Nathenial F. Early History of the University of Virginia
as Contained in the Letters of Thomas Jefferson and James C.
Cabell. Richmond: J.W. Randolph, 1956.

2649 Carey, John P. "Influences on Thomas Jefferson's Theory and
Practice of Higher Education." Doctoral dissertation, University of Michigan, 1969.

2650 Culbreth, David M. The University of Virginia: Memories of Her
Student-Life and Professors. New York and Washington: Neale,
1908.

2651 Davis, John S. "History of the Medical Department of the University of Virginia, 1825-1914." University of Virginia Alumni
Bulletin 3d series 7 (1914): 299-320.

2652 Fisher, Regina B. "Coeducation at the University of Virginia
1920-1940." Master's thesis, University of Virginia, 1942.

2653 Freeman, Anne H. "Mary Munford's Fight for a College for
Women Co-ordinate with the University of Virginia." Virginia
Magazine of History and Biography 78 (1970): 481-491.

VIRGINIA

2654 Isbell, Egbert R. "The Universities of Virginia and Michigan." Michigan History 21 (1942): 39-53.

2655 Little, Bryan. "Cambridge and the Campus: An English Antecedent for the Lawn of the University of Virginia." Virginia Magazine of History and Biography 79 (1971): 190-201.

2656 Malone, Dumas. Edwin A. Alderman, A Biography. New York: Doubleday, 1940. [Alderman was President, 1904-1931.]

2657 Minor, Berkeley. Legislative History of the University of Virginia as Set Forth in the Acts of the General Assembly of Virginia, 1802-1927. Charlottesville: University Press of Virginia, 1928.

2658 Moore, James. "The University and the Readjusters." Virginia Magazine of History and Biography 78 (1970): 87-101.

2659 Patton, John S. Jefferson, Cabell, and the University of Virginia. New York and Washington: Neale, 1906.

2660 Patton, John S. Jefferson's University: Glimpses of the Past and Present of the University of Virginia. Charlottesville: V. Michie Co., 1915.

2661 Snavely, Tipton R. The Department of Economics at the University of Virginia, 1825-1956. Charlottesville: University Press of Virginia, 1967.

2662 Tanner, Carol M. "Joseph C. Cabell, 1778-1856." Doctoral dissertation, University of Virginia, 1948.

2663 Thornton, William M. "Gildersleeve the Teacher." University of Virginia Alumni Bulletin 3d series 27 (April 1924): 118-129. [Gildersleeve was Professor of Greek, 1850-1876.]

2664 Thornton, William M. "The Honor System at the University of Virginia in Origin and Use." Sewanee Review 15 (1907): 41-57.

2665 Tope, Melancthon. William Holmes McGuffey. Bowerston, Ohio: Phrenological Era Printing Co., 1929. [McGuffey was Professor of Moral Philosophy, 1845-1873.]

2666 Venable, Elizabeth M. Venables of Virginia. New York: Printed Exclusively for Members of the Family, 1925. [Charles S. Venable was Professor of Mathematics, 1865-1896.]

2667 Yates, R.C. "Sylvester at the University of Virginia." American Mathematical Monthly 44 (1937): 194-201. [Sylvester was Professor of Mathematics, 1841-1842.]

WASHINGTON AND LEE UNIVERSITY

2668 Crenshaw, Ollinger. <u>General Lee's College: The Rise and Growth of Washington and Lee University</u>. New York: Random House, 1969.

2669 Britt, Samuel S., Jr. "Henry Ruffner, Nineteenth Century Educator." Doctoral dissertation, University of Arizona, 1962. [Ruffner was President, 1836-1848.]

2670 Hoyt, William D., Jr. "A Crisis in Education, 1834 (Washington College)." <u>Virginia History Magazine</u> 48 (1940): 1-11, 130-140, 243-252, 307-314; 49 (1941): 62-73.

2671 Riley, Franklin L., ed. <u>General Robert E. Lee After Appomattox</u>. New York: Macmillan, 1922. [Lee was President, 1866-1870.]

2672 Ruffner, Henry. "Early History of Washington and Lee University." <u>Washington and Lee Historical Papers</u> 1 (1890): 1-105.

WESLEYAN FEMALE SEMINARY

2673 Brown, Charles K. "The Wesleyan Female Institute: A College for Young Women Under the Auspices of the Baltimore Conference of the Methodist Episcopal Church, Staunton, Virginia, 1846-1897." Master's thesis, University of Virginia, 1936.

WILLIAM AND MARY, COLLEGE OF

2674 Adams, Herbert B. <u>The College of William and Mary: A Contribution to the History of Higher Education with Suggestions for Its National Promotion</u>. Washington, D.C.: U.S. Bureau of Education, 1887.

2675 Canby, Courtland. "A Note on the Influence of Oxford University upon William and Mary College in the 18th Century." <u>William and Mary Quarterly</u> 2d series 21 (1941): 243-247.

2676 Ewing, Galen W. <u>Early Teaching of Science at the College of William and Mary in Virginia</u>. Williamsburg: n.p., 1938.

2677 Hemphill, William E. "George Wythe, the Colonial Briton." Doctoral dissertation, University of Virginia, 1937. [Wythe was Professor of Law, 1779-1790.]

2678 Hughes, Robert M. "William and Mary, the First American Law School." <u>William and Mary Quarterly</u> 2d series 2 (1922): 40-48.

2679 Jennings, John M. "The First Hundred Years of the Library of the College of William and Mary in Virginia, 1693-1793." Master's thesis, American University, 1948.

2680 Motley, D.E. "Life of Commissary James Blair." Johns Hopkins Studies in History and Political Science 14 (1901), no. 10. [Blair was First President, 1693-1743.]

2681 Thomson, Robert P. "The Reform of the College of William and Mary, 1763-1780." Proceedings of the American Philosophical Society 115 (1971): 187-213.

2682 Tucker, Nathaniel B. "The Honor System at William and Mary College." William and Mary Quarterly 1st series 18 (1910): 165-170.

2683 Tyler, Lyon G. "Early Presidents of William and Mary." William and Mary Quarterly 1st series 1 (1892): 63-75.

2684 Tyler, Lyon G. "William and Mary College." Tyler's Quarterly and General Magazine 16 (1935): 218-227. [About re-establishment and author's presidency, 1888-1919.]

2685 Tyler, Lyon G. "William and Mary College as Expressing the American Principle of Democracy." William and Mary Quarterly 2d series 15 (1935): 282-293.

2686 Watson, Joseph, and Watson, David. "Letters from William and Mary College, 1798-1801." Virginia Magazine of History and Biography 39 (1921): 129-179.

2687 Watson, Thomas S. "William and Mary Letters from 1795-1799." Virginia Magazine of History and Biography 30 (1922): 223-249.

Washington

GENERAL REFERENCES

2688 Bolton, Frederick E., and Bibb, Thomas W. History of Education in Washington. Washington, D.C.: U.S. Government Printing Office, 1935.

2689 Spencer, Lloyd. A History of the State of Washington. New York: American Historical Society, 1937. [Vol. 2, ch. 24, pp. 294-307, about higher education.]

2690 U.S. Bureau of Education. Survey of Higher Education in the State of Washington. Washington, D.C.: U.S. Government Printing Office, 1916.

INSTITUTIONAL HISTORIES

CENTRAL WASHINGTON STATE COLLEGE

2691 Mohler, Samuel R. The First Seventy-Five Years: A History of Central Washington State College, 1891-1966. Ellensburgh: Central Washington State College, 1967.

EASTERN WASHINGTON STATE COLLEGE

2692 Dryden, Cecil P. Light for an Empire: The Story of Eastern Washington State College. Cheney: Eastern Washington State College, 1965.

2693 Oliphant, J. Orin. History of the State Normal School at Cheney. Spokane: Inland-American Printing Co., 1924.

GONZAGA UNIVERSITY

2694 Schoenberg, Wilfred P. *Gonzaga University: Seventy-Five Years, 1887-1962.* Spokane: Gonzaga University, 1963.

2695 Weibel, George. *Gonzaga's Silver Jubilee: A Memoir.* Spokane: Gonzaga University, 1912.

PACIFIC LUTHERAN UNIVERSITY

2696 Schnackenberg, Walter C. *The Lamp and the Cross, Sagas of Pacific Lutheran University, 1890-1965.* Tacoma: Pacific Lutheran University Press, 1965.

SEATTLE PACIFIC COLLEGE

2697 Hedges, Richard G. "A Historical Study of Seattle Seminary and Seattle Pacific College, 1891-1906." Master's thesis, University of Washington, 1962.

WALLA WALLA COLLEGE

2698 Walla Walla College. *Sixty Years of Progress: The Anniversary History of Walla Walla College.* College Place: The College Press, 1952.

WASHINGTON STATE UNIVERSITY

2699 Bryan, Enoch A. *Historical Sketch of the State College of Washington, 1890-1925.* Spokane: The Alumni Association and the Associated Students, 1928.

2700 Landeen, William. *E.O. Holland and the State College of Washington, 1916-1944.* Pullman: Washington State University Press, 1958.

2701 Lindsey, Ernest E. "The State College of Washington, a Land-Grant College." *Americana* 34 (1940): 179-219.

2702 Murdock, Patrick M. "A Critical History of the College of Agriculture, State College of Washington, 1892-1916." Doctoral dissertation, Washington State University, 1955.

2703 Neill, Thomas. *Incidents in the Early History of Pullman and the State College of Washington.* Pullman: The Pullman Herald, 1922.

WASHINGTON, UNIVERSITY OF

2704 Gates, Charles. The First Centennial of the University of Washington, 1861-1961. Seattle: University of Washington Press, 1961.

2705 Harrison, Joseph B. Vernon Louis Parrinton, an American Scholar. Seattle: University of Washington Press, 1929. [Parrington was Professor of History, 1908-1929.]

2706 Lawrence, Cora. "University Education for Nursing in Seattle, 1912-1950: The University of Washington School." Doctoral dissertation, University of Washington, 1972.

2707 Leggett, Glenn. "A Conservative View." In The New Professors, edited by Robert O. Bowen, pp. 155-181. New York: Holt, Rinehart, and Winston, 1960. [Author was Director of Freshman English.]

2708 McCaffrey, Frank. Campus Memories: A Sentimental Stroll Through the University of Washington Campus With Professor Edward S. Meany. Seattle: Dogwood Press, 1933.

2709 Meany, Edward S. "Early Records of the University." Washington Historical Quarterly 8 (1917): 114-123.

2710 Odegaard, Charles E. The University of Washington: Pioneering in Its First and Second Century. New York: Newcomen Society in North America, 1964.

2711 Potter, Jessica. A History of the University of Washington Library. Rochester, N.Y.: University of Rochester Press, 1956. ACRL microcard series #56.

WESTERN WASHINGTON STATE COLLEGE

2712 MacDonald, Gary. "Growth By Fire." In Five Experimental Colleges, edited by Gary MacDonald, pp. 196-228. New York: Harper and Row, 1973. [About Fairhaven.]

WHITMAN COLLEGE

2713 Penrose, Stephen B. Whitman, An Unfinished Story. Walla Walla: Whitman Publishing Co., 1935.

WASHINGTON

WILLAMETTE UNIVERSITY

2714 Matthews, James T. Turn Right to Paradise. Portland: Binfords
      and Mort, 1942.

West Virginia

GENERAL REFERENCES

2715 Machesney, John. "The Development of Higher Education Governance and Coordination in West Virginia." Doctoral dissertation, University of West Virginia, 1972.

2716 Whitehill, Alexander R. <u>History of Education in West Virginia</u>. Washington, D.C.: U.S. Government Printing Office, 1902.

2717 Woods, Roy C. "History of Teachers' Institutes in West Virginia." <u>West Virginia History</u> 16 (1955): 107-125.

2718 Woods, Roy C. "Private Normal Schools in West Virginia, 1890-1926." <u>West Virginia History</u> 15 (October 1953): 68-88.

INSTITUTIONAL HISTORIES

BETHANY COLLEGE

2719 Morrison, John L. "Alexander Campbell and Moral Education." Doctoral dissertation, Stanford University, 1966. [Campbell was Founder.]

FAIRMONT STATE COLLEGE

2720 Turner, William P. <u>A Centennial History of Fairmont State College</u>. Fairmont: Fairmont State College, 1970.

2721 Boughter, Isaac F. <u>Fairmont State Normal School: A History</u>. Fairmont: Fairmont State Normal School, 1929.

WEST VIRGINIA

MARSHALL UNIVERSITY

2722 Marshall College. One Hundred Years of Marshall College. Huntington: Centennial Committee of Marshall College, 1937.

2723 Smith, Victoria A. "A Social History of Marshall University During the Period as the State Normal School, 1867-1900." West Virginia History 25 (October 1963): 32-41.

SALEM COLLEGE

2724 Bond, Sirus O. The Light of the Hills: A History of Salem College. Charleston: Education Foundation Inc., 1960.

SHEPHERD COLLEGE

2725 Slonaker, Arthur G. A History of Shepherd College. Parsons: McClaim Printing Co., 1967.

2726 Ghiselin, Charles. "Joseph McMurran, Founder and First President of Shepherd College." Magazine of the Jefferson County Historical Society 5 (December 1939): 16-23.

WEST LIBERTY STATE COLLEGE

2727 Reuter, Frank T. West Liberty State College: The First 125 Years. West Liberty: West Liberty State College, 1963.

2728 Regier, C.C. West Liberty Yesterday and Today. West Liberty: West Liberty State Teachers College, 1939.

WEST VIRGINIA UNIVERSITY

2729 Dawson, James. West Virginia University: An Early Portrait. Morgantown: n.p., 1971.

2730 Munn, Robert F. "West Virginia University Library, 1867-1917." Doctoral dissertation, University of Michigan, 1961.

WEST VIRGINIA WESLEYAN COLLEGE

2731 Plummer, Kenneth M. A History of West Virginia Wesleyan College, 1890-1965. Buckhannon: West Virginia Wesleyan College Press, 1965.

2732 Haught, Thomas W. West Virginia College: The First Fifty Years, 1890-1940. Buckhannon: The College, 1940.

Wisconsin

GENERAL REFERENCES

2733 Allen, W.F., and Spencer, David F. <u>Higher Education in Wisconsin</u>. Washington, D.C.: U.S. Bureau of Education, 1891.

2734 Bailey, Richard P. "The Wisconsin State Colleges, 1875-1955, with Respect to the Function of Preparing Secondary School Teachers." Doctoral dissertation, University of Wisconsin, 1959.

2735 Smith, Ronald A. "Athletics in the Wisconsin State University System, 1867-1913." <u>Wisconsin Magazine of History</u> 55 (1971): 2-23.

2736 Smith, Ronald A. "From Normal Schools to State Universities: A History of the Wisconsin State University Conference." Doctoral dissertation, University of Wisconsin, 1969.

2737 Woerdehoff, Frank J. "Doctor Charles McCarthy: His Educational Views and Influence upon Adult Education in Wisconsin." Doctoral dissertation, University of Wisconsin, 1955.

2738 Wyman, Walker, ed. <u>History of the Wisconsin State Universities</u>. River Falls: River Falls State University, 1968.

INSTITUTIONAL HISTORIES

BELOIT COLLEGE

2739 Ballard, Lloyd. <u>Beloit College, 1917-1923: The Brannon Years</u>. Beloit: Beloit College, 1971.

2740 Eaton, Edward D. <u>Historical Sketches of Beloit College</u>. New York: A.S. Barnes & Co., 1928.

2741 Pearsons, Daniel K. *Daniel K. Pearsons, His Life and Works.* Elgin, Ill.: Brethren Publishing House, 1912. [Pearsons was Benefactor.]

2742 Richardson, Helen L. "The Beloit College Agency." *Wisconsin Magazine of History* 40 (1956): 247-260.

2743 Richardson, Robert K. "The Mindedness of the Early Faculty of Beloit College." *Wisconsin Magazine of History* 19 (1935): 31-70.

2744 Richardson, Robert K. "The Non-sectarian Clause in the Charter of Beloit College." *Wisconsin Magazine of History* 22 (1938): 127-155.

CARDINAL STRITCH COLLEGE

2745 Flahive, Robert F. "Cardinal Stritch College." Doctoral dissertation, Marquette University, 1973.

DOMINICAN COLLEGE

2746 Kohler, Mary H. *Rooted in Hope: The Story of the Dominican Sisters of Racine, Wisconsin.* Milwaukee: Bruce Publishing Co., 1962.

LAKELAND COLLEGE

2747 Jaberg, Eugene C. *A History of Mission House-Lakeland.* Philadelphia: Christian Education Press, 1962.

LAWRENCE UNIVERSITY

2748 Crouch, Barry A. "Amos A. Lawrence, 1814-1886." Doctoral dissertation, University of New Mexico, 1968.

2749 Kieckhefer, G.N. *The History of Milwaukee-Downer College, 1851-1951.* Milwaukee: The College, 1951. [Merged with Lawrence.]

2750 Plantz, Samuel. "Lawrence College." *Wisconsin Magazine of History* 6 (1922): 146-164.

MARQUETTE UNIVERSITY

2751 Hamilton, Rapheal N. *The Story of Marquette University: An Object Lesson in the Development of Catholic Higher Education.* Milwaukee: Marquette University Press, 1953.

WISCONSIN

2752 Dittman, V.W. "History of the Marquette Law School." Marquette Law Review 8 (June 1924): 298-304.

2753 Garraghan, Gilbert J. "Marquette University in the Making." Illinois Catholic Historical Review 2 (1920): 417-436.

MILTON COLLEGE

2754 Whitford, William C. An Historical Sketch of Milton College. Milton: Milton College Alumni Association, 1916.

MILWAUKEE COLLEGE

2755 Kellogg, Louise P. "The Origins of Milwaukee College." Wisconsin Magazine of History 9 (1926): 386-408.

2756 Norton, Minerva B. A True Teacher: Mary Mortimer. New York: F.H. Revell Co., 1894.

MILWAUKEE TECHNICAL COLLEGE

2757 Staff, Public Relations Division. Six Decades of Service, 1903-1963. Milwaukee: Milwaukee School of Engineering, 1963.

MOUNT MARY COLLEGE

2758 Mount Mary College. The Autobiography of a College, by the President, Faculty, and Students of Mount Mary College, Milwaukee, Wisconsin. Milwaukee: The College, 1939.

RACINE COLLEGE

2759 Chitty, Arthur B. "Racine College, Racine, Wisconsin, 1852-1933." History Magazine of the Protestant Episcopal Church 37 (1968): 135-139.

RIPON COLLEGE

2760 Keeton, Morris, and Hilberry, Conrad. Struggle and Promise: A Future for Colleges. New York: McGraw-Hill, 1969, pp. 243-280.

2761 Merrell, Edward H. Ripon College: An Historical Sketch. Ripon: Ripon Free Press, 1893.

2762 Pedrick, Samuel M. "Early History of Ripon College." Wisconsin Magazine of History 8 (September 1924): 22-37.

WISCONSIN, UNIVERSITY OF, AT MADISON

2763 Curti, Merle, and Carstensen, Vernon. *The University of Wisconsin*. 2 vols. Madison: University of Wisconsin Press, 1959.

2764 Anderson, Rasmus B. *Life Story*. Madison: Privately Printed, 1917. [Author was Professor of Scandinavian Languages, 1875-1883.]

2765 Carstensen, Vernon. "The Wisconsin Regents: Academic Freedom and Innovation, 1900-1925." *Wisconsin Magazine of History* 48 (1964): 101-110.

2766 Clark, Paul F. *The University of Wisconsin Medical School, 1848-1948*. Madison: University of Wisconsin Press, 1967.

2767 Commons, John R. *Myself*. New York: Macmillan, 1934. Reprinted by University of Wisconsin Press, 1963. [Author was Professor of Economics, 1904-1932.]

2768 Content, Mary. "The National Impact of the 'Wisconsin Idea': A Bibliographic Study." Master's thesis, George Washington University, 1964.

2769 Cook, John F. "History of Liberal Education at the University of Wisconsin, 1862-1918." Doctoral dissertation, University of Wisconsin, 1970.

2770 Ely, Richard T. *Ground Under My Feet: An Autobiography*. New York: Macmillan, 1938. [Author was Professor of Economics, 1892-1925.]

2771 Fine, Sydney. "Richard T. Ely, Forerunner of Progressivism, 1880-1901." *Journal of American History* 37 (1951): 599-624.

2772 Frost, R.E. *Beloved Professor: The Life and Times of William D. Frost*. New York: Vantage, 1961. [W.D. Frost was Professor of Biology, 1902-1938.]

2773 Galpin, Charles J. *My Drift into Rural Sociology*. University, La.: Louisiana State University Press, 1938. [Author was Professor of Agricultural Economics, 1911-1919.]

2774 Glover, William H. *Farm and College: The College of Agriculture of the University of Wisconsin*. Madison: University of Wisconsin Press, 1952.

2775 Green, James M. "Alexander Meiklejohn, Innovator in Undergraduate Education." Doctoral dissertation, University of Michigan, 1970.

WISCONSIN

2776 Hawkes, James H. "Antimilitarism in State Universities: The Campaign Against R.O.T.C., 1920-1940." Wisconsin Magazine of History 49 (1965): 41-54.

2777 Herfurth, Theodore. Sifting and Winnowing: A Chapter in the History of Academic Freedom at the University of Wisconsin. Madison: University of Wisconsin Press, 1949.

2778 Ingraham, Mark H. Charles Sumner Slichter: The Golden Vector. Madison: University of Wisconsin Press, 1972. [Slichter was Professor of Mathematics, 1886-1925.]

2779 Johnson, William R. "The University of Wisconsin Law School, 1868-1930." Doctoral dissertation, University of Wisconsin, 1972.

2780 Larsen, Lawrence. "How Glenn Frank Became President of the University of Wisconsin." Wisconsin Magazine of History 46 (Spring 1963): 197-205. [Frank was President, 1925-1937.]

2781 Levin, Alexandra. "The Jastrows in Madison: A Chronicle of University Life, 1888-1890." Wisconsin Magazine of History 46 (1962): 243-256.

2782 McGrath, Sylvia W. Charles Kenneth Leith, Scientific Advisor. Madison: University of Wisconsin Press, 1971. [Leith was Professor of Geology, 1902-1945.]

2783 Muir, John. The Story of My Boyhood and Youth. Boston: Houghton Mifflin, 1913. [Muir was Student, 1856-1860.]

2784 Olin, Helen Maria. The Women of a State University. New York and London: G.P. Putnam's, 1909.

2785 Penn, John S. "Earl Melvin Terry, Father of Educational Radio." Wisconsin Magazine of History 44 (Summer 1961): 252-257.

2786 Rader, Benjamin G. The Academic Mind and Reform: The Influence of Richard T. Ely in American Life. Lexington, Ky.: University of Kentucky Press, 1966.

2787 Rosentreter, Frederick M. "The Boundaries of the Campus: A History of the Extension Division of the University of Wisconsin." Doctoral dissertation, University of Wisconsin, 1954.

2788 Ross, Edward A. Seventy Years of It. New York: Appleton-Century-Crofts, 1936. [Author was Professor of Sociology, 1906-1937.]

2789 Sachse, Nancy D. "The University of Wisconsin Arboretum." Wisconsin Magazine of History 44 (1960): 117-131.

2790 Schlabach, Theron. "The Case of Richard T. Ely." Wisconsin Magazine of History 47 (1963): 146-159.

2791 Sellery, George C. E.A. Birge. Madison: University of Wisconsin Press, 1956. [Birge was Professor of Biology, 1879-1917, and President, 1918-1925.]

2792 Sellery, George C. Some Ferments at Wisconsin, 1901-1947. Madison: University of Wisconsin Press, 1960.

2793 Smith, Charles F. Charles Kendall Adams: A Life Sketch. Madison: Regents of the University of Wisconsin, 1924. [Adams was President, 1892-1901.]

2794 Townley, Sidney D. Diary of a Student of the University of Wisconsin, 1886-1892. Stanford, Calif.: n.p., 1940.

2795 Vance, Margaret M. "Charles Richard Van Hise." Doctoral dissertation, University of Wisconsin, 1960. [Van Hise was President, 1903-1915.]

2796 Weaver, Warren. Scene of Change: A Lifetime in American Science. New York: Scribner's, 1970. [Weaver was Professor of Biology.]

WISCONSIN, UNIVERSITY OF, AT MILWAUKEE

2797 Klotsch, J. Martin. The University of Wisconsin at Milwaukee: An Urban University. Milwaukee: University of Wisconsin at Milwaukee, 1972.

WISCONSIN, UNIVERSITY OF, AT PLATTVILLE

2798 Gamble, Richard D. From Academy to University, 1866-1966. Plattville: Wisconsin State University, 1966.

WISCONSIN, UNIVERSITY OF, AT RIVER FALLS

2799 Lankford, John. "Founding the Fourth State Normal School." Wisconsin Magazine of History 47 (1963): 26-34.

WISCONSIN, UNIVERSITY OF, AT WHITEWATER

2800 Bohi, Mary. A History of Wisconsin State University, Whitewater, 1868-1968. Whitewater: Wisconsin State University Foundation, 1967.

Wyoming

GENERAL REFERENCES

2801 Bartlett, Ichabod. <u>History of Wyoming</u>. Chicago: S.J. Clarke, 1918. [Vol. 1, ch. 27, pp. 428-449, about higher education.]

2802 Verhallen, Roman J. "Legislation Affecting the Government of Higher Education." <u>University of Wyoming Publications</u> 16 (1951): 249-255.

INSTITUTIONAL HISTORIES

CASPER COLLEGE

2803 McCollom, Stewart F. "A History of Casper College, with References to Selected Historical Aspects of the Junior College Movement in the United States and Wyoming." Doctoral dissertation, University of Wyoming, 1964.

WYOMING, UNIVERSITY OF

2804 Clough, Wilson O. <u>A History of the University of Wyoming, 1887-1964</u>. Laramie: University of Wyoming, 1965.

2805 Michelet, Maren. <u>Glimpses from the Life of Agnes Mathilde Wergeland</u>. Minneapolis: Folkebladet Publishing Co., 1916. [Wergeland was Professor of History, 1902-1914.]

2806 Woodward, George R. "History of the College of Education, University of Wyoming, 1887-1945." Doctoral dissertation, University of Wyoming, 1971.

Index

Abilene Christian College, 2484
Academic freedom, 66, 77, 187, 393, 819, 1294, 1467, 1468, 1890, 2098, 2342, 2375, 2472, 2539, 2548, 2645, 2765, 2777, 2788, 2790
Academic honesty. See Honor systems
Accreditation, 65
Adams, Charles K., 2793
Adams, Henry, 913, 991
Adams, Henry C., 1723
Adams, Herbert B., 909
Adams, John Q., 1836
Adams State College, 203
Adelphi University, 1612
Adler, Cyrus, 1776
Administration, 633, 1079. See also Presidency, office of
Admissions, 87, 299, 1291, 2168, 2585
Adrian College, 1205, 1206
Adult education. See University extension
Agassiz, Louis, 1018, 1052, 1056
Agnes Scott College, 391
Agricultural education, 41, 237, 291, 697, 943, 1123, 1237, 1353, 1355, 1483, 1724, 1918, 2043, 2124, 2215, 2524, 2563, 2582, 2586, 2702, 2774
Akron, University of, 2004, 2005
Alabama, State of, 1, 2
Alabama, University of, 3, 4
Alaska, State of, 29
Alaska, University of, 30

Albany State College, 392
Albany, State University of New York at, 1613-1615
Albion College, 1207-1209
Albright College, 2194, 2195
Alcohol, use of. See Drugs, use of
Alcorn A & M College, 1376
Alderman, Edwin A., 2656
Alfred University, 1616
Allegheny College, 2196
Alma White College, 1530
Alumni, 250, 259, 387, 1054, 1090, 1113, 1273, 1510
American Association of University Professors, 1355
American International College, 946, 947
American University, 315
Amherst College, 948-965
Ancient languages, 177, 684, 876, 901, 964, 1062, 1248, 1296, 1340, 1710, 1764, 2053, 2663
Anderson, Martin B., 1838
Anderson, Rasmus B., 2764
Andreen, Gustav, 463
Andrews, Charles M., 1247
Andrews, Elisha B., 2342, 2343
Andrews University, 1210, 1211
Angell, James B., 1249, 1286, 1293
Angelo State University, 2485
Anna Maria College for Women, 966
Anthropology, 94, 1562, 2277
Antioch College, 2006-2011
Architectural education, 828

INDEX

Architecture, campus, 51, 110, 547, 960, 1046, 1250, 1552, 1678, 1950, 2289, 2340, 2655
Arizona, State of, 32-35
Arizona State University, 35
Arizona, University of, 36
Arkansas A & M College, 41
Arkansas College, 42
Arkansas, State of, 37-40
Arkansas, University of, at Fayetteville, 43-51
Arkansas, University of, at Little Rock, 52
Armstrong, Samuel C., 2604
Armstrong State College, 393
Arnett, Trevor, 494
Art education, 1413, 1823, 1865
Articulation. See Admissions
Arts and sciences. See Liberal arts
Asbury College, 795
Ashe, Samuel A., 935
Ashland College, 2012
Astronomy, 500, 994, 1039, 1899, 1904, 2281
Athenaeum, 2013
Athletics, 307, 796, 916, 1275, 1393, 1394, 1716, 1956, 2089, 2093, 2411, 2412, 2735. See also by specific sport
Atlanta Medical College, 394, 395
Atlanta University, 396-398
Attudac College, 78
Auburn Community College, 1617
Auburn University, 6,7
Augsburg College, 1326
Augusta College, 796
Augustana College (Ill.), 463
Augustana College (S.D.), 2395
Augustana Hospital School of Nursing, 464
Austin College, 2486, 2487
Averett College, 2592
Aydelotte, Frank, 2317

Babbitt, Irving, 1055
Baker, James H., 207
Baker, Ray S., 1238
Baker University, 761
Baldwin, James M., 1544
Baldwin, Simeon E., 276
Baldwin-Wallace College, 2014

Ball State University, 594-596
Baltimore College of Dental Surgery, 894
Bangor Theological Seminary, 871, 872
Bark College, 1618, 1619
Barker, Lewellys F., 899
Barnard, Frederick A.P., 1657, 1668
Barnard College, 1620-1626
Barrow, David C., 420
Barrows, John H., 2072
Bascom, Henry B., 846
Bascom, John, 1173
Basketball, 760
Bateman, Newton, 559
Bates, Katherine L., 1161
Bates College, 873, 874
Battle, Kemp P., 1945
Baylor University, 2488-2490
Beadle, William H., 2403
Beaver College, 2197
Becker, Carl, 1738
Belmont Abbey College, 1919
Beloit College, 2739-2744
Bemidji State College, 1327, 1328
Bemis, Edward W., 487
Benjamin, Simeon, 1747
Bennington College, 2571, 2572
Benton Harbor College, 1212
Berea College, 797-805
Bessey, Charles, 1491, 1492
Bethany College, 2719
Bethany Nazarene College (Okla.), 2128
Bethany Nazarene College (Tex.), 2491
Bethel College (Ind.), 597
Bethel College (Kan.), 762, 763
Bethel College (Minn.), 1329
Bethune, Mary M., 365
Bethune-Cookman College, 365
Bevier, Isabel, 525
Biology, 268, 491, 1018, 1023, 1052, 1056, 1116, 1163, 1281, 1491, 1492, 1669, 1698, 1846, 1862, 2280, 2321, 2347, 2407, 2772, 2789, 2791, 2796
Birge, E.A., 2791
Birmingham Southern College, 8, 9
Bishop, Robert H., 2044
Black, Arthur D., 570
Black, Greene V., 570

Black higher education, 18, 20, 39, 311, 352, 365, 387, 389, 392, 396, 429, 442, 793, 856, 1021, 1376, 1395, 1883, 1890, 1914, 1917, 1972, 2073, 2113, 2252, 2364, 2369, 2430, 2481, 2609
Black Mountain College, 1920-1922
Blackburn, Gideon, 465
Blackburn College, 465
Blair, James, 2680
Blanchard, Charles A., 585
Blinn Memorial College, 2492
Bloomfield College, 1533
Blount College, 2463
Blue Mountain College, 1377
Bluemont Central College, 770
Bluffton College, 2015
Boating, 1084, 1739
Boggs, William E., 418
Boise State College, 452, 453
Bond, Elizabeth, 2319
Boring, Edwin G., 1007
Boston College, 967, 968
Boston University, 969-975
Botany. See Biology
Bowdoin, James, 885
Bowdoin College, 875-885
Bowling Green State University, 2016, 2017
Bowman, John B., 825
Boyd, Thomas D., 864
Boyden, Albert G., 978
Bradley University, 466-468
Brandeis University, 976
Breckinridge, Robert J., 811
Bridgewater College, 2593
Bridgewater State College, 977-980
Brigham Young University, 2561, 2562
Broadcasting, 541, 1801, 2785
Brockport, State University of New York College at, 1627, 1628
Brookings, Robert S., 1457
Brooklyn College, 1629
Brooks, Charles, 942
Brown, Charles R., 252
Brown, George W., 912
Brown, Rollo, 1010
Brown, Thomas M., 2251
Brown, William A., 1876
Brown, William L., 7
Brown University, 2335-2354
Bryn Mawr College, 2198-2202
Buchanan, Joseph, 840

Bucknell University, 2203-2205
Buffalo, State University of New York at, 1632-1636
Buffalo, State University of New York College at, 1630, 1631
Burgess, John W., 1653, 1676
Burleson, Rufus C., 2490
Business education, 1019, 1796, 2136, 2192, 2282, 2283
Butler, Howard C., 1562
Butler, Nicholas M., 1655, 1713
Butler University, 598, 599

Cabell, James C., 2648, 2659, 2662
Caldwell, Charles, 843
Caldwell, Joseph, 1946
California Baptist College, 79
California Institute of Technology, 80, 81
California State College at Long Beach, 82
California, State of, 62-77
California State Polytechnic College at San Luis Obispo, 83
California, University of, at Berkeley, 84-104
California, University of, at Los Angeles, 105-112
California, University of, at Santa Barbara, 113-115
California, University of, at Santa Cruz, 116, 117
California, University of, Medical School at Loma Linda, 118
Calvin College, 1213, 1214
Camp, David N., 235
Camp, Walter, 297
Campbell, Alexander, 2719
Campbell, Prince L., 2170
Campus planning. See Architecture, campus
Cane Hill College, 53
Canisius College, 1637, 1638
Canterbury College, 600
Canton College, 469
Capen, Samuel P., 1636
Cardinal Stritch College, 2745
Carleton, Charles, 2493
Carleton College, 1330, 1331
Carlisle Indian School, 2206
Carlton College, 2493
Carnegie, Andrew, 2209

INDEX

Carnegie-Mellon University, 2207-2209
Carroll, John, 346
Carson-Newman College, 2423
Carter, Thomas M., 1209
Carthage College, 470
Carver, Thomas N., 1013
Cary, Freeman, 2043
Case-Western Reserve University, 2018-2027
Casper College, 2803
Catawba College, 1923
Catholic higher education, 15, 65, 68, 70, 126, 127, 133, 146, 159, 316, 341, 509, 940, 1193, 1448
Catholic University of America, 316-329, 644
Cedar Crest College, 2210
Cedarville College, 2028
Centenary College of Louisiana, 858
Central College, 676
Central Connecticut State College, 234, 235
Central Michigan University, 1215, 1216
Central Missouri State College, 1404, 1405
Central Normal College, 601
Central University, 806, 807
Central Washington State College, 2691
Centre College, 808, 809
Certification, 33, 65. See also Teacher education
Chamberlin, Thomas C., 481, 499
Chambers, Will G., 2182
Chapman College, 119
Charleston, College of, 2365, 2366
Chase, George C., 874
Chase, Harry W., 1798
Chatham College, 2211, 2212
Cheating. See Honor systems
Chemistry, 265, 340, 655, 691, 778, 910, 1016, 1083, 1095, 1253, 2027, 2094, 2296, 2297
Chicago State College, 471-473
Chicago Theological Seminary, 474
Chicago, University of, 475-501
Chicano higher education, 203
Chico State College, 120
Chittenden, Russell H., 256
Chowan College, 1924
Christian College, 2150, 2151

Church and state, relations between, 69, 545, 1188, 1189, 1197, 1912, 2362, 2583
Cincinnati, University of, 2029-2035
Citadel, The, 2367, 2368
City College of New York, 1639-1645
Claflin College, 2369
Clap, Thomas, 304
Claremont Men's College, 121, 122
Clarion State College, 2213, 2214
Clark University, 981-986
Clarkson College of Technology, 1646, 1647
Clemson University, 2370
Cleveland State University, 2036
Clinch Valley College, 2594
Cocke, Charles L., 2615
Coe College, 677
Coeducation, 423, 721, 1268, 1272, 2080, 2652. See also Women's higher education
Coffin, James H., 2245
Coffman, Lotus D., 1344
Colby College, 886-888
Colby Junior College, 1505
Colgate University, 1648, 1649
Colorado College, 204
Colorado, State of, 199-202
Colorado State University, 205
Colorado, University of, 206-213
Columbia College (Iowa), 678
Columbia College (S.C.), 2371-2373
Columbia Seminary, 2374, 2375
Columbia University, 1273, 1650-1716
Columbian Institution, 330
Commons, John R., 2767
Community and junior colleges, 38, 52, 63, 72, 128, 200, 226, 227, 363, 411, 453, 461, 467, 736, 822, 834, 1192, 1200, 1225, 1228, 1323, 1396, 1401, 1411, 1473, 1505, 1603, 1617, 1916, 1965, 2002, 2230, 2506, 2519, 2523, 2556, 2803
Compton, Arthur, 1455
Comstock, Anna, 1725
Conant, James B., 1016, 1095
Conaty, Thomas J., 322
Concordia College (Minn.), 1332
Concordia College (Mo.), 1406, 1407

Concordia Teachers College (Calif.), 123
Concordia Teachers College (Ill.), 502
Concordia Teachers College (Neb.), 1475, 1476
Connecticut College, 236
Connecticut, State of, 232, 233
Connecticut, University of, 237, 238
Consulting, faculty. See Faculty activism
Continuing education. See University extension
Converse College, 2376
Cooley, Mortimer E., 1254, 1265
Cooper, Peter, 1717
Cooper, Thomas, 2388
Cooper Memorial, 764
Cooper Union, 1717
Copeland, Charles T., 992
Corlett, William T., 2021
Cornell, Ezra, 1726
Cornell College, 679
Cornell University, 1718-1739
Cortland, State University of New York College at, 1740-1743
Coulter, John M., 491
Counseling. See Student personnel services
Court cases, 1517, 1519, 1520, 2104, 2590
Courtney, Charles E., 1739
Cox, Jacob D., 2031
Craven, Braxton, 1930
Crawshaw, William H., 1649
Credit system. See Elective system
Crehore, Albert C., 1509
Cross, Wilbur L., 258
Crothers, George E., 174
Crowell, John F., 1929
Cubberley, Elwood P., 180, 189
Culver-Stockton College, 1408
Cumberland College, 810
Cumberland Female College, 2424
Cumberland University, 2425, 2426
Curriculum, 220, 231, 246, 303, 305, 383, 488, 495, 669, 689, 755, 959, 989, 1452, 1547, 1584, 1773, 2006, 2019, 2030, 2321, 2775
Cushing, Harvey, 1093

Dabney, Robert L., 2635
Dagg, John L., 428
Dakota State College, 2396
Dakota Wesleyan University, 2397
Dallas College, 2152
Dana, James D., 268
Dana College, 1477
Danville Theological Seminary, 811
DaPonte, Lorenzo, 1703
Darby, Edwin T., 2284
Dartmouth College, 1506-1522, 2123
Davidson College, 1925, 1926
Davie, William R., 1955
Davis, Alexander J., 1250
Davis, Jesse B., 1229
Dayton, University of, 2037-2041
Dean, academic, 1010, 1622, 1653, 1711
Dean of students, 1554, 2349
Dean of women, 496, 1263
Defferrari, Roy J., 319, 320
Delaware Military Academy, 310
Delaware State College, 311
Delaware, University of, 312-314
Delaware Valley College of Science and Agriculture, 2215
Delta State College, 1378
Denison University, 2042
Dental education, 570, 874, 1030, 2023, 2284
Denver, University of, 214-225
DePauw University, 602-605, 978
Deputy, Manfred W., 1328
Des Moines University, 680, 681
Desegregation, 437, 438, 834, 1073, 1386, 1416, 1422, 2137
Detroit, University of, 1217, 1218
Dewey, John, 903
Dickey, John M., 2252
Dickinson College, 2216-2220
Dickinson State College, 1983
Dillard University, 859
Diman, J. Lewis, 2346
Dixon, Edward H., 1610
Dodd, William E., 498
Dominican College, 2746
Doney, Carl G., 2178
Dormitories, 1051, 1089, 1870
Dos Passos, John, 1002
Douglass College, 1532
Downstate Medical Center, 1744
Drake, Daniel, 2087
Drake University, 682-685

INDEX 301

Draper, Andrew S., 530, 535, 1806
Drew University, 1529, 1530
Drexel Institute of Technology, 1535
Drexel University, 2221
Drugs, use of, 1020
Drury College, 1409
DuBois, W.E.B., 1021
DuBose, William, 2454
Dubuque, University of, 686
Duer, William A., 1660
Duke, James B., 1934
Duke University, 1927-1935
Dunn, Esther C., 1145
Duns Scotus College, 1219
Dunshee, Norman, 684
Dunster, Henry, 1014
Duquesne University, 2222
Durant, Henry F., 1167
Dutton, Samuel T., 1688
Dwight, John S., 1017
Dwight, Timothy, 263

Earlham College, 606-608
East Tennessee College, 2463
East Tennessee University, 2464
East Texas State University, 2494-2497
Eastern Baptist College, 2223
Eastern Illinois University, 503, 504
Eastern Kentucky University, 812, 813
Eastern Mennonite College, 2595
Eastern Michigan University, 1220-1223
Eastern Nazarene College, 987
Eastern New Mexico University, 1594
Eastern Washington State College, 2692, 2693
Eastman, George, 1835
Eaton, Amos, 1831
Economics, 479, 487, 2661, 2767, 2770
Edgcumbe, George S., 1212
Edinboro State College, 2224
Education (as discipline), 107, 112, 168, 178, 180, 188, 189, 212, 253, 476, 492, 1029, 1078, 1260, 1278, 1655, 1672, 1673, 1680, 1688, 1702, 1706, 1709, 1713, 1820, 2090, 2165, 2806
Egan, Maurice F., 640
Eleutherian College, 609
Eliot, Charles W., 902, 1034, 1038
Eliot, William G., 1456
Elizabeth College, 2596
Elizabethtown College, 2225
Elliott, Edward C., 650
Elmhurst College, 505
Elmira College, 1745-1749
Ely, Richard T., 2770, 2771, 2786, 2790
Emory and Henry College, 2597
Emory University, 399, 400
Engineering education, 704, 918, 1120, 1254, 1265, 1398, 1430, 1551, 1663, 1699, 1727, 2091, 2267
English (as discipline), 258, 416, 490, 640, 914, 992, 1055, 1076, 1145, 1161, 1162, 1354, 1564, 1649, 1719, 1731, 1898, 1952
Erskine, John, 1779
Eugene Bible College, 2157
Eureka College, 506
Evans, John, 221, 222
Evelyn College, 1536

Faculty activism, 1016, 1095, 1455, 2768, 2786
Fairclough, Henry R., 177
Fairleigh Dickinson University, 1537
Fairmont State College, 2720, 2721
Farmers College, 2043, 2044
Fayetteville State University, 1936
Federal City College, 331, 332
Fee, John G., 799
Ferris State College, 1224
Fiction about higher education, 998
Financing higher education, 543, 544, 601, 670, 686, 743, 796, 950, 961, 1006, 1026, 1032, 1035, 1071, 1279, 1288, 1511, 2184, 2185, 2279, 2292, 2309, 2420
Finch College, 1750
Finley, John H., 556, 557, 1641, 1643
Finney, Charles G., 2076, 2079, 2085
Fisher, Daniel W., 614
Fisk University, 2430, 2431
Flexner, Abraham, 905, 907

Flint Community College, 1225
Flipper, Henry O., 1883
Florence State University, 10
Florida Agricultural and Mechanical University, 366
Florida Presbyterian College, 367
Florida, State of, 360-364, 417
Florida State University, 368-370
Florida, University of, 371-373
Flowers, John G., 2516
Flynt, Henry, 1022
Folwell, William W., 1342
Football, 297, 493, 645, 759, 997, 1000, 1879, 2370
Ford, Guy S., 1347
Fordham University, 1751-1754
Foreign influence on American higher education, 1256, 2655, 2675
Foreign students, 449, 1271
Forensics, 707, 1266, 1267, 1521
Forestry education, 1862, 1867, 1869
Fort Hays Kansas State College, 765
Fox, George H., 1666
Framingham State College, 988
Franconia College, 1523
Frank, Glenn, 2780
Frankfurter, Felix, 1027
Franklin, Benjamin, 2273, 2301
Franklin and Marshall College, 2226
Franklin College of Indiana, 610, 611
Franklin Institute, 2227
Fraternities and sororities: honorary, 217, 1077; social, 1283
Fredonia, State University of New York College at, 1755-1757
Freeman, Alice, 1165, 1168
Frelinghuysen, Theodore, 1577
Fresno State College, 124
Friends University, 766
Frieze, Henry S., 1248
Frost, William D., 2772
Frost, William G., 800
Fuerbringer, Ludwig E., 1406
Furman, James C., 2378
Furman, Richard, 2379
Furman University, 2377-2380

Gailor, Thomas F., 2457
Gale, George W., 558
Gallaudet, Edward M., 335
Gallaudet College, 333-338
Galpin, Charles J., 2773
Gammon Theological Seminary, 984
Gaston, William, 348
Gatch, Thomas M., 2161
Gates, George A., 690
Gauss, Christian F., 1554
Geddes, James, 971
General Motors Institute, 1226, 1227
General Theological Seminary, 1758
Geneseo, State University of New York College at, 1759-1761
Geology, 86, 268, 1008, 1566, 2097, 2782, 2795
George Peabody College for Teachers, 1282, 2432-2438
George Washington University, 339, 340
George Williams College, 507, 508
Georgetown College, 814-817
Georgetown University, 341-351
Georgia Institute of Technology, 401, 402
Georgia, State of, 378-390
Georgia, University of, 403-424
Gettysburg College, 2228, 2229
Gibbons, Cardinal, 328
Gibbs, Willard, 300
Gildersleeve, Basil L., 901, 2663
Gildersleeve, Virginia C., 1622
Gilman, Daniel C., 96, 902, 906
Girardeau, John L., 2374
Goddard College, 2573, 2574
Golden State College, 125
Gonzaga University, 2694, 2695
Goodell, Henry H., 1126
Goshen College, 612
Goucher College, 895, 896
Graceland College, 687
Graduate education, 111, 164, 266, 712, 917, 938, 1593, 1701, 1736, 1794, 2437
Graham, George M., 861
Grand Rapids Junior College, 1228, 1229
Grand Valley State College, 1230
Graves, Frank P., 1807
Gray, Asa, 1023
Green, Lewis W., 2600
Gregory, John M., 536
Griggs, Edward H., 178

INDEX

Grinnell College, 688-691
Griswold College, 692
Gross, Samuel D., 2237
Guilford College, 1937
Gustavus Adolphus College, 1333-1335

Hadley, Arthur T., 270
Hale, George E., 500
Hall, G. Stanley, 983, 986
Hallowell, Benjamin, 922
Hamilton College, 1762-1764
Hamlin, Cyrus, 2575
Hamline University, 1336, 1337
Hampden-Sydney College, 2598-2603
Hampshire College, 989
Hampton Institute, 2604-2609
Hanover College, 613-615
Hanus, Paul, 1029
Hardin-Simmons University, 2498, 2499
Harding College, 55, 56
Hardy, Arthur S., 1512
Hare, Robert, 2296
Harker, Joseph, 550
Harkness, Edward S., 1715
Harper, William R., 480, 483, 485
Harris, John H., 2204
Harris, William, 2373
Harris Teachers College, 1410
Harrisburg Area Community College, 2230
Harshberger, John, 2280
Hartsville College, 616
Hartwick College, 1765
Harvard University, 990-1102
Hastings College, 1478
Haven, Erastus O., 1296
Haverford College, 2231-2234
Hawaii, University of, 446-449
Hawkes, Herbert E., 1711
Hebrew Union College, 2045, 2046
Hedge, Frederick H., 1049
Heidelberg College, 2047
Henderson, Joseph L., 2544
Henderson State College, 57
Hendrix College, 58
Henrico College, 2610-2612
Henry, Joseph, 1572
Hersey Junior College, 2230
Hetherington, Clark W., 170
High Point College, 1938
Hill, D.H., 45
Hill David J., 1840

Hill, Thomas, 1045
Hille, Walter B., 419
Hillsdale College, 1231
Hiram College, 2048
History (as discipline), 909, 991, 1004, 1178, 1247, 1665, 1671, 1719, 1731, 1738, 1841, 1864, 1895, 2291, 2538, 2705, 2805
Hitchcock, Edward, 957
Hitchcock, Embury A., 2091
Hobart and William Smith Colleges, 1766-1769
Hofstra University, 1770
Holland, E.O., 2700
Holley, Joseph W., 392
Hollingworth, Leta S., 1673
Hollins College, 2613-2616
Holy Cross, College of the, 1103, 1104
Holy Names, College of the, 126
Home economics, 496, 525, 1115, 1631
Honor systems, 2664, 2682
Hope, John, 432
Hope College, 1232-1234
Hopkins, Mary, 1172, 1175
Horsford, Eben N., 1083
Houghton College, 1771, 1772
Houston, David F., 2529
Howard, O.O., 356
Howard College, 11, 12
Howard Payne College, 2500
Howard University, 352-357
Hoy, Carl B., 2412
Hughes, John, 1752
Humanities, 160
Hunter College, 1773-1775
Huntington, William E., 972
Huntington College (Ala.), 13
Huntington College (Ind.), 617
Hurst, John F., 315
Huston-Tillotson College, 2501, 2502
Hutchins, Harry B., 1292
Hyde, Ammi B., 219

Iberia Junior College, 1411
Idaho, State of, 450, 451
Idaho State University, 454
Idaho, University of, 455
Illinois Benedictine College, 509
Illinois College, 510-514
Illinois Institute of Technology, 515

Illinois, State of, 457-462
Illinois State University, 516-523
Illinois, University of, 524, 548
Illinois Wesleyan University, 549
Illinois Women's College, 550
Illustrated histories, 90, 93, 98, 224, 531, 573, 821, 860, 1252, 1555, 1954, 2467, 2641
Immaculate Conception Seminary, 1412
Immaculate Heart College, 127
Incarnate Word College, 2503
Indiana Central College, 618
Indiana Central Medical College, 619
Indiana, State of, 587-593
Indiana State University, 620, 621
Indiana University, 622-636
Indiana University of Pennsylvania, 2235
Indians, higher education for. See Native Americans, higher education for
Iowa College, 693-695
Iowa, State of, 668-675
Iowa State University, 696-701
Iowa, University of, 702-726
Iowa Wesleyan College, 727-730

Jackson State College, 1379
Jacksonville University, 374
Jacobs, Thornwell, 435
Jacobs, William P., 2383
James, Edmund, 543, 546
James, William, 993
Jastrow, Morris, 2781
Jefferson, Thomas, 2643, 2645, 2648, 2649, 2659, 2660
Jefferson College, 1380
Jefferson Medical College, 2236-2238
Jesse, Richard H., 1423
Jewish Theological Seminary, 1776
John and Mary's College, 2239
John Brown University, 59
Johns Hopkins University, 897-918
Johnson, Alvin S., 1789
Johnson, Burgess, 1898
Johnson, Charles E., 2167
Johnson, Emory R., 2282
Johnson, Samuel, 1704
Johnson, Samuel W., 291
Johnson C. Smith University, 1939

Jordan, David S., 171, 182, 626, 628
Journalism about higher education, 458
Jubilee College, 551, 552
Juilliard School, 1777-1779
Juniata College, 2240, 2241

Kalamazoo College, 1235
Kansas City Art Institute, 1413
Kansas, State of, 757-760
Kansas State Teachers College, 767-770
Kansas State University, 771-774
Kansas, University of, 775-780
Keep, Rosalind, 129
Kemper College, 1414
Kendall, Amos, 338
Kent State University, 2049, 2050
Kentucky, State of, 787-794
Kentucky, University of, 818-825
Kenyon College, 2051-2054
Kephart, Ezekial B., 751
Keuka College, 1780, 1781
Keyes, Charles H., 1860
Kidd-Key College, 2504
Kilgo, John C., 1931
King, Henry C., 2083
King, William F., 679
King's College, 2242
Kinley, David, 540
Kirk, John, 1433
Kleinsmid, Rufus B., 166
Kliewer, John W., 763
Knoles, Tully, 139
Knox, Warren B., 2160
Knox College, 553-560
Kober, George M., 351
Koos, Leonard, 476
Kroeber, Alfred, 94
Kuntz, Frank A., 323
Kutztown State College, 2243

Lafayette College, 2244-2247
LaGrange College, 425, 426
Lakeland College, 2747
Lamar University, 2505-2507
Lambuth College, 2439
Land grants, 544, 696, 1374, 1472, 2001, 2090, 2190, 2480
Lane College, 2440
Lane Seminary, 2055
Langdell, Christopher C., 1086

INDEX

Larsen, Laure, 733
Larson, Laurence M., 537
LaSalle College, 2248
Lasell Junior College, 1105
Lawrence, Amos A., 2748
Lawrence University, 2748-2750
Lebanon Valley College, 2249
LeConte, Joseph, 86, 410
Lee, Robert E., 2668, 2671
Lee College, 2441, 2442
Legal education, 48, 239-241, 264, 271-274, 276, 301, 831, 845, 847, 995, 1024, 1027, 1086, 1092, 1097, 1100, 1911, 1992, 2031, 2278, 2623, 2677, 2678, 2752, 2779
Lehigh University, 2250, 2251
Leith, Charles K., 2782
LeMoyne College, 1782
Leonard, Arthur G., 1990
Leverett, John, 1041
Lewis, Henry C., 827
Lewis Sinclair, 269
Lewis, Wilmarth S., 283
Lewis and Clark College, 2153
Liberal arts, 926, 928, 1082, 1793, 2006, 2321, 2769, 2775
Libraries, 100, 390, 791, 850, 927, 995, 1050, 1087, 1682, 2679, 2711, 2730
Library education, 532, 1658, 2608
Lieber, Francis, 1667
Limestone College, 2381, 2382
Lincoln, Robert T., 1028
Lincoln College, 786
Lincoln University (Mo.), 1415, 1416
Lincoln University (Pa.), 2252-2254
Lindsay, Philip, 2447, 2451
Linfield College, 2154, 2155
Lipscomb, Andrew A., 415
Lipscomb College, 2427-2429
Litchfield Law School, 239-241
Literary societies, 563, 667, 725, 1521, 1545
Little, Clarence C., 1298
Lock Haven State College, 2255
Log College, 2256, 2257
Lon Morris College, 2508
Long Island University, 1783, 1784
Loras College, 731
Lord, Eleanor, 896
Lord, Livingston C., 504

Lotteries, 1071, 2292
Louisiana, State of, 854-857
Louisiana State University, 860-864
Louisville, University of, 826-831
Lovett, R.M., 489
Low, Seth, 1681, 1686
Lowell, Abbott L., 1042, 1101
Lowell Institute, 1106-1108
Loyola College, 919
Luce, Stephen B., 2355
Luther Academy, 1479
Luther College, 732-735
Lycoming College, 2258
Lyon, Mary, 1128, 1129

Macalester College, 1338-1340
MacArthur, Douglas, 1888
McBride, James, 2062
McCarthy, Charles, 2737
McConnell, Francis J., 604
McCosh, James, 1557
McGuffey, William H., 2665
McIlwaine, Richard, 2601
McIver, Charles D., 1961
McKendree College, 561
McKenzie College, 2510
McMurran, Joseph, 2726
McNeely Normal School, 2056
McVey, Frank L., 819
Macy, Jesse, 691
Madison College, 2616, 2618
Magill, Edward H., 2320
Mahan, Alfred T., 935
Mahan, Asa, 2084
Mahan, Dennis H., 1887
Maine, State of, 868-870
Maine, University of, 889
Maine, University of, at Farmington, 890
Malone College, 2057
Manchester College, 637
Manhattan College, 1785
Mann, Horace, 2010
Manual training, 20-28, 73, 114, 756, 1454
Marian College, 638
Marietta College, 2058-2060
Marillac College, 1417
Marion College, 1418
Marquette University, 2751-2753
Mars Hill College, 1940
Marsh, James, 2580, 2602
Marshall University, 2722, 2723

Martha Washington College, 2443
Mary Baldwin College, 2619, 2620
Mary Hardin-Baylor College, 2509
Mary Washington College, 2621
Maryland, State of, 891-893, 2238
Maryland, University of, 920-923
Marymount College, 2622
Maryville College of the Sacred Heart, 1419
Massachusetts General Hospital, 1109
Massachusetts Institute of Technology, 1110-1122
Massachusetts, State of, 941-945
Massachusetts, University of, 1123-1126
Mathematics, 477, 994, 1122, 1512, 1946, 2245, 2666, 2667, 2778
Mather, Cotton, 287
Matthews, Brander, 1693
Maxcy, Jonathon, 2386
Mays, Benjamin, 431
Mayville State College, 1984
Mecklin, John M., 1516
Medical education, 118, 351, 353, 378, 382, 394, 395, 413, 593, 685, 720, 824, 829, 843, 863, 893, 898, 899, 900, 1031, 1093, 1116, 1277, 1299, 1348, 1402, 1452, 1507, 1578, 1610, 1666, 1705, 1712, 1744, 1846, 1932, 1933, 1975, 2000, 2024, 2087, 2146, 2236, 2275, 2295, 2444, 2541, 2546, 2558, 2570, 2579, 2651, 2766
Meharry Medical School, 2444
Meiklejohn, Alexander, 2775
Mendenhall, Thomas C., 1182
Menlo Junior College, 128
Mercer University, 427, 428
Meredith College, 1941
Miami University, 2061-2066
Michigan, State of, 1185-1204
Michigan State University, 1237-1244
Michigan, University of, 1089, 1245-1304, 2654
Middle Tennessee State University, 2445
Middlebury College, 2575, 2576
Military education, 228, 244, 310, 388, 572, 719, 933, 1599, 1878, 2264, 2355, 2367, 2446, 2637
Miller, Kelly, 357

Millersville State College, 2259, 2260
Millikan, Robert A., 81
Millikan University, 772
Mills, Cyrus, 131
Mills, Susan L., 131, 132
Mills College, 129-132
Milton College, 2754
Milwaukee College, 2755, 2756
Milwaukee-Downer College, 2749
Milwaukee Technical College, 2757
Minnesota, State of, 1320-1325
Minnesota, University of, 1341-1356
Minnesota, University of, at Morris, 1357
Mississippi College, 1381
Mississippi, State of, 1372-1375
Mississippi State University, 1382-1384
Mississippi, University of, 1385-1391
Mississippi Valley State College, 1392
Missouri, State of, 1397-1403
Missouri, University of, at Columbia, 1420-1427
Missouri, University of, at Kansas City, 1428
Missouri, University of, at Rolla, 1429, 1430
Mitchell, Maria, 1899, 1904
Modern languages, 303, 971, 1049, 1061, 1094, 1096, 1703, 2764
Monmouth College, 562-564
Montana, State of, 1464, 1465
Montana, University of, 1466-1468
Montclair State College, 1538
Monticello Female Seminary, 1431
Montieth, John, 1251
Montieth College, 1305
Mood, Francis A., 2520
Moore, Benjamin, 1689
Moravian College, 2261, 2262
Morehead State University, 832
Morehouse College, 429-432
Morley, Edward W., 2027
Morris, George S., 1300
Morris Brown College, 433
Mortimer, Mary, 2756
Mosher, Eliza, 1263
Moton, Robert R., 22
Moulton, Richard G., 490
Mount Angel College, 2156
Mount Holyoke College, 968, 1127-

1134
Mount Mary College, 2758
Mount Saint Mary's College, 924
Mount Union College, 2067
Muensterberg, Hugo, 1070
Muhlenberg, William A., 2631
Muhlenberg College, 2263
Muir, John, 2783
Munford, Mary, 2653
Murchison, Carl A., 985
Murlin, Lemuel H., 974
Music education, 255, 456, 953, 1017, 1091, 1756, 1777, 2032, 2034
Muskingum College, 2068-2070

Nash, John A., 680
Nashville, University of, 1282, 2446-2451
Native Americans, higher education for, 1964, 2206
Naval War College, 2355, 2356
Nebraska College, 1480
Nebraska, State of, 1470-1474
Nebraska, University of, 1481-1492
Nebraska Wesleyan University, 1493
Needham Law School, 2623
Neill, Edward D., 1338
Neill, William, 2220
Neilson, W.A., 1150
Nelson, Simon, 2290
Nevada, State of, 1500
Nevada, University of, 1501-1503
New Hampshire, State of, 1504
New Hampshire Technical College, 1524
New Hampshire, University of, 1525
New Jersey, State of, 1527-1529
New Mexico Military Institute, 1599
New Mexico, State of, 1594-1597
New Mexico State University, 1600
New Mexico, University of, 1601, 1602
New Paltz, State University of New York, College at, 1786-1788
New School for Social Research, 1789, 1790
New York, State of, 1603-1611
New York, State University of (whole system), 1799-1802
New York University, 1791-1798
New York, University of the State of (Regents), 1803-1810
Newark State College, 1539
Niagara University, 1811-1813
Nichols, Roy F., 2291
Nichols, Stewart B., 962
Normal schools, 41, 71, 73, 157, 205, 234, 516, 521, 594, 610, 621, 870, 892, 942, 945, 988, 1203, 1369, 1494, 1615, 1741, 1819, 1949, 2017, 2056, 2125, 2187, 2235, 2259, 2307, 2328, 2435, 2693, 2718, 2723, 2736
Norsworthy, Naomi, 1672
North, S.N., 1764
North Carolina, State of, 1889, 1908-1918
North Carolina State University, 1942
North Carolina, University of, at Chapel Hill, 1943-1959
North Carolina, University of, at Greensboro, 1960-1962
North Carolina, University of, at Raleigh, 1963
North Central College, 565
North Dakota, State of, 1979-1982
North Dakota State University, 1985
North Dakota, University of, 1986-1992
North Iowa Area Community College, 736
North Park College, 566
North Texas State University, 2511, 2512
Northeast Missouri State College, 1432-1434
Northeastern University, 1135
Northern Illinois University, 567
Northern Iowa, University of, 737-740
Northern Michigan University, 1306
Northrup, Cyrus, 1345
Northwest Missouri State College, 1435
Northwestern Christian College, 2157
Northwestern College, 741, 742
Northwestern Female College, 568
Northwestern University, 569-573
Norwich University, 2577
Notre Dame, College of, 133
Notre Dame of Maryland, College of, 925
Notre Dame, University of, 639-647

Nott, Eliphalet, 1873
Nursing education, 358, 464, 1109, 2019, 2299, 2706
Nutt, Cyrus, 634

Oakland University, 1307, 1308
Oberlin College, 2071-2086
Occidental College, 134
O'Connell, Denis J., 318
Ogden College, 833
Ogelthorpe University, 434-436
Ohio Medical College, 2087
Ohio, State of, 1994-2003
Ohio State University, 2088-2099
Ohio University, 2100-2105
Ohio Wesleyan University, 2106
Oklahoma Baptist University, 2129
Oklahoma Christian College, 2130
Oklahoma City University, 2131 2132
Oklahoma Presbyterian College, 2133
Oklahoma, State of, 2122-2127
Oklahoma State University, 2134
Oklahoma, University of, 2135-2138
Old High Gate College, 2139
Old Westbury, State University of New York College at, 1814-1816
Oliver, John R., 915
Oneonta, State University of New York College at, 1817
Oread Collegiate Institute, 1136
Oregon College of Education, 2158
Oregon, State of, 2144-2149
Orègon State University, 2159-2163
Oregon, University of, 2164-2170
Osborn, Henry F., 1698
Osgood, Herbert L., 1665
Oswego, State University of New York College at, 1818-1820
Ottawa University, 781, 782
Otterbein College, 2107-2109
Ozarks, College of the, 60

Pacific College, 136
Pacific Lutheran University, 2696
Pacific Union College, 137
Pacific University, 2171
Pacific, University of the, 138, 139
Packard, Silas S., 1821

Packer Collegiate Institute, 1821, 1822
Paducah Junior College, 822, 834
Page, David P., 1615
Paine College, 437, 438
Palmer, Alice Freeman. See Freeman, Alice
Palmer, George H., 1074, 1165
Park College, 1436, 1437
Parker, Francis W., 471
Parker, Horatio, 255
Parrington, Vernon L., 2705
Parsons College, 743-746
Parsons School of Design, 1823
Pasadena College, 140
Paterson State College, 1540
Patrick, Thomas W., 716
Patterson, James K., 823
Payne, Daniel A., 2114, 2115
Payne, William H., 1278
Paynter, John H., 2254
Peabody, Andrew P., 1075
Peabody, Selim H., 528
Pearsons, Daniel K., 2741
Peattie, Roderick, 2097
Peirce, Benjamin, 994
Peirce, Charles S., 904
Peirce, Cyrus, 988
Pembroke College, 2345
Pembroke State University, 1964
Pennsylvania Military College, 2264
Pennsylvania, State of, 2179-2193
Pennsylvania State University, 2265-2268
Pennsylvania, University of, 547, 2269-2303
Pepper, William, 2302
Perkins, Dexter, 1841
Perry, Arthur L., 1178
Perry, Bliss, 1076, 1564
Peru State College, 1494, 1495
Pfeiffer College, 1965
Pharmacy education, 1714, 1953, 2304
Phelps, William L., 293
Philadelphia College of Pharmacy, 2304, 2305
Philadelphia College of Textiles, 2306
Philadelphia Normal School for Girls, 2307
Philander Smith College, 61
Philanthropy, 88, 174, 950, 1048, 1167, 1457, 1715, 1726, 1835,

INDEX

1897, 1934, 2201, 2209, 2311, 2471, 2741. See also Financing higher education
Phillips, Ulrich B., 422
Phillips University, 2140, 2141
Philomath College, 2172
Philosophy (as discipline), 178, 716, 903, 904, 1074, 1081, 1085, 1300, 2665
Physical education, 170, 1130, 1152, 1802, 2035
Physics, 81, 300, 1509, 1572
Piedmont College, 439
Pierce, John D., 1194
Pikeville College, 835
Pittsburgh, University of, 2308-2311
Plattsburgh, State University of New York College at, 1824, 1825
Plymouth State College, 1526
Political science, 104, 699, 1013, 1342, 1546, 1653, 1667, 1676
Polytechnic Institute of Brooklyn, 1826
Pomona College, 141, 142
Potomac, College of the, 2624
Potsdam, State University of New York College at, 1827
Powell, T.S., 395
Pratt Institute, 1828
Presbyterian College, 2383
Presidency, office of, 1067, 2160, 2167
Princeton University, 1273, 1541-1573
Principia College, 574
Pritchett, Henry S., 1114
Pritchett College, 1438
Professional education, 1685, 1878, 1887, 2266. See also by specific profession
Providence College, 2357
Providence Hospital School of Nursing, 358
Pryor, Joseph W., 824
Psychology, 326, 571, 715, 840, 915, 983, 985, 993, 1007, 1070, 1544, 1673, 1680
Public relations, 542
Puerto Rico, University of, 2331, 2332
Pugh, Evan, 634
Pupin, Michael I., 1699
Purdue University, 648-655

Queens College, 1966
Quincy College, 575

Racine College, 2759
Radcliffe College, 1137-1139
Radford College, 2625, 2626
Rainey, Homer P., 2539, 2548
Rammelkamp, Charles H., 510, 511, 513
Randall, Eugene, 1353
Randolph-Macon Woman's College, 2627, 2628
Redlands, University of the, 143
Reed College, 2173
Reese, Michael, 88
Reinhardt, Aurelia H., 130
Religion and higher education, 267, 288, 586, 948, 1053, 1258, 1303, 1561, 1687, 1995, 2071, 2077, 2472, 2744
Remson, Ira, 910
Rendall, Isaac N., 2253
Rendall, John B., 2253
Rensselaer Polytechnic Institute, 1829-1832
Research, place of, 492, 1707
Rhees, Rush, 1844
Rhode Island College, 2358, 2359
Rhode Island, State of, 2333, 2334
Rhode Island, University of, 2360
Rice, John A., 1922
Rice University, 2513
Richard, Gabriel, 1217, 1284
Richards, Ellen H., 1115
Richards, Robert H., 1120
Richmond, University of, 2629
Ricks College, 456
Rider College, 1570
Ripon College, 2760-2762
Rittenhouse, David, 2281
Roanoke College, 2630
Robinson, Ezekiel G., 2350
Robinson, James H., 1671
Rochester Institute of Technology, 1833
Rochester, University of, 1834-1845
Rockefeller University, 1846
Rockford College, 576, 577
Rockne, Knute K., 645
Rogers, William B., 1121
Rollins College, 375
Rosary Hill College, 1847
Rose-Hulman Institute of Technology, 656

Ross, Edward A., 187, 193, 2788
R.O.T.C., 572, 2166, 2776
Ruffner, Henry, 2669
Ruggles, Samuel, 1708
Rush, Benjamin, 2217, 2276
Russell, James E., 1702, 1709
Russell Sage College, 1848-1850
Rutgers, Henry, 1581
Rutgers, The State University, 1575-1585
Ruthven, Alexander G., 1281, 1297
Ryan, James H., 329
Ryan, Thomas J., 321

Sacramento State College, 144, 145
Sacred Heart Seminary, 1309
Saint Andrew's College, 1967
Saint Augustine's College, 1968, 1969
Saint Benedict, College of the, 1358
Saint Bernard College, 14
Saint Bonaventure University, 1851-1853
Saint Cloud State College, 1359, 1360
Saint Elizabeth, College of, 1586
Saint Francis College, 657
Saint John, Lynn W., 2089
Saint John's College (Calif.), 146
Saint John's College (Md.), 926-930
Saint John's College (N.Y.), 1854
Saint John's Seminary, 1140
Saint John's University, 1361, 1362
Saint Joseph's College, 2312
Saint Lawrence University, 1855, 1856
Saint Louis College of Pharmacy, 1439
Saint Louis University, 1440-1447
Saint Mary-of-the-Woods College, 658, 659
Saint Mary's College of California, 147, 148
Saint Mary's Seminary, 1448
Saint Olaf College, 1363-1365
Saint Paul's College, 2631
Saint Rose, College of, 1857
Saint Thomas College, 836
Saint Thomas, College of, 1366-1368
Salem College (N.C.), 1970, 1971
Salem College (W. Va.), 2724
Salem State College, 1141
Salisbury State College, 931

Salmon, Lucy M., 1895
San Diego State College, 149
Sanford, Maria, 1354
San Francisco State College, 150-154
San Jose State College, 155-157
San Luis Obispo Junior College, 158
Santa Clara, University of, 159
Santayana, George, 1085
Sarah Lawrence College, 1858
Scholarships and fellowships, 2588
Schuylkill College, 2195
Science education, 256, 1108, 2676
Science in higher education, 284, 1005, 1324, 2246, 2339
Scott, Walter D., 571
Scott, William B., 1566
Scripps College, 160
Scripps Institute of Oceanography, 161
Scudder, Vida D., 1162
Sears, Barnas, 2353
Sears, Jesse B., 188
Seattle Pacific College, 2697
Sedgwick, William T., 1116
Seeds, Corinne, 112
Seelye, Laurenus C., 1148
Seton Hall University, 1587, 1588
Sewall, Joseph A., 211
Sharswood, George, 2278
Shaw University, 1972, 1973
Sheldon, Edward A., 1820
Sheldon Jackson College, 31
Shepherd College, 2725
Shields, Thomas E., 326
Shields, T.T., 681
Shipp, Albert M., 2391
Shippen, William, 2275
Shippensburg State College, 2313, 2314
Shorter College, 440, 441
Shurman, Jacob G., 1729
Shurter, Edwin D., 2543
Shurtleff College, 578
Shuster, George N., 1775
Shyder, Henry N., 2392
Siena College, 1859
Sill, Anna P., 577
Silliman, Benjamin, 265, 1108
Sills, Kenneth, 876
Simmons College, 1142-1144
Simpson College, 747
Sioux Falls College, 2398, 2399

Skidmore College, 1860
Slaught, Herbert E., 477
Slichter, Charles S., 2778
Small, Albion W., 486
Smith, Henry L., 627
Smith, William, 2273, 2274, 2279, 2287, 2294, 2298
Smith College, 1145-1150
Smithson College, 660
Snedden, David S., 1706
Snyder, Jonathan L., 1241
Social sciences, 1011, 1015, 1723
Social work education, 1201, 2020
Sociology, 193, 278, 290, 486, 1516, 2272, 2337, 2351, 2773, 2788
Sonoma State College, 162
Sororities, social. See Fraternities and sororities, social
South Carolina, State of, 2361-2364
South Carolina, University of, 2384-2389
South Dakota School of Mines, 2400, 2401
South Dakota State University, 2402-2404
South Dakota, University of, 2405-2413
South, University of the, 2452-2458
Southeast Missouri State College, 1449
Southeastern Louisiana University, 865
Southeastern Massachusetts University, 1151
Southern California, University of, 163-168
Southern Illinois University, 579-582
Southern Methodist University, 2514
Southern Mississippi, University of, 1393, 1394
Southern Oregon College, 2174-2176
Southwest Missouri State College, 1450
Southwest Texas State University, 2515-2518
Southwestern at Memphis, 2459
Southwestern Junior College of the Assemblies of God, 2519
Southwestern State College, 2142

Southwestern University, 2520, 2521
Sparrow, William, 2054
Speech education, 592, 1700
Spelman College, 442
Spellman, Cecil L., 366
Spencer, Cornelia P., 1947
Spokane University, 2157
Sprecher, Samuel, 2118
Spring Arbor College, 1310
Spring Hill College, 15-17
Springfield College, 1152, 1153
Stagg, Amos A., 493
Stanford, Leland, 172, 181
Stanford University, 169-193
State control, 364, 379, 386, 405, 421, 670, 778, 779, 857, 1119, 1202, 1260, 1312, 1398, 1400, 1602, 1609, 1799, 1803, 1805, 1979, 2002, 2144, 2184, 2185, 2186, 2482, 2540, 2548, 2657, 2715, 2802
State systems, 64
Steele, Joel D., 1749
Steffens, Cornellius M., 686
Steffens, Lincoln, 101
Steidle, Edward, 2268
Stephens College, 1451, 1452
Stetson, John B., 376
Stetson University, 376, 377
Stevens Institute of Technology, 1589
Stiles, Ezra, 285, 286
Stille, Charles J., 2300
Stockbridge, Levi, 1124
Stone, James K., 2053
Stone, Winthrop E., 654
Stonewall Jackson College, 2632
Stowe, Calvin E., 880
Straight, Henry H., 1495
Student activism, 75, 92, 95, 152-154, 513, 572, 632, 1003, 1044, 1047, 1065, 1243, 2050, 2055, 2086, 2160, 2167, 2605, 2776
Student life, 44, 101, 249, 262, 307, 323, 408, 414, 459, 527, 845, 952, 956, 958, 962, 1006, 1021, 1060, 1068, 1087, 1198, 1238, 1244, 1407, 1515, 1567, 1573, 1882, 1883, 1893, 1951, 1989, 2328, 2348, 2537, 2650, 2783, 2794
Student organizations, 699, 1266, 1267, 1555, 1670, 1697, 1770. See also Fraternities and

sororities, Literary societies, and Student life
Student personnel services, 596, 1191, 1257, 1487, 1685, 2033, 2070
Sturtevant, Julian M., 514
Suffolk University, 1154, 1155
Summer sessions, 1190, 1486, 1949, 2125
Summerskill, John, 153
Sumner, William G., 278, 290
Susquehanna University, 2315
Swarthmore College, 2316-2321
Sweet Briar College, 2633, 2634
Syracuse University, 1861-1870

Tabor College, 783-785
Talbot, Marion, 496
Talledega College, 18
Talmadge, Eugene, 405
Tappan, Henry P., 1276, 1304
Tarleton, John, 2522
Tarleton State College, 2522
Tayloe, Edward T., 1035
Taylor, Albert R., 769
Taylor, Creed, 2623
Taylor, James M., 1896
Taylor, Joseph W., 2201
Taylor University, 661
Teacher education, 10, 19, 34, 65, 115, 120, 123, 232, 262, 377, 406, 471, 478, 502, 520, 534, 621, 726, 740, 792, 855, 1153, 1186, 1302, 1315, 1375, 1390, 1471, 1596, 1605, 1606, 1611, 1634, 1659, 1757, 1818, 1868, 1997, 2149, 2180, 2181, 2182, 2191, 2418, 2434, 2483, 2543, 2566, 2591, 2717, 2734. See also Normal schools
Technical education, 6, 7, 41, 80, 81, 83, 401, 402, 466, 515, 539, 648, 656, 1110, 1181, 1200, 1226, 1524, 1535, 1589, 1646, 1826, 1829, 1833, 1998, 2207, 2221, 2460, 2524, 2531, 2639, 2757
Temple Buell College, 226
Temple Junior College, 2523
Temple University, 2322
Tennessee, State of, 2417-2422
Tennessee Technological University, 2460
Tennessee, University of, 2461-2467

Tennessee Wesleyan College, 2468
Terry, Earl M., 2785
Texas A and M University, 2524-2529
Texas Christian University, 2530
Texas, State of, 2478-2483
Texas Technological University, 2531-2533
Texas, University of, 2534-2549
Texas Wesleyan College, 2550, 2551
Texas Woman's University, 2552, 2553
Theological education, 251, 252, 277, 280, 811, 871, 880, 1075, 1099, 1549, 1563, 1758, 2262, 2374, 2426, 2635
Thomas, Theodore, 1712
Thomas, M. Carey, 2200
Thomas More College, 837, 838
Thompson, William O., 2099
Thorndike, Edward L., 1680
Thornwell, James H., 2389
Thurston, Robert H., 1727
Thwing, Charles F., 2018
Ticknor, George, 1094, 1096
Tift College, 443
Toledo, University of, 2110
Tougaloo College, 1395
Towson State College, 932
Transylvania University, 839-851
Trenton State College, 1586, 1587
Trinidad State Junior College, 227
Trinity College (Conn.), 242, 243
Trinity College (D.C.), 359
Trinity University, 2554, 2555
Troy State University, 19
Trustees, 711, 825, 912, 1270, 1709, 1803, 2540, 2765
Tucker, William J., 1522
Tufts University, 1156-1159
Tuition and fees. See Financing higher education
Tulane University, 866, 867
Tulsa, University of, 2143
Turner, Frederick J., 1004
Turner, Henry M., 433
Turner, Hulbert, 1710
Turner, Jonathan B., 512
Tusculum College, 2469
Tuskegee Institute, 20-28
Tyler, Lyon G., 2684
Tyler, Moses C., 1719, 1731
Tyler, William S., 964

INDEX

Union College (Ky.), 852
Union College (Neb.), 1496, 1497
Union College (N.Y.), 1871-1875
Union Seminary, 2635
Union Theological Seminary, 1876, 1877
United States Air Force Academy, 228-231
United States Coast Guard Academy, 244
United States Military Academy, 1878-1893
United States Naval Academy, 933-939
University extension, 108, 445, 1654, 2737, 2787
Upper Iowa College, 748, 749
Upsala College, 1588
Utah, State of, 2556, 2557
Utah State University, 2563
Utah, University of, 2564-2566
Utica Junior College, 1396

Valdosta State College, 444
Valentine, Alan, 1845
Valley City State College, 1993
Valparaiso University, 662
Vaughan, Victor C., 1299
Vanderbilt, Cornelius, 2474
Vanderbilt University, 2470-2475
Van Hise, Charles R., 2795
Vassar, Matthew, 1897
Vassar College, 1894-1904
Veblen, Thorstein, 479
Venable, Charles S., 2666
Veterinary medicine, 2293
Villanova University, 2323, 2324
Vincennes University, 663-665
Vineland Training School, 1589
Virginia Commonwealth University, 2636
Virginia Military Institute, 2637, 2638
Virginia Polytechnic Institute, 2639, 2640
Virginia, State of, 2583-2591
Virginia, University of, 2641-2667
Vocational education, 62, 1200, 1833

Wabash College, 666, 667
Waco University, 2489
Waddel, John N., 1391

Wagner Free Institute, 2325
Wake Forest University, 1974-1976
Walker, Francis A., 1112, 1117
Walla Walla College, 2698
Wallace, James, 1340
War and higher education, 1255, 1301, 2495
Ward, Joseph, 2414
Ward, Lester F., 2337, 2351
Wartburg College, 750
Washburn University of Topeka, 786
Washington and Jefferson College, 2326, 2327
Washington and Lee University, 2668-2672
Washington College, 2476
Washington, State of, 2688-2690
Washington State University, 2699-2703
Washington University, 1453-1459
Washington, University of, 2704-2711
Watts, Isaac, 298
Wayland, Francis, 2338
Wayne State College, 1499
Wayne State University, 1311-1314
Weaver, Warren, 2796
Webster, Daniel, 1517
Wellesley College, 1160-1169
Wells College, 1905
Wergeland, Agnes M., 2805
Wesbrook, Frank F., 1348
Wesleyan Female Seminary, 2673
Wesleyan University, 245-247
West Chester State College, 2328
West Georgia College, 445
West Liberty State College, 2727, 2728
West Los Angeles College, 194
West Virginia, State of, 2715-2718
West Virginia University, 2729, 2730
West Virginia Wesleyan College, 2731, 2732
Western Carolina University, 1977
Western College, 751
Western College for Women, 2111
Western Illinois University, 583
Western Kentucky University, 853
Western Michigan University, 1315-1319
Western Montana College, 1469
Western Washington State College, 2712

Westfield State College, 1170
Westmar College, 752
Westminster College (Mo.), 1460-1462
Westminster College (Penn.), 2329
Westminster College (Utah), 2567
Wheaton College (Ill.), 584-586
Wheaton College (Mass.), 1171
Wheeler, Benjamin I., 103
Wheelock, Eleazer, 1514, 1515
White, Andrew D., 902, 1720, 1733, 1737
White, Emerson, 649
White, James W., 2295
Whitman College, 2713
Whitney, Josiah D., 1008
Whittaker, Johnson, 1890
Whittier College (Calif.), 195-198
Whittier College (Iowa), 753
Wickersham, James P., 2260
Wiener, Norbert, 1122
Wilberforce University, 2112-2116
Wiley, Harvey W., 340, 655
Willamette University, 2177, 2178, 2714
Willard, Emma, 1848
William and Mary, College of, 2674-2687
William Jewell College, 1463
William Penn College, 754, 755
Williams, Walter, 1427
Williams College, 1172-1179
Williston, Samuel, 1100
Wilson, Woodrow, 46, 526, 1543, 1546, 1570
Winona State College, 1369-1371
Wisconsin Idea. See Faculty activism
Wisconsin, State of, 2733-2738
Wisconsin, University of, at Madison, 1004, 1173, 2763-2796
Wisconsin, University of, at Milwaukee, 2797
Wisconsin, University of, at Plattville, 2798
Wisconsin, University of, at River Falls, 2799
Wisconsin, University of, at Whitewater, 2800
Wittemberg Manual Labor College, 756
Wittenberg University, 2117, 2118
Wofford College, 2390-2392
Women's higher education, 129-132, 191, 282, 368, 568, 576, 875, 1127, 1137, 1149, 1160, 1171, 1272, 1431, 1451, 1505, 1532, 1536, 1620, 1745, 1780, 1785, 1858, 1860, 1894, 1905, 1913, 1960, 2022, 2111, 2198, 2211, 2261, 2345, 2424, 2552, 2571, 2589, 2627, 2633, 2653, 2673, 2784. See also Coeducation
Woodhouse, James, 2297
Woodrow, James, 2375
Woods, Leonard, 883
Woodstock College, 940
Woolley, Mary E., 1131
Wooster, College of, 2119
Worcester College for the Blind, 1180
Worcester Polytechnic Institute, 1181-1184
Wriston, Henry M., 2352, 2354
Wyandanch College, 1906
Wylie, Andrew, 635
Wyoming, State of, 2801, 2802
Wyoming, University of, 2804-2806
Wythe, George, 2677

Xavier University, 2120, 2121

Yadkin College, 1978
Yale University, 248-307, 404, 1273
Yankton College, 2414-2416
Yeshiva University, 1907
Y.M.C.A., 2644
York College, 1498
Young, Ella F., 472

Zoology. See Biology